MW01659760

I Am Not a Monk "Sponging Off" Buddhism

我不是「呷教」的和尚

I Am Not a Monk “Sponging Off” Buddhism

我不是「呷教」的和尚

（英文版）

Venerable Master Hsing Yun
English Translation by Robert H. Smitheram

Fo Guang Shan International Translation Center

© 2021 Fo Guang Shan International Translation Center

English translation by Robert H. Smitheram
Edited and proofread by Fo Guang Shan International Translation Center
Cover and book designed by Yin Chiu

Fo Guang Shan International Translation Center
3456 Glenmark Drive
Hacienda Heights, CA 91745, U.S.A.
Tel: (626) 330-8361 / (626) 961-9697
Fax: (626) 330-8363
E-mail: info@fgsitc.org
Website: www.fgsitc.org

All rights reserved.
Protected by copyright under the terms of the International Copyright Union. Except for fair use in book reviews, no part of this book may be reproduced for any reason by any means, including any method of photographic reproduction, without permission of the publisher.

Printed in Taiwan.

Library of Congress Cataloging-in-Publication Data

Names: Xingyun, 1927- | Smitheram, Robert, translator.
Title: I am not a monk "sponging off" Buddhism = Wo bu shi "xia jiao" de he shang / Venerable master Hsing Yun ; Fo Guang Shan International Translation ; English translation by Robert Hale Smitheram.
Other titles: Wo bu shi "xia jiao" de he shang. English
Description: Los Angeles : Fo Guang Shan International Translation Center, 2022. | Translated from Chinese.
Identifiers: LCCN 2021049148 | ISBN 9781943211425 (paperback)
Subjects: LCSH: Xingyun, 1927- | Buddhist priests--China--Biography.
Classification: LCC BQ9800.F6392 X5574513 2022 | DDC 294.3/92092 [B]--dc23/eng/20211012
LC record available at https://lccn.loc.gov/2021049148

Table of Contents

DILIGENT EFFORTS WILL NOT BE WASTED

POSTSCRIPT

Author's Preface

"Buddhism depends upon me" has been a guiding light for my entire life.

I was born during the chaos of war, and although I experienced hardships in my life, I give thanks to my parents for bestowing a compassionate nature upon me. Even as a child, I cared for and protected little animals, and I enjoyed helping others. After I joined the monastic order at the age of twelve, the strict and domineering education of the monastery instilled in me an accommodating personality: I do not fear difficulty or adversity in doing anything. I am now ninety-three years old [2019] and have been a monastic for more than eighty years. If I were to sum up my life, I think the phrase "born into tribulation, raised in adversity, yet experienced a lifetime of joy" would serve as an adequate account of it.

I have spent my entire life promoting Humanistic Buddhism, and I always encouraged myself with the words "live three hundred years' worth of life," so I have never ceased in my efforts for Buddhism. However, the world is the combination of causes and conditions. Aging, sickness, death, and rebirth are natural phenomena; so too will the body of flesh experience times when sicknesses must be healed. At the end of 2016, owing to over-exhaustion, I suffered a brain hemorrhage and underwent an operation. I am grateful to Chen Chao-Long, honorary director of the Kaohsiung Chang Gung Memorial Hospital, who helped me by leading the medical treatment team. I am also grateful for the blessings invoked by all the people connected to me throughout the world, for it was by such means that I was restored to health. I have made sickness my friend and taken patience as my strength throughout this life; I really do not feel I have suffered any pain, only some inconveniences. Nothing hinders my heart, and I remain free and at ease, for there is only joy and happiness.

During my convalescence, my disciples told me that everybody warmly received the *Complete Works of Venerable Master Hsing Yun* as soon as it was published, and it has now already gone into its third printing. But a work that encompasses a total of three hundred and sixty-five volumes is really too enormous, and it is unclear with which volume one should begin. My disciples wondered if it were possible for me to select a few articles from the collection that focus on my own experiences and publish them as a separate volume, serving as a standard upon which their practice of Buddhism could rely. What I have spent my entire life saying and writing is also what I have been doing myself. If it can be of benefit to everyone and is helpful to Buddhism, then, of course, I would happily see it accomplished. I have heard from the editor Miss Tsai Meng-Hua that this work, *I Am Not a Monk "Sponging Off" Buddhism*, is ready for publication.

The term "Sponging off Buddhism" means making a living through a dependence upon Buddhism. More than seventy years ago [1949], Venerable Chenkong wrote me a letter from Mount Putuo in Zhejiang Province, and he asked Venerable Zhuyun to deliver it into my hands. He wrote, "Now we Buddhist youth must let 'Buddhism depend upon us,' and not give any thought to how 'we depend upon Buddhism.'" This passage made a deep impression upon me.

Yes, I hope Buddhism depends upon me, for I do not want to depend upon Buddhism, which means that I do not want to be a monk who "sponges off" Buddhism. I promised myself to be someone who repays kindness; furthermore, I vowed "to give to others and not expect others to give to me." "Buddhism depends upon me" is a phrase that has become a guiding light in my heart, and I am always encouraged by it, for it makes my heart shine more brightly and enhances the power of my faith.

Indeed, Humanistic Buddhism is the future light and hope of Buddhism. I have benefited from the kindness and generosity of the Triple Gem:[1] I never received a formal education and had never even seen a school during my childhood, yet I became an elementary school principal, established five universities throughout the world, and received honorary doctorates from more than thirty universities as well as many honorary professorships from numerous educational institutions. On five continents, I have established three hundred temples, in which more than one thousand three hundred disciples engage in propagating the Dharma through culture, education, charity, and Dharma services, respectively. I am grateful to everyone who has supported my work to promote Humanistic Buddhism, for it has allowed the Buddhism of sutra chanting and repentance services during the Ming [1368–1644 CE] and Qing [1644–1911 CE] dynasties to develop into the Humanistic Buddhism accepted by people in the 21st century.

Based on the belief that Humanistic Buddhism holds true to the original intent of the Buddha, I have made propagating Buddhism my mission in life and placed the assembly before myself, so I humbly offer this book, *I Am Not a Monk*

1 The Buddha, the Dharma (the teachings of the Buddha), and the Sangha (the Buddhist monastic community).

"Sponging Off" Buddhism, to all readers. If anyone were to ask me again what I wish for in this lifetime, I would give my blessing to everyone: "May peace and happiness brighten the five continents."

—Hsing Yun, Founder's Hall at Fo Guang Shan
February 2019

Foreword by Charles Kao

Giving is Venerable Master Hsing Yun's initial resolve and his life's practice — I don't wish for Buddhism to raise me, I wish for Buddhism to progress.

I. The Venerable Master Speaks; He Remembers; and He Is Writing.

This is Venerable Master Hsing Yun's first book to come out after his recovery, something truly precious and so incredible. It is just like August of last year when the Venerable Master exhibited his *One-Stroke Calligraphy*[2] *After Illness* for the first time in Nanjing. He surprised and delighted everyone.

I was indeed fortunate to attend. Nanjing, where this exhibition took place, is the place where I was born, and this new book is being published by Global Views-Commonwealth Publishing Group, which gives me the pleasure of being the first among its readers.

Looking back to October 30th, 2016, Venerable Master Hsing Yun gave me his consent to undertake the important tasks of making his speech and presenting awards at our 14th Global Views Leaders Forum. On the night before I was to

2 At age 70, Venerable Master Hsing Yun's vision began to blur, and his hands started to shake. Nevertheless, he focused his mind and continued to write. From that time forward, he has done his calligraphy in one continuous stroke, for if he raised his brush, he would not be able to see where to continue. Thus, his work came to be known as "one-stroke calligraphy."

The Venerable Master and Charles Kao at Dajue Temple.

present his speech, I received a phone call from one of his disciples, who said the Venerable Master was to undergo immediate surgery due to a brain hemorrhage. This truly was an overwhelming turn of events. Venerable Chueh Pei hurried over and made a last-minute appearance at the auditorium to explain the Venerable Master's ideas in a clear and moving way, prompting an enthusiastic response.

The *United Daily News* even reported how, on October 31st, the Venerable Master "had suffered a stroke and was in the hospital for surgery, the blood clot being as big as a fist" in its lead story on the front page. As a longtime reader of the *United Daily News*, I have never read about any other popular leader being treated with such a degree of importance. For a long time now, Venerable Master Hsing Yun has been on the level of a national treasure, a guiding teacher and so well respected by everyone.

The Venerable Master, who for many years now has "made a friend out of sickness," already looks upon sickness as a friend in peaceful coexistence; he also looks upon death as cause and effect,[3] for he has already placed death and rebirth beyond his

3 One of the teachings of the Buddha: once a cause is generated, when appropriate, necessary conditions are present, its effect will come to fruition; cause and effect govern all things.

sphere of consideration. However, the major brain operation on this occasion was no small matter, and after the success of the operation, everyone felt a sense of relief, but the road to recovery was not something we dared think about. If the Venerable Master were able to live on but lose his ability to remember and speak, then what kind of torment would it be for him since he has always enjoyed working throughout his life?

The speed of the Venerable Master's recovery far exceeded the most optimistic estimations of the medical treatment team lead by Dr. Chen Chao-Long at Chang Gung Memorial Hospital. This is a miracle in medical history. A few months after the operation, the progress of his rehabilitation was accelerating daily.

"The Venerable Master is speaking"; "the Venerable Master remembers"; and "the Venerable Master is writing"; every time his disciples passed on such good news, I was overcome with excitement and wished to pay him a visit.

During the summer of last year, a disciple of his called me on the phone to pass on some words from the Venerable Master: "You tell Professor Kao that I really long to see him." This helped me overcome my hesitation of not daring to disturb the Venerable Master, and I hurriedly went up to visit him.

During the Venerable Master's recuperation, I made close to ten visits; I further made a special trip to Dajue Temple at Yixing in mainland China, along with the publisher Cora Wang and a few colleagues. The Venerable Master was resting and recuperating in the serene and spacious seat of his lineage,[4] with its bamboo-covered hills in the back and a lake reflecting the clouds in the front. Truly, it was like a scene in

4 The temple where a monastic's master originally came from; the foundational seat of one's Buddhist lineage and practice, from which other temples are connected and supported.

paradise. Every time I visited, I always came away with priceless photographs and observations.

II. One "Small Book" Is yet Again Another "Great Work."

The thickness of this new book constitutes a "small book" when compared with the Venerable Master's other written works, which amount to more than thirty million characters over the course of his lifetime, but in terms of the ideas being promoted here, it is a "great work." Everything has its source. The Venerable Master is asking himself, "What was my initial resolve for becoming a monk? Where is my fundamental motivation?"

Whether he is at Fo Guang Shan in Kaohsiung or at Dajue Temple in Yixing, during the early dawn or after sunset, how has the Venerable Master, at over ninety years of age, managed to become a Buddhist leader who has established an abundance of Buddhist temples, universities, middle schools, primary schools, and art galleries, as well as founded media platforms, such as *The Merit Times*[5] and Beautiful Life Television,[6] and even basketball teams? Putting it in more direct terms, how has the Venerable Master been able to create something out of nothing, constantly expanding both at home and abroad?

The Venerable Master's nonchalant answer is "I took part in all of these things, but none of them belongs to me. I never want what individuals give to me, nor have I ever possessed a single dollar; I am always willing to let go. Money belongs to everyone; it just gets exchanged from here to there and back again."

5 A daily newspaper founded by Venerable Master Hsing Yun in 2000.
6 A non-profit television station in Taiwan founded by Venerable Master Hsing Yun in 1997; it was originally known as Buddha's Light Television (1997–2002).

In 1949, he came to Ilan from Yangzhou as a twenty-three-year-old monk, and his initial resolve was that he did not want to rely on Buddhism financially but rather that Buddhism would progress through his own efforts.

The strength of his initial resolve is something I can completely understand because in 1949, I myself was thirteen years old when I accompanied both of my parents from Shanghai to Taiwan. As a youth, I cultivated a self-striving personality in a village for military dependents and went to the United States to study at the age of twenty-three; it was during these younger days that I developed complete self-reliance. In the face of the "fortuitous little pleasures" that have spread all over Taiwan in recent decades, I exclaim: seek out one's own job oneself; set up one's own family oneself; search for one's own stage oneself; and attend to one's own old age oneself!

The Venerable Master has probably never read the eighteenth century work *The Wealth of Nations* by Adam Smith, nor has he read *The Competitive Advantage of Nations* by the contemporary [Michael E.] Porter. In no way do these influence his judgments pertaining to wealth, human nature, markets, the state of the world, internationalism, and so on. With his retentive memory, his self-taught understanding, and his learning by analogy, he has his own definite views and holds his own breadth of vision.

III. Where There Is Dharma, There Is a Way: Where There Is the Venerable Master, There Is Great Achievement.

Throughout his life, the words and deeds of the Venerable Master are the most concrete demonstration of his great achievement: "giving" is the initial resolve; it is unconstrained by form, and it has no end.

The Venerable Master gives people confidence, gives people joy, gives people hope, and gives people convenience; and the Venerable Master promotes doing good deeds, speaking good words, and thinking good thoughts. The Venerable Master has passed on compassion, wisdom, and non-attachment.

Such formless wholesome thoughts move many people and then transform into physical beauty, one after the other, when he sets about establishing Buddhist temples, schools, and art galleries. Everyone becomes the beneficiary of the humanistic bounty.

Having followed the Venerable Master for half a century, Venerable Tzu Jung makes this acute observation: the Venerable Master does not make use of the donations toward Buddhism; instead, he relies on the sums of money from his own writings, author's compensation, and copyright royalties as well as his *One-Stroke Calligraphy*. That would be enough for him, but he takes all of that money and donates its entirety to society and Fo Guang Shan. Not only does he not want it, but he also enjoys giving it away and is happy to give it to others. The people to whom he has provided financial assistance number far more than the hundreds of thousands; the people he supports every day number far more than the hundreds of thousands; but what he has given to society amounts to far more than the thousands of millions. He has neither a bank account, nor does he save any change; he does not even have a desk to call his own.

As for a detailed accounting of the Venerable Master's work, it includes such areas as the educational, cultural, and charitable, but for all of these numerous projects, he does not do them because he "wants" them: they all come about from his giving. It is because of giving that he is able to let go, and it is because of his letting go that he is able to obtain. The poor monk is, on the contrary, not poor but rich instead. It is only that the Venerable Master "treats not having as having" and "treats emptiness as joy."

Venerable Tzu Jung further stated that over the past sixty years, she has seen how the master has often encountered difficulties, but it really seems that the Buddha is protecting him. When it is obvious "after endless mountains and rivers, one doubts there is a path out" yet one can still find "by going through the shade of a willow and the brightness of flowers, there is a lovely village," he will often say, "Where there is Dharma, there is a way," and the disciples also feel that "Where there is a Venerable Master, there is a great achievement."

Throughout his entire life, the Venerable Master has always firmly grasped the original intention of his initial resolve. Giving is better than receiving, for he does not wish that "everybody does things for him"; rather, he wants to change it into "I do things for everybody." He does not want to depend upon Buddhism; rather, he wants to devote his entire strength to propagating Buddhism.

Forty years earlier, he borrowed the popular saying from [Milton] Friedman winner of the Nobel Memorial Prize in Economic Science "There's no such thing as a free lunch in this world" and called upon his fellow countrymen to strive for themselves. No one could have known that this phrase from a great religious teacher of the Chinese world would develop into "realizing the power of the vow of the human world."

I can only say, "Our Venerable Master is so amazing."

Founder of the Global Views-
Commonwealth Publishing Group

Foreword by Jude Thomas Manzo

A Lifetime of Giving through Humanistic Buddhism: Venerable Master Hsing Yun and His Global Contributions

In 1997, I experienced Humanistic Buddhism firsthand through Hsi Lai Temple in Los Angeles, California with my wife Shujan Cheng. Prior to this, I had experienced Buddhism as a solitary activity, only reading texts about Buddhism.

At Hsi Lai Temple, the monastics and lay devotees embodied the daily practices of Venerable Master Hsing Yun's approach, encouraging everyone to learn about and practice Humanistic Buddhism by offering weekly classes on meditation, lectures on the Buddhist approach to life, vegetarian lunches, and numerous cultural and volunteer activities, culminating in a short-term monastic retreat and taking refuge.

While at Hsi Lai Temple, my wife and I also met Venerable Yi Chao, Executive Director of the Fo Guang Shan International Translation Center, who encouraged us to volunteer in translation and editing; these include *The Flower Adornment Sutra's Practices and Vows of Samantabhadra Bodhisattva Chapter*; and Venerable Master's *Humble Table, Wise Fare; Infinite Compassion, Endless Wisdom: The Practice of the Bodhisattva Path; Pearls of Wisdom: Prayers for Engaged Living*, volumes 1 and 2; *Traveling to the Other Shore: Buddha's Stories on the Six Perfections*; and the text before you.

As Venerable Master nears the age of ninety-five (2021), this collection may serve as an introduction and overview for anyone who wishes to learn more about and to practice Humanistic Buddhism. Venerable Master wishes, "May peace and happiness brighten the five continents." From a Chinese cultural perspective, our planet consists of five continents, so his wish for peace and happiness is directed to all of us across the globe, whatever our spiritual, national, ethnic, or geographic background, whatever our current conditions may be at the present moment, since we all are interconnected.

Gifts

Venerable Master's connection to Buddhism has always been plain and simple. He states, "Buddhism depends upon me." His aspiration is "to live three hundred years' worth of life," making every day of his life a gift to humanity through his daily practices of Humanistic Buddhism.

From the age of twelve in 1939, despite all of the traumatic and life-and-death experiences in the China of World War II and its subsequent Civil War, and all of the social hostility he later faced when moving to Taiwan in 1949 to spread the Dharma, Venerable Master has served as a humble monk, continuously asking himself, "Am I acting like a monk?" using skillful means to teach the Dharma to individuals from all walks of life, successfully recruiting them to assist in renewing Buddhism through the founding of more than three hundred temples as well as children's homes, primary and middle schools, senior homes, art galleries, television and other media platforms, and colleges and universities throughout the world. He has thereby created opportunities for monastics, lay devotees, and anyone interested in Buddhism to participate in and create new Humanistic Buddhist activities and to study Buddhism at any level, up to and including the undergraduate and graduate levels.

This edition, requested by his devotees, culls from over sixty years of his writings and life experiences, and with quick brush strokes takes us through the initial years of war's effects upon society, of manual labor in Chinese temples, cooking, cleaning, chopping firewood, reading and studying the sutras, and balancing chanting for hours with meditating for hours in temples without electricity; of seriously considering simply serving as a cooking monk or retreating completely from society and dedicating himself exclusively to either studying sutra or to meditation for the rest of his life; of the years of social struggle in Taiwan to ensure that civil authorities would permit the construction of temples requested by the Taiwanese people, of the manual labor in the actual construction of those temples, of preserving them during times of flooding, and of the managerial skills required to ensure their maintenance; of years of skillful writing and promoting the publication of Buddhist texts and translation in numerous languages, bringing the Dharma to diverse audiences; of the most recent years of seriously declining health, of his *One Stroke Calligraphy After Illness*, and of his declaration, "I have made sickness my friend."

Venerable Master's own life experiences, deep spiritual practice, basic humility, and willingness to give to and serve mankind have led to his belief that we should balance the humility of chanting, in which individuals rely upon the Buddha, with meditation, in which individuals learn to rely upon themselves, and can lead to a practice of giving to humanity that can become almost a daily, continual meditation. In *The Core Teachings* he suggests: "Once we become accomplished at sitting meditation, we will begin to see that it is possible to meditate while standing, or walking, or doing just about anything." This "doing just about anything" might include his own practice of giving and might explain how he has been able to give so very much for so very long, to so very many of us around the world.

For those of us who might not reach this level of meditative giving, Venerable Master emphasizes the "Four Givings," which we can perhaps grasp more readily: "giving people confidence, giving people joy, giving people hope, and giving people convenience." For Venerable Master, giving is his initial resolve, his aspiration, and his vow: it is unconstrained by form, and it has no end.

Benefits

To benefit all of us, Venerable Master has given his life to providing educational opportunities, sponsoring cultural events, engaging in community service, and writing and teaching extensively about the Buddhist path of wisdom and compassion.

Each of the articles in this collection is written in a very straightforward and easy to follow style; Venerable Master does not assume that the reader has a background in Buddhism; instead, the collection serves as a skillful introduction, with a broad perspective that can lead to further study at any level, including the undergraduate and graduate levels.

Moving Forward

Venerable Master's gifts continue to be available to us on a daily basis through his numerous writings. In addition, the monastics and lay devotees of many of the temples he has founded, rather than allowing the pandemic to reduce or completely eliminate interactions and practices, have increased their offerings via the internet. As a result, anyone who wants to learn more about Humanistic Buddhism can attend temples in the United States, Taiwan, Canada, etc. online, and can attend an expanding number of classes on meditation, sutra study, vegetarian cooking, the tea ceremony, and many other innovative classes brought about by the monastics and lay devotees of the temples.

Whatever our daily life, profession, or our current spiritual practices, may we still take his spirit and practice of "I am not a monk, 'sponging off' Buddhism" to heart in our everyday life and spiritual practices, giving to mankind through our spiritual and other daily practices rather than simply expecting to receive. I hope that reading these excerpts from a monk who has given over eighty years of his life to spreading Humanistic Buddhism can spur you on to develop or refine your own spiritual practices, and to include some of the activities and attitudes described by Venerable Master in this text.

Jude Thomas Manzo
PhD, Yale University

Editor's Note

To retain as much of the content and quality of the original Chinese text as possible, contextual information not in the original, such as years and dates, has been added in brackets.

Readers may notice that the age of Venerable Master Hsing Yun varies throughout the text, reflecting the timeline leading up to this publication: The articles "I Am Not a Monk 'Sponging Off' Buddhism" (I, II, and III) were originally published in *The Merit Times* in 2016, when the Venerable Master was ninety years old. These, along with other essays about his life and thoughts, were published together in 2019, when he was ninety-three years old. The only content added to the English translation in 2021 are the foreword by Jude Thomas Manzo and footnotes.

When writing Chinese names and words in English, we use the Hanyu Pinyin romanization system. However, when names already have an accepted common spelling in English, such as Dr. Sun Yat-sen or Kaohsiung, we use that instead.

Chinese names are written last name (family name) first and first name (given name) second. When anglicized, names are written given name first and family name second. For example, Han Kuo-yu was changed to Daniel Han.

In Chinese, 佛光 (Fo Guang) means "Buddha's Light"; both appear throughout the text, depending on conventional usage.

For Buddhism

There is no free lunch in this world—vowing to benefit the world

I often think to myself, that if I had come into the world only to engage in self-cultivation in some mountain forest and be unable to be of service to people as a whole, then what would be the point of coming into the world at all?

Venerable Rongzhai once gave me this instruction: "As one who has not yet realized enlightenment, make the aspiration to liberate sentient beings first; this is the aspiration made by the bodhisattvas."[1] Consequently, I made the vow to become a bodhisattva. I also remember with reverence Venerable Zhifeng's phrase "Do not become a burned and ruined seed," for I do not want to become Buddhism's burned and ruined seed. I cannot make a living from exploiting Buddhism by using the name of spiritual cultivation, and I cannot live my life frivolously by relying upon the name of spiritual cultivation; nor would I choose of my own accord such an aimless and dissipated life. Since I was born into this life of mine for Buddhism, I ought to work for Buddhism; I ought to look to Buddhism and not look to the wealth of gold and silver in society.

---

1 Those who vow to liberate all sentient beings from suffering and attain Buddhahood; a bodhisattva practices all perfections and helps sentient beings achieve enlightenment.

I Am Not a Monk "Sponging Off" Buddhism

(Part I)

At the many places I engaged in practice and study—at places such as Qixia in Nanjing, Jinshan and Jiaoshan in Zhenjiang, and Tianning in Changzhou, where I was brought up experiencing spring breezes, summer rains, autumn frosts, and winter snows—I studied silently and grew up quietly. I was always thinking as to how I could repay Buddhism's kindness. I could not make a living by depending on Buddhism over the long term. I ought to make some contributions to Buddhism—this was the idea that developed in me from a young age.

Jiagao means "to eat off religion" in Taiwanese.

After Taiwan's liberation from the Japanese, life was poor and simple owing to the earlier Japanese oppression. Some religions were able to give you some milk powder and give you some clothing and necessities, but you had to believe in their religion. Everybody set about changing their beliefs in order to eat and survive. Therefore, some people said that they were jiagao.

"Jiagao" is to make a living through a dependence upon Buddhism.

After I gained my own understanding of Buddhism, I was always hoping that Buddhism would depend upon me. Sixty-seven years ago [1949], Venerable Chenkong wrote me a letter from Mount Putuo in Zhejiang Province, and he asked Venerable Zhuyun to deliver it into my hands. It began: "Now we Buddhist youth must let 'Buddhism depend upon us' and not give any thought to how 'we depend upon Buddhism.'" This letter of his was a voluminous and fluent piece of writing.

As for my relationship with Venerable Chenkong, he was the teacher, and I was the student. We only had the opportunity to meet once, and that was in 1947 when I met him at Jiaoshan's first training class for staff members of the Chinese Buddhist Association. "Buddhism depends upon me," is a phrase that has become a guiding light in my heart, and I am always encouraged by it, for it makes my heart shine more brightly and enhances the power of my faith.

Repaying Kindness, Dedicating Everything to Buddhism

My family was a poor one, and when I was young, about seven or eight years of age, I lived at home and depended upon

Venerable Master Zhikai, the Venerable Master's tonsure master.

my parents for food. I wanted to do some work in order to make some money and help out with the family expenses. Later on, I would get up early in the morning to collect dog droppings, and then at dusk I would head out to gather cow dung. Making these into piles would then produce fertilizer that could be sold for money. The adults were happy, and I myself felt elated as well.

After I left home and joined the monastic order, Buddhism raised and taught me, which is why I was not bothered by all the beating, scolding, and humiliation I received. At the many places I engaged in practice and study—at places such as Qixia in Nanjing, Jinshan and Jiaoshan in Zhenjiang, and Tianning in Changzhou, where I was brought up experiencing spring breezes, summer rains, autumn frosts, and winter snows—I studied silently and grew up quietly. I was always thinking as to how I could repay Buddhism's kindness. I could not make a living by depending on Buddhism over the long term. I ought to make some contributions to Buddhism—this was the idea that developed in me from a young age.

I promised myself to be someone who repays kindness, and furthermore I vowed "to give to others and not expect others to give to me." Therefore, the kindness of "a half bowl of salted vegetables" from my teacher Abbot Zhikai [1911–1979] while I was sick allowed me to make the aspiration to propagate the Dharma and benefit sentient beings. This is my natural disposition.

During my life of practice and study, cloistered in the monastery for ten years, it seemed that I did the hard jobs such as being the vegetable and rice cook, vegetable steward, and water carrier year after year. These many tasks were not necessarily something I had to do, but I made up my mind to undertake them of my own accord. I never rested a single day, for I was conscious of having some small, special aptitude, and that was delighting in cooking the vegetables and rice as an offering to the monastic assembly. As a matter of fact, when I initially joined the monastic order, I really did not possess any sort of aspiration; I only wanted to be the monk who cooks the vegetables and rice, and nothing more. In no way did I ever imagine I would become the "Venerable Master" of whom everybody speaks. I felt that being the monk who cooks the

In his quest for the Dharma in 1938, the Venerable Master became a monastic under Venerable Master Zhikai at Mount Qixia.

vegetables and rice would perhaps become the greatest enjoyment of my life.

After ten years of life in the monastery, I had a chance to return to Dajue Temple, the seat of my lineage. This was also a poor and simple Buddhist monastery, but it did have a farm, and as I had originally come from a family of farmers, I thought I could earn a living by engaging in agriculture. There was an elementary school near the monastery, and I was fortunate enough to teach there. In my mind, I had become a monastic, yet I also wanted to produce something so that I would not be criticized as one of society's consumers. I did not want to make a living by depending upon Buddhism, and even less did I want society to come and provide me with relief. I wanted to live through my own efforts and earn my own living.

I do not know what reasons took me from the poor and simple job of a vegetable and rice cooking monk so that I could wander here to Taiwan. The kindheartedness of the Taiwanese people and the simple fare of Taiwan nurtured me into maturity. They even showed deference to me with my status as a monastic, and they wanted me to teach the Dharma. At first I thought, there is a saying: "The Dharma is universal, neither high nor low"; giving teachings on the Dharma and cooking vegetables as an offering to the monastic assembly are the same thing, so there is no point to making distinctions between them. Thus, I slowly took the route of propagating the Dharma, establishing temples, securing the monastic community, and liberating sentient beings. But frankly speaking, now that I am ninety years old [2016], were you to ask me if I have any regrets, it would be my inability to become the vegetable and rice cooking monk I initially wanted to be.

When the Venerable Master (*second row, seventh from the left*) first arrived in Taiwan, Venerable Master Miaoquo of Yuanguang Temple in Chungli permitted him to stay, which formed the conditions for the Venerable Master to be established in Taiwan and to propagate the Dharma throughout the world. This is a group photo for the Seven-Day Amitabha Chanting Retreat. Seated in the front row (*center*) is Venerable Master Miaoquo, with Householder Sun-Chang Ching-yang (*fifth from the right*), and (*from the left*) Venerable Zhuyun, Venerable Lühang, and others.
October 11, 1950

In the Service of Liberating Sentient Beings, Not Becoming a Burned and Ruined Seed

Thinking back to the time when I first arrived in Taiwan, I served as a water carrier at Yuanguang Temple in Zhongli. Every day I would draw six hundred buckets of water to supply the needs for the entire temple of eighty people. Early in the morning before it was light, I would pull the cart to the market to buy goods needed by the resident monastics. I never declined any task at the temple, whether it be sweeping, cleaning the latrines, carrying loads, collecting the rent in grain, keeping watch at the temple, and so on. I promised myself to keep the spirit of offering so as to help everyone manage the tasks and to perform every kind of service. I think that having an outlook of serving everyone means not failing oneself in life.

I also considered that since I had already joined the monastic order, I might as well make the effort with spiritual cultivation, and as I wanted to carry on with my studies, I must have an environment conducive to study. There were also devoted lay members of the temple who said they wanted to support my going on a retreat, which would allow me to devote myself to essay writing. I once had the thought as well of going to the temple at Lingyan Mountain to spend all my life reciting the name of [Amitabha] Buddha, and I would also have willingly spent my remaining years sitting in meditation in a meditation hall. Yet when I reflect that if I had been successful with my spiritual cultivation in retreat and would go on to rebirth in the Western World of Ultimate Bliss[2] or the Eastern World of Pure Crystal,[3] all those many people who had supported me and

Having stepped forth into the public, monastics are able to become Dharma masters who guide the multitudes.
Photo by Qiu Liyue

2 In a past life, when Amitabha Buddha was Dharmakara Bhiksu, he made forty-eight vows to establish and adorn a Pure Land. After mindfully cultivating for five kalpas, he finally attained Buddhahood, and the realm he adorned became the Western Pure Land of Ultimate Bliss. Bodhisattvas who are reborn there will not regress on their path, and many will become Buddhas in one more rebirth.

3 "The Land of Pure Crystal," where the "Medicine Buddha of Pure Crystal Radiance" presides.

provided me with food would still be in this Saha world;[4] what would be done about them?

Upon giving it some thought, such would still be selfish acts that would be unable to benefit people as a whole. So I gave up on those kinds of ideas that made no consideration for others and were only concerned with my own success. Venerable Rongzhai (fl. 1939) once gave me this instruction: "As one who has not yet realized enlightenment, make the aspiration to liberate sentient beings first; this is the aspiration made by the bodhisattvas." Consequently, I made the vow to become a bodhisattva. I also remember with reverence Venerable Zhifeng's [1901–1971] phrase "Do not become a burned and ruined seed," for I do not want to become a burned and ruined seed of Buddhism.

Human Life Is Precious, It Cannot Be Carelessly Frittered Away

I have my own character, in that I delight in going up and down mountain forests, and I enjoy the kind of detachment that comes from leaving the world behind and living independently, the freedom of being one with heaven and earth. Engaging in spiritual cultivation while living in the mountains means having nothing else to do, and except for the chanting services in the morning and evening at the main hall, one could describe it as being free and at ease, which would also be very satisfying. But I often think to myself, that if I had come into the world only to engage in self-cultivation in some mountain forest and be unable to be of service to people as a whole, then what would be the point of coming into the world at all?

4 In Sanskrit, Saha means "endurance." The Saha world refers to our world; the world in which Sakyamuni Buddha teaches the Dharma; although this world is tormented by suffering, human beings have the power to endure it.

Within Buddhism, there are a good number of people who depend upon and avail themselves of sutra chanting and repentance services to chant sutras for the sake of others, thereby making a living by collecting donations (gifts of money). Since giving talks on the sutras is not easy, sutra chanting is relatively easier. Were I to go off and chant sutras even during that turbulent time when living was not easy, that would still be living off the Buddha. Then again, as my voice is unable to carry a tune, I have no wish whatsoever to do sutra chanting. In my mind, human life is something so very precious: my parents raised me, giving me this opportunity to act in this world; how can I possibly let my own life slip away so blithely?

I also have seen many monastics who do nothing all day long, as they wander about far and wide. I have no idea where their travel expenses are coming from, and neither do I have any idea what their travels here and there are for. Of course, I too would like to travel and study, expanding my knowledge, but I cannot just have people come and help me: they pay, and I go traveling; is this fair?

I also have seen people living in small temples and shrines where the doors are shut every day. It is only on the first and fifteenth of the lunar month that they open the main gate and allow the devotees to come and burn some incense. The money they collect from donations is quite enough to maintain their lives for three meals a day. But then, is it possible for me to become such a monastic? In 1952, Venerable Yinshun [1906–2005] once told me at the Taiwan Buddhist Seminar in Hsinchu: "Spiritual cultivation, spiritual cultivation—people who say such words under the pretext of this term are actually turning it into a synonym for laziness." Therefore, I cannot make a living from exploiting Buddhism by using the name of spiritual cultivation, and I cannot live my life frivolously by relying upon the name of spiritual cultivation; nor would I choose of my own accord such an aimless and dissipated life.

I also worried about how I was to spend my life. The meaning of life's existence cannot be separated from everyone as a whole, and it cannot be separated from contributions to society; otherwise, one is nothing but a rice bucket[5] or a clothes rack.[6] What value is there in that?

The Meaning of Life Lies in Contributing to the World

There are often people who ask me, "Are there times when you felt discouraged and disappointed?" I have never felt this way, but the road ahead is a long one such that I did not know what I could do—this kind of thought I have had often. This is especially true in Taiwan, where kitchen work in the temple was mainly the responsibility of the female monastics. As a young monk, it was impossible for me to serve as monastic cook in the kitchen, which led to the biggest regret of my entire life. As for what is called "spiritual cultivation," isn't boiling rice and cooking vegetables with the spirit of offering a good form of spiritual cultivation? Aren't those engaged in the many arduous ascetic practices cultivating the practice of "being in the present"? No one understands the spiritual cultivation of living, which is precisely why Buddhism is out of touch with society!

Thinking back to when Fo Guang Shan had just been founded, its facilities were extraordinarily crude and rudimentary, but there were already a good number of readers of

5 Chinese slang meaning someone who is incompetent.

6 Chinese slang meaning someone who is superficial, looking good on the outside but having no depth of character.

Fo Guang Shan held the Festival of Light and Peace during the Chinese New Year period, exhibiting Buddhist cultural items and various lanterns. About 100,000 devotees came to pay homage to the Buddha. Seeing the great crowd of people coming into Fo Guang Shan, the Venerable Master quickly set about cooking noodles in the kitchen of the Guole Vegetarian Cafeteria at the Non-duality Gate so that devotees could enjoy a great meal.
Photo by Gao Quanfu, Jan. 25, 1982

the *Awakening the World* periodical who came having heard the news. Finally, this gave me the opportunity to distinguish myself: At that time, all the devotees knew that if they could not find me upon arriving at Fo Guang Shan, they could most likely see me busily coming and going were they to approach the kitchen.

During the Spring Festival one year, I was cooking noodles at the Guole[7] Vegetarian Cafeteria and became so busily engaged in my task, that I set a record for cooking twenty batches of noodles in a single noon hour. It was only then that my disciples realized that besides being a carpenter and a bricklayer, their teacher had all along been able to boil a fine bowl of noodles and cook a fine dish of vegetables, for which they gave me lavish praise. Chang P'ei-keng, who served as secretary-

7 In Chinese, 果樂 (guole) means "fruits of happiness."

general for the National Salvation Corps in the city of Kaohsiung has said that eating a bowl of noodles that I cooked remains an indelible memory even after twenty years.

However, my circumstances did not give me such an opportunity to serve the public. That was all right, for besides being the chief cook at the monastery, I discovered that I possessed another capability: I could write articles.

Although the conditions in Taiwan early on were difficult, I wrote for such Buddhist magazines as *Human Life*, *Bodhi*[8] *Tree*, and *Awakening Living Beings.* Most of these did not offer any author's compensation, yet I still continued to supply them with articles for publication. I was even willing to forgo any compensation, in that I did not wish to write articles for those many magazines and periodicals that offered author's compensation. Since I was born into this life for Buddhism, I ought to work for Buddhism; I ought to look to Buddhism, and not look to the wealth of gold and silver in society.

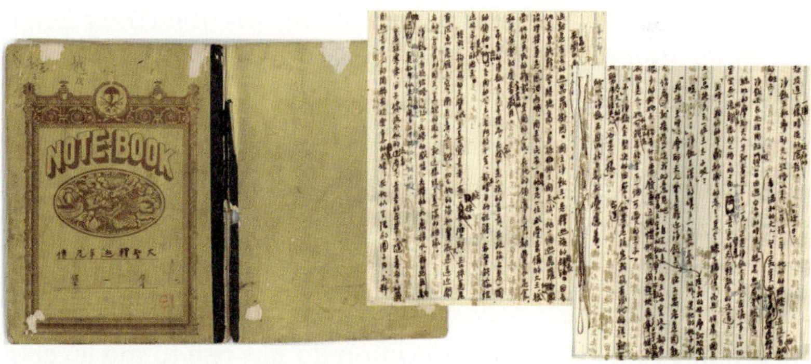

The cover (*left*) and text (*right*) of the Venerable Master's handwritten manuscript of *The Biography of Sakyamuni Buddha.*

8 In Sanskrit and Pali, "awakening" or "enlightenment"; one's mind of original intention at the start of an undertaking, such as the vow to become a Buddha or a bodhisattva.

I do not remember clearly which publishing house was soliciting articles, but I wrote an article and received one hundred and fifty [Taiwan] dollars. Taiwan during the 1950s was a society in which material goods suffered widespread shortages. I was extraordinarily happy to use this sum of money to buy a copy of *Cihai*.[9] Moreover, upon its first page I inscribed: "This volume, a silent teacher, will be keeping me company through the countless months and years, enabling me to broaden my knowledge of the world and even to bestir myself into soaring upward." I felt that I was extremely fortunate, in that besides labor service and meal preparation, I was now adding a place where I could make contributions to Buddhism—to use my article writing in order to protect and support Buddhism.

After the age of twenty-four or twenty-five and despite my lack of relevant reference materials, I still completed a series of books, one volume after the other: *The Biography of Sakyamuni Buddha*; *The Universal Gate: A Commentary on Avalokitesvara Bodhisattva's Universal Gate Sutra; Bells, Gongs, and Wooden Fish; National Master Yulin; The Ten Great Disciples of the Buddha; and The Great Realizations: A Commentary on the Eight Realizations of a Bodhisattva Sutra.* Thinking back on these many little volumes, I am struck by their immaturity and dare not browse through them now. But my disciples tell me that there are some professors who still employ the contents of these early works in order to conduct their literary research. Putting it that way makes me feel ashamed, for indeed these many exercises in composition do not rise to the level of those with refined tastes. However, it was not until I learned that these many books were now circulating in their tens of

9 Renowned Chinese dictionary of words and phrases known as the "ocean of words."

Fo Guang Shan Chief Construction Engineer Hsiao Ting-shun recounted those days: "Working completely in accordance with the geographical contours, wherever we went, the master would use a piece of bamboo and sketch in the dirt. Discussing with gesturing, we would plan out how to work with the land."
1968

thousands and even their millions that I somewhat comforted myself with the thought: Wasn't this also propagating the Dharma? Wasn't this "Buddhism depends upon me"?

Turning Nothing into Something: Limitless and Immeasurable Resolve

Having called myself a "humble monk" my entire life, although I have built several hundred temples and dozens of universities, middle schools, primary schools, kindergartens, Chinese schools, and so on—none of these belong to me. These many institutions all belong to the masses of society, and they all belong to Buddhist believers who protect the Dharma. This "humble monk character" of mine has remained unchanged for my entire life, but neither is it something innate, and for this I ought to thank my compassionate teacher for the excellent education he gave me. In mainland China, I spent more than ten years with him, but he as a matter of course never gave me a single article of clothing, and he never gave me a single dollar, nor did he permit me to go out for travel and study. Having joined the monastic order and become a monk, the days I spent were more impoverished than living at home.

With such a great monk who is so awe-inspiring as one's teacher, how can one be so shabby and miserable? Only now do I realize how this compassionate and great teacher raised me, ensuring that my life later on would be free of the habit of buying things and be free of the desire for material things. Therefore, I always talk about the concept of "turning nothing into something." "Nothing" does not mean the absence of something; after gaining some understanding of it, within "nothing" there is only a resolve that is infinite and inexhaustible, limitless and immeasurable.

The first tonsure ceremony held in the Huai-en Hall.
September 19, 1968

From this point onward, I explained the sutras and taught the Dharma, promoting the recitation of [Amitabha] Buddha's name and promoting education, and I threw myself into literary pursuits. I set up tutoring classes for young people and organized [Amitabha] Buddha's name recitation centers for older folks. I felt that in doing such work, I would probably not become someone who "sponges off" Buddhism for one's entire life.

During this time, there were also many young people who came and indicated that they wanted to learn Buddhism with me by leaving home and joining the monastic order. At first, I had no choice either, as they took the tonsure on their own without obtaining my permission. So I simply had to set up a small-scale Buddhist college for them. Later on, as student enrollment increased year after year, we moved from Shoushan Temple in Kaohsiung's downtown area to Fo Guang Shan on a hill covered with thorny bamboo; and that was how Fo Guang Shan was founded.

When Fo Guang Shan was initially founded, there were gullies and ditches everywhere, while the topsoil had been scoured away long ago by the rains. There was not even a single mountain byroad, so one could only go on foot by following the gullies and riverbeds. Where precisely could a temple possibly be built? One of the devotees looked around and exclaimed, "Not even ghosts would come to a place like this." But I thought to myself, "I'm building a temple here. As long as the Buddha comes, it is fine. It does not matter if the ghosts don't come." I am indebted to Mr. and Mrs. Chu Bosi, overseas Chinese from Vietnam, for their good suggestion that I take over this parcel of land. As I figured it, I could proceed slowly if I did have the money, and if I did not have the money, putting the project on hold would not matter.

That was how work began on the monastery. Students were increasing day by day, and the number of disciples requesting to join the monastic order was also increasing with each passing day. Devotees were also coming in droves to participate in various kinds of construction work as well as activities for propagating the Dharma. For more than fifty years, the Buddhist college has never stopped enrolling students; and that is not including the other universities and middle schools. The number of students in the Buddhist college alone once exceeded more than six hundred, and I had promised to supply their room and board, their pocket money and stipend. It was only then I realized that I was really facing some difficulties.

Having been consistently unwilling to conduct sutra chanting and repentance services on behalf of others, it suddenly occurred to me that it did not matter. I could go to the funeral parlors to conduct all-night chanting vigils for others, since donations for all-night vigils would be slightly more, which could be used to subsidize the expenses for the Buddhist college. That was how the present Fo Guang Shan Tsung-Lin University became the first Buddhist college in the history of Buddhism to remain in operation for more than fifty years while enrolling students every single year.

Turning a Withdrawal into an Advance: Dharma Waters Flow Steadily across the Five Continents

I cannot endorse in any way the idea that once monastics undertake some duty, they would be unwilling to step down after assuming the position. Holding the position of temple administrator is temporary, and serving as the venerable abbot is

In 1985, the Venerable Master stepped down and Venerable Hsin Ping, who joined the monastic order in 1957, was inaugurated as the second generation abbot of Fo Guang Shan.

also temporary. No matter what kind of institution there is in society today, they all have a term of office for their positions; that is, the new are constantly replacing the old as one wave drives the previous one. If you do not step down, then how are those behind you going to advance?

At the beginning of Fo Guang Shan's founding, I instituted a system whereby an abbot would serve a six-year term and could be reappointed for another term. At the end of twelve years, one must leave that office and step down. Later on, I was unable to resist the request of the disciples, and as this also occurred just as the founding of Fo Guang Shan was facing some difficulty, I had no choice but to serve again for another term. Eighteen years after the founding of Fo Guang Shan, I invited one thousand three hundred seniors to celebrate their sixtieth birthday together at Fo Guang Shan. It was at this time that I firmly resigned and withdrew from the abbot position of Fo Guang Shan.

In order to dissuade the disciples from developing a habit for dependence, I came up with the idea of traveling the world to propagate the Dharma. The earliest manifestation of this was the establishment of Hsi Lai Temple in the United States, and later there was the establishment of Nan Tien Temple and Chung Tian Temple in Australia. This was followed by the opening of Buddhist centers in such regions as Europe, Africa, and South America. In addition, a series of affiliate temples were also founded in Hong Kong, Thailand, Malaysia, Japan, Singapore, Korea, and so on across Asia. In this way, all the devotees worked hard together with me in setting up the two hundred to three hundred Buddhist centers around the globe by adapting to the local conditions.

I could not have imagined that the withdrawal from my position as abbot would mean turning a withdrawal into an advance instead, allowing Humanistic Buddhism to head outward. There are many scholars who have said to me that the Buddha of the past brought Buddhism to the five regions of India, while Fo Guang Shan has brought Buddhism to the five continents, becoming the first religious group to internationalize Chinese Buddhism.

In all fairness, when I initially began building Buddhist centers, it was not entirely the result of making the great vow to propagate the Dharma for the benefit of sentient beings either. I only was thinking about how the devotees and disciples had become more numerous: Where would they all go to take their meals? If I were to take some number of devotees to a neighboring Buddhist temple for meals, it would be an embarrassment if we did not make donations to the temple; and it would be an embarrassment even if we did. In the face of such a dilemma, it would be better to build a temple in places that are often visited. This would allow all the people who came with me to have something to eat.

Among these was Fushan Temple situated in Changhua, which was built because every time we traveled back and forth between Kaohsiung and Taipei propagating the Dharma to the northern and southern parts of Taiwan, stopping for a meal was no easy matter, and that was the problem. (At the time the expressway had not yet been built.) That temple was built from the slow saving up of the small profits obtained from environmental-friendly recycling. I once even thought of naming the temple, the "Environmentally-Friendly Temple," or perhaps "Offering Temple," but in the end I went with the majority view and named it "Fushan Temple."[10]

In this human world, I hope that everyone will depend upon me for their meals and livelihood, but I too would be unable to exist without a dependence upon everyone. This is the law of dependent origination[11] according to Buddhism. Everybody coexists together in oneness within positive affinity. It is much like during the initial founding of Fo Guang Shan: When people came to make donations, most people hoped that the devotees would make larger donations, but I hoped they would make somewhat smaller donations because only a scant amount of water will flow on steadily. Making too large of a donation will on the contrary create a burden for people; it is for this reason as well that I have consistently advocated how I would rather partake of meals from myriad families, rather than enjoy a meal from just one.

10 Ch. 福山寺 (fushansi); literally, "Blessed Mountain Temple."

11 This is the Buddhist concept that all phenomena arise and cease due to causes and conditions. Thus, no phenomena possess an inherent nature.

The noble image of Venerable Master Jianzhen brought back from Toshodai-ji in Japan is now housed in Jianzhen Library at Yangzhou, Jiangsu, so that people may pay homage to him.

Protecting the Dharma and Defending the Faith: Bravely Speaking Out and Making a Stand

Besides vowing to "not sponge off Buddhism," I was also determined to protect the Dharma and defend the faith. I remember it was during the 1950s when the famous Peking opera star Ku Cheng-chiu [1929–2016] was performing "Fire Burns Honglian Temple" at the Yung-Le Theater. Its contents to some extent were a vilification of Buddhism, and I wrote a letter in protest. This was at a time when Chiang Ching-kuo[12] was romantically pursuing Ku Cheng-chiu, so all she needs to do was say the word, and I would probably have suffered the tragic fate of being killed. But for the sake of Buddhism, I paid no regard to such matters. I would rather sacrifice my life to protect the faith than become an ignorant monk for Buddhism, one who hides from the public, tail between the legs.

With their position so authoritative within Buddhist circles, the lay Buddhists Li Bingnan [1889–1986] and Zhu Fei [b. 1921] took over the management of the *Awaken the Masses* magazine and tried to transform it into a periodical specializing in the Pure Land teachings,[13] but I strongly objected. In order to

12 1910–1988; president of the Republic of China in Taiwan from 1978–1988.

13 The Pure Land School encourages the recitation of Amitabha Buddha's name. Through this practice, one is able to achieve single-minded concentration and maintain a continuum of pure thoughts. Then, at the time of death, the practitioner will be received by Amitabha Buddha and be reborn in the Western Pure Land.

preserve the mission of *Awaken the Masses* as founded back then by Venerable Master Taixu [1890–1947], I wrote a letter in protest of their action. In publishing my original letter, they felt that I was opposing the Pure Land practice of reciting [Amitabha] Buddha's name, which left me practically shunned in Taiwan. In fact, I have participated in no less than a hundred or more seven-day retreats over the course of my lifetime; add to that the morning and evening recitation of [Amitabha] Buddha's name and the weekend group practice, and that number would be even greater. I have been a consistent advocate of "an understanding that encompasses all the Dharma, and a practice that simultaneously follows both Chan and Pure

The faculty and students at the Taiwan Buddhist Seminar at Ching Tsao Hu, Hsinchu. *Front row, from the left*: venerables Zhiding, Xingding, Huiding, and (*on the right*) Shanding; *back row, from the left*: venerables Xinran, Xinwu, Zhuyun, and the Venerable Master (Dean of Academic Affairs at that time).
1951

Land," and I once had the experience of both the body and mind dissolving away during a session of reciting [Amitabha] Buddha's name. So how could I oppose the Pure Land practice? However, if you were to ask where the Pure Land is located, as I see it, the Pure Lands of the Buddhas throughout the ten directions are located in the human world.

My faith has been this simple throughout my life, and it has never ever changed. Now that I am living in a Buddhist temple and what I have received is the nurturing of Buddhism and the faithful support of the devotees, I shall live for Buddhism and die for Buddhism, for I cannot do without fairness and justice. It is equivalent to what a fellow countryman of a

Venerable Ci Hang and the Kanjurwa-Mergen-Nomun-Khan visiting the teachers and students of the Taiwan Buddhist Seminar at Ling Yin Temple at Hsinchu. *Front row, from the left*: Guan Kaitu (teacher for Japanese language), venerable Huansheng; the Venerable Master; venerables Wushang, Lühang, the Kanjurwa-Mergen-Nomun-Khan, Ci Hang, Yan Pei, and others.
October 9, 1952

much earlier generation, Venerable Master Jianzhen,[14] stated as he was departing for Japan to propagate the Dharma: "It is all for the sake of this great mission, so of what value is my life?"

In relating the many events of the past, I am not announcing to the world that "I am not sponging off Buddhism," it is just that my conscience quite naturally compels me to act in this way. Now that I have joined the monastic order and become a monk, I will "continue to strike the bell for each day that I remained a monk"; otherwise, what am I doing draping myself in Buddhist robes?

When I first started working on behalf of Buddhism, I felt that my own education level was not enough, so I approached a succession of many great worthies and Dharma masters so as to learn from them. In this respect, I felt that I had benefited considerably from doing so. I eventually came to realize that if young monastics have not practiced and studied with more than one hundred Dharma masters and wise advisors, they cannot be called dedicated spiritual practitioners. The Youth Sudhana[15] made fifty-three study pilgrimages in *The Flower Adornment Sutra*,[16] while the great worthies of the Chan School in the past also became the so-called "travelers to Jiang or Hu," in order to seek the Dharma in Jiangxi and Hunan by drawing near Mazu [Daoyi (709–788 CE)] and [Shitou] Xiqian [700–709 CE], Chan masters who were held in high esteem for their moral integrity. As to how such great worthies offered

14 688–763 CE; he achieved his aspiration to bring the Dharma to Japan; however, it took him six attempts and cost him his eyesight.

15 The "Entry into the Dharma Realm" chapter of *The Flower Adornment Sutra* describes how the young Sudhana asked for instruction from fifty-three good Dharma friends so that he could learn to practice the bodhisattva path.

16 Among all Buddhist sutras, it is known as the "king of sutras"; it is the greatest and most profound among the Buddha's teachings. It has become fully integrated into Chinese Buddhism.

The Venerable Master accompanying a Buddhist visiting group to Beeh Low Temple in Singapore. Group picture in front of the Main Shrine.
August 4, 1963

teachings, and how esteemed monastics gave instruction, if you do not remember the guidance of these many advisors, then how can you call what you are doing "practice and study"?

I was also very fortunate that I had much in the way of meritorious causes and conditions for the future, so I could draw near many senior monastics, Dharma masters, great worthies, and young venerables as well as some Taiwanese great worthies of the laity from every region of the world.

If someone were to ask me now what they had talked about and what instruction they had given, I could tell you all of it, point by point. Even today after several decades, I have not forgotten anything. In Buddhism, humility and respect are very important: To enjoy drawing near to such advisors makes it possible to absorb their rich experiences of life. Being able to retain one or two good words or phrases that are like the Buddha's or Confucius' sayings, we will be able to benefit from them throughout our lives.

Cherishing the Words of the Teachers Brings a Lifetime of Benefits

I do not hold with sectarianism, and I do not think in terms of separate schools. My feeling is that Buddhism is an integral whole, not something to be split up or broken apart. The family on my father's side had grown sparse, and after I joined the monastic order, it too had grown sparse. Therefore, whenever I heard of a teacher and great worthy at some location, I always went there to pay a visit and request instruction, irrespective of school or sect. But I am ashamed to say that I was only able to go visit and learn outside of my lineage, for I was not even clear about the names of my lineage holders of the past, and I feel regret over why my teacher never mentioned them. Clearly, even though we were master and disciple, it was difficult to make the connection. Therefore, if important words pop up in conversation, they all must be cherished to an extraordinary degree.

During those difficult times when material goods were in short supply, I too encountered a lot of setbacks in approaching the many older, middle-aged, and younger advisors. For example, I was rejected outside the gate by Venerable Bai Sheng, so I was not permitted to register as a visiting monastic and was unable to attend a conference. I was also once caught off balance by a question posed by Venerable Nan Ting. He said, "Will you be eating here?" I was young at the time and very shy. The noon hour was approaching, and I plainly wanted to go and eat something, but I was ashamed to answer "I will," so I only said "I won't" and then departed feeling so disappointed. Venerable Dong Chu with whom I was on the closest terms sat at the dining table and, pointing to the only two dishes on the table, said, "These dishes were cooked especially for you!" I really felt ashamed of myself for putting the senior monastic through such trouble.

Positive Enthusiasm: Establishing the Four Givings Creed

I feel ashamed of myself: I dare not become arrogant and dare not become conceited. In being able to receive the instructions of so many senior monastics and wise advisors, I only feel more modest and deferential. We cannot succeed on our own, for all of us slowly mature over time while being nourished by the kind rains and sweet dew of the community as a whole. Now that I have not become a monastic in order to "sponge off Buddhism," I ought to make contributions through sacrifice "for Buddhism" and propagate the Dharma to benefit sentient beings "for Buddhism."

Now that I am over ninety in age, I too have suffered from diabetes for more than fifty years. For a diabetes sufferer to be able to live such a long time should be something rarely seen in the history of medicine. What causes have created this condition? Thinking back over the past, I experienced privation under Buddhism: so much humiliation, so much resignation, so much misery, and so much bitterness. It was just like how Tao Yuanming [365–427 CE] put it in his poem:

> *Having meals nine times in a month,*
> *Wearing the same cap for ten years;*
> *Longing for the cock to crow by evening,*
> *Wishing for the crows to roost at dawn.*

In my mind, the major cause of my suffering from diabetes and heart disease is probably the result of such conditions of severe malnutrition.

However, I have made a friend out of illness, and I feel no resentment whatsoever. Moreover, having made the vow to "widely open the Universal Gate," not only do I give people food to eat, for Buddhism I have established the creed of "giving people confidence, giving people joy, giving people hope, and giving people convenience." This was done as a way of encouraging myself to move forward, act positively, and exert myself as a lifetime optimist. This is known as:

My mind embraces the vow of compassion to liberate all beings;
My body floats like an untethered boat in the Dharma sea;
If you ask what wish I hold for my life:
May peace and happiness shine upon the five continents.

I have lived my life in this way right up to today.

Reflecting on the past, if there were any honor and glory, then all of that was brought about by the Buddha; if there were some successes, then all of that was achieved with the help of the devotees; and if I have taught others through my example, then all of my efforts as a model or exemplar for others was brought about by the many great worthies and wise advisors. Having written to this point, I recall how in January of 2012, I accepted an invitation to return to the Shah Alam Stadium in Malaysia, and propagate the Dharma. At the time there were two thousand Malaysian young people who, with their loud

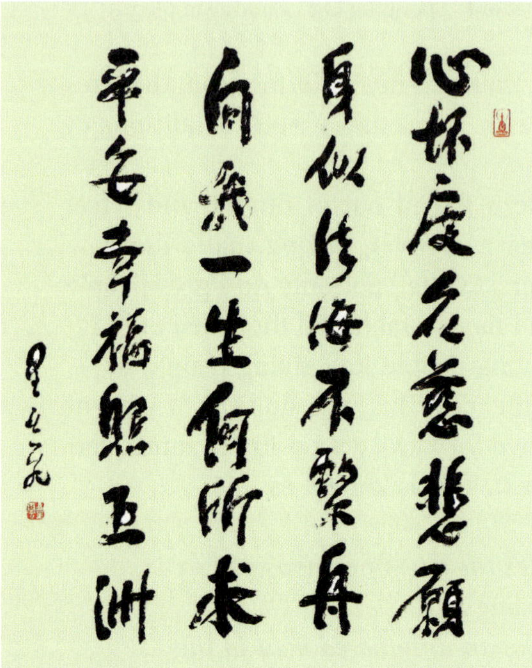

The Venerable Master's calligraphy: Please see English translation on page 29.

(June 8, 2015)

voices, led the audience of eighty thousand people in singing together: "Buddhism depends upon me." This could not help but leave my eyes brimming with tears.

In November of last year [2015], they again held the Marvelous Malaysia [Buddhist] Music Concert, but since my age made it impossible for me to attend, I could only give them my blessing via a recorded video message. My disciples told me there were eight thousand young Malaysians there amid the torrential rains as they sang "Buddhism depends upon me" with spirit, undaunted by wind and rain. Their faces filled with enthusiasm and their voices loud and clear were deeply moving, echoing back to everyone loudly singing "The Rhythm of the Buddhist Youth" on an earlier occasion in Ilan. It is in this way that Buddhism is handed down from generation to generation. In the future, it will continue on unbroken and forever, oriented toward "Buddhism depends upon me."

These words of mine today have no other purpose, for I only hope that my teachers and friends in Buddhist circles who have resolved to join the Buddhist order and become monastics will do so for the sake of Buddhism, and not come to "sponge off" Buddhism. I look forward to everyone accepting Humanistic Buddhism and practicing Humanistic Buddhism, to become bodhisattvas of the human world. Commit [yourself] to letting "Buddhism depend upon [you]," and do not become a monastic who "sponges off" Buddhism. That then would fulfill my wish.

The Venerable Master attending the Marvelous Malaysia Music Concert at the Shah Alam Stadium in Malaysia, in celebration of his fifty years of Dharma propagation. There were 80,000 people in attendance.

November 24, 2012

I Am Not a Monk "Sponging Off" Buddhism

(Part II)

It is enough for most monks to only have the ability to chant and teach the Dharma, and of course I too can chant sutras and teach the Dharma. But only being this kind of monk was not something I was willing to do. I wanted to become a monk who was able to engage in propagating the Dharma in a multifaceted way: There is nothing I would not do, as long as I am capable of doing it and as long as it is related to Buddhism.

On January 23, 2016, *The Merit Times* published the article, "I Am Not a Monk 'Sponging Off' Buddhism." After doing so, the response over the past few days has been warm and enthusiastic. Some people said that they wanted to cry after reading it; some people said that they wanted to learn more; and some people said that they felt very happy and at ease after reading it. The point here is that there were people who delighted in reading this sort of article.

This elicited thoughts in my mind about this topic. There are many other issues in this regard that are worthwhile pointing out to everyone. So now I am going to say something more about "I Am Not a Monk 'Sponging Off' Buddhism."

In saying that I am not a monk "sponging off" Buddhism, I am not bragging about myself. I am ninety years old [2016] this year and have already become a disabled old man, advanced in age. What more is there for me to seek from the human world? I have my faults, though everyone may not acknowledge them; and I am confident about the strong points I do have, so by writing them out everyone can examine them.

Winning Glory for Buddhism, Pressing Ahead with Localization

There are a lot of charitable people in this world. Of the readers sixty years ago, many of them criticized me, and there were many who praised me as well—what is called "as much censure as praise." For example, when I wrote *The Biography of Sakyamuni Buddha*, there was one venerable who criticized it by saying, "A certain Hsing Yun has depicted the Buddha as a person, which actually goes too far in blaspheming against the

Buddha. He has committed an act of showing no respect to such an exalted figure, so the Buddhist Federation should hold a meeting to investigate him!" When I heard, I paid no attention to it.

When I began building Fo Guang Shan, there was a shipping magnate Shen Chie-chen who lived in New York, in the United States. When he learned that I wanted to establish a monastery fifty years ago, he was ready to offer me a donation of fifty million [Taiwan] dollars to cover the building costs. At that time, I figured that building Fo Guang Shan would not require fifty million [Taiwan] dollars. Moreover, were such a great donor to help me in building Fo Guang Shan, then everyone would say that Kaohsiung's Fo Guang Shan was donated at the behest of the lay Buddhist Shen Chie-chen in the United States. Consequently, I politely declined the kind offer of the fifty million. I would rather accept the financial aid of money in the tens or twenties that ordinary people in Taiwan had given me. Then they could share the glory of supporting the temple's establishment.

Being Self-Aware of Shortcomings, Redoubling Efforts in Striving for Progress

Now I say that I myself did not want to become a monk who "sponges off" Buddhism, but strictly speaking, even my qualifications for becoming a monk are not entirely complete. Within the Buddhist monastic tradition, one must possess the ability to chant, so how could someone like me whose voice is unable to carry a tune find a place to settle down and pursue my calling within the Buddhist monastic tradition? Besides my faith in Buddhism, in no way did I possess the basic requirements for becoming a monk.

The Venerable Master commencing the "Love and Peace" prayers for world peace at the Buddha Museum. Twelve religious leaders officiated the event together, which was attended by over 30,000 people.

Photo by Venerable Hui Yan, Aug. 23, 2011

I knew I was tone deaf, for there was one time when Yang Yung-p'u, a music teacher at Ilan High School, came for a visit. I had entrusted him with the task of composing music for the song lyrics I had written, so I went on to explain to him the meaning of the many phrases in the song. After listening to my explanation, he suddenly said to me, "Most people speak using the four tones of 'even, rising, falling, and entering'; how come you are lacking the 'entering tone' when you speak?" I was quite surprised when I heard this; for all along having not excelled in the five-note scale of *do, re, mi, so, la*; I was now incomplete in even the four tones of speaking. How come I only had three tones? Would this mean that I would not even be able to talk later on?

This brings to mind an opportunity I had in recent years to return to my hometown of Yangzhou, in which I was honored by the elders and relations of Yangzhou who all said, "Your Yangzhou accent has not changed a bit." As it happens, the Yangzhou dialect only has three tones as well. A monk unable to chant in tune would have no redeeming quality whatsoever even if he attempted to become a monk who "sponges off" Buddhism.

I am fortunate in knowing my own shortcomings and frustrations, so I simply must do all I can in striving for the best and redoubling my efforts: I supplement my own strengths by using other methods. In becoming a monk who does not "sponge off" Buddhism, I want to ensure that everyone is able to accept me, recognizing that "Buddhism depends upon me."

Cultivating Cultural Education, Doing Good with Compassion

Since I understood my own failings, I did my best to improve myself. Consequently, when I saw that few people cultivated the cultural aspects of Buddhism, I became determined to become a cultural monk. I also noticed that few people went on to promote Buddhist education, so I thought I could increase my effort in this area and become an educational monk. As for charity work, even though Buddhism has already done a lot in this area, I also wanted to encourage myself to not withdraw and be absent from this work, so I was also determined to become a monk doing good with compassion.

I am constantly aware of how I am only a Buddhist devotee, the same as ordinary *upasakas* and *upasikas*;[1] not only did I want to become a monk, but I wanted to become a "monastic devotee," joyously giving and contributing various kinds of merits for Buddhism.

It is enough for most monks to only have the ability to chant and teach the Dharma, and of course I too can chant sutras and teach the Dharma. But only being this kind of monk was not something I was willing to do. I wanted to become a monk who was able to engage in propagating the Dharma in a multifaceted way: There is nothing I would not do, as long as I am capable of doing it and as long as it is related to Buddhism. In the area of education, during the several decades of my career as a monk, I have set up five universities and a dozen or more Buddhist colleges in addition to the middle schools, elementary schools, and kindergartens; so I certainly should be called an "educational monk," but I have never heard anyone ever say that I am an "educational monk."

---

1 In Sanskrit, male and female members of the Buddhist laity, respectively.

Venerable Master with the five university presidents of the Fo Guang Shan International University Consortium. *From the left*: Lin Tsong-ming , President of Nanhua University; Stephen Morgan, President of University of the West in the USA; the Venerable Master; Helen Correa, President of Guang Ming College in the Philippines; Yung Chaur-shin, Chief of Fo Guang Shan University Consortium; and Bill Lovegrove, President of Nan Tien Institute in Australia.

October 2, 2016

In the area of culture, my disciples inform me that I have written articles totaling more than thirty million words and published more than two hundred and seventy books. I have also run many journals, magazines, art workshops, and exhibitions, but no one has ever called me a "cultural monk." I care about philanthropic work and make sure I do not lag behind others in this, and I have also immersed myself in providing disaster relief the same as my devotees. I have emulated Avalokitesvara[2] Bodhisattva's relieving of suffering and distress, yet no one has ever said that I am a "philanthropic monk."

2 In Sanskrit, "Observing the Sounds of the World"; translated into Chinese as 觀世音 (guanshiyin) or "Guanyin"; he is a representation of great compassion and resides in the Western Pure Land.

However, there is one name I do dislike hearing, the one people actually speak about in many cases, and that is "political monk."

Caring about Society, Voicing the Aspirations of the People

In talking about this term, "political monk," I am aware of how unqualified I am to do so. Moreover, I was also unwilling to be known as a political monk because I am not interested in politics. But the more I was unwilling to do so, the more some people in society began talking about it; added to that, it was circulated by the media, so the name of "political monk" was constantly being spread all around. It seemed that only this name suited me in their estimation. I undertook my own self-examination: Why did I suddenly change from a "monk who does not 'sponge off' Buddhism" into a "political monk"?

Later on, I learned the reason: Since I cared about society, sometimes in my articles I would inevitably give some voice to the aspirations of society and its people about the hardships being faced. In addition, some political figures would often come and visit me: Mr. Chiang Ching-kuo alone was received by me on four occasions, and he also once invited me to attend a conference and partake of a light meal at the Presidential Office. Later on, his successor President Lee Teng-hui came on many occasions to Fo Guang Shan, where he received a grand reception. President Chen Shui-bian once stayed overnight at Fo Guang Shan, and he said he was willing as well to sweep the courtyard in front of the Great Buddha Hall for us. He even invited me to attend the monthly meeting at the Presidential Office and give a talk about Buddhism to the senior officials at the top of the governmental departments.

Since Mr. Chiang Ching-kuo had visited Fo Guang Shan, those that served in a succession of offices, such as the commanders of the armed forces, the heads of the Five Yuan, and the senior officials of various departments, also felt that they could come to the monastery for a visit whenever they had some free time. Within the guidelines for members of the Buddha's Light International Association (BLIA),[3] there is one particular item for association members: "Greeting people when they come and bidding farewell when they go." These guests who have traveled far should be received by me after all. Once reporters knew, they would announce in the newspapers how these many political figures had come to Fo Guang Shan to pay a visit, and they would further say how I personally received them. It was probably in this way that I indeed became a "political monk."

I experienced the period of the White Terror,[4] and I also experienced the heavy fire and hail of bullets during the War of Resistance Against Japan [1937–1945]; and it was during the Chinese Civil War period [1945–1949] that I also suffered much in the way of gross injustices. I was even abducted and hauled off to court, so I had the experience of facing execution by firing squad. What else is there for me to fear? During those times when my life was in great peril, I was not frightened at all. As for whatever honor or disgrace, praise or blame may come, what worries would I still have about them? There is no need to discuss any of these, but what I found unavoidable was how society at large would still insist that politics was placed above my faith and stubbornly assert that I was a

3 A lay Buddhist organization founded by Venerable Master Hsing Yun as a way for lay people to become involved in propagating Humanistic Buddhism. The BLIA serves social, religious, and charitable functions around the world.

4 February 27, 1947–July 15, 1987; the suppression of political dissidents in Taiwan.

"political monk." I cannot help sighing in regret, for this too is really unfair!

As a matter of fact, I do not accept this at all, because my engagement in the work of propagating the Dharma is far more abundant and more important when compared to receiving those political VIPs. So why can't I become some other "monk not 'sponging off' Buddhism," instead of being called a "political monk" so insistently? Later on, the film director Mr. Liu Wei-bin said to me, "Being a political monk is not that bad! There are those who try to become political monks but fail to do so. Calling you a political monk indicates that you are quite resourceful and powerful!" As soon as I heard this, I thought to myself, "Is the meaning of 'political monk' really like this?" Then I thought, "Oh well, never mind; I am not going to worry about whether it is good or bad. Then again, what has this to do with me? If it's good, it is still not mine, and if it's bad, then it has nothing to do with me. So I am not going to worry about it!"

Politically Active but Not Politically Involved Is the Principle for Action

Thinking of the past, after victory in the Sino-Japanese War [1937–1945], Venerable Master Taixu put forth the declaration of "being politically active but not politically involved," which is a proposition I can cherish with extraordinary admiration. I think Buddhism can indeed care about the welfare of society, the welfare of the nation, and the welfare of people (being politically active), but it is not necessary to go on and hold an official position in government (administering the affairs of state). Later on, Mr. Chiang Kai-shek [1887–1975] once invited

Fo Guang Shan's temple registration application took over ten years to be approved. Each year several million people have visited the temple, ever since it opened more than 50 years ago. No admission fee has ever been collected. Pictured are the Buddhas in the Main Shrine at Fo Guang Shan.

Photo provided by Commonwealth Publishing

Venerable Master Taixu to serve as a member of the National Assembly as well, and Venerable Master Taixu raised this demand: "Please permit Buddhism to have a quota of twenty National Assembly members."

At the time, Mr. Ch'en Li-fu was serving in the Organization Department of the Nationalist Party [Kuomintang/KMT], and he did not approve of Venerable Master Taixu's idea. He believed that if Buddhism wanted a quota of twenty National Assembly members, then what about other religions? Could it be that all the National Assembly representatives were to become representatives of religion? Venerable Master Taixu said that in other religions such as Protestantism and Catholicism, they are religious adherents, but they all have other occupations, so even if they become members of the National Assembly, that is entirely the result of the qualifications for being a representative produced by their other occupations. But Buddhist monks have no other occupation, so they cannot become representatives via some other occupational organizations, and therefore they have this special kind of situation. However, this did not meet with Mr. Ch'en Li-fu's agreement at that time, and Venerable Master Taixu did not do anything more in advancing his case, so he did not become a member of the National Assembly either.

I identify with "being politically active but not politically involved," as this is the best principle for taking action between Buddhism and politics. I remember how more than fifty years ago when Fo Guang Shan had not yet been established, Mr. Chi Lü-k'e of the Kaohsiung City Chapter of the KMT once came to Shoushan Temple and asked me, "Are you willing to become a legislator?" If I had followed Venerable Master Taixu's way of thinking at that time, then I could have become a legislator; all that was needed was for me to nod my head and I would have had the KMT's nomination. So I should have already had the qualifications for a legislator fifty years ago.

That was the time when Taiwan had just started implementing elections, yet the common practices for elections had already become extraordinarily bad. I said to Mr. Chi, "Chairman Chi, this is absolutely impossible. If I were to put myself forward in an election for legislator, it wouldn't matter to me if people were to criticize and malign my ancestors. But if I were to bring dishonor to the founder of my faith, Sakyamuni Buddha, such that people would say this is what Buddhism is like, and that is what monks are like, then that would be something I could not bear. Please select some other superb individual for this position of legislator!"

In Taiwan, except for my having given a speech at the Presidential Office and served as lecturer for the Taiwan Provincial Government's Provincial Training Corps, I have never been to any other governmental organization, nor have I requested the government do anything for me. It even reached the point after Fo Guang Shan was built, that I was quite unable to successfully register the temple within the ten-year time period. Ultimately, I still had to rely upon the assistance of Mr. Ch'en P'o-fen, a friend from Ilan, in order to obtain the registration. At the time, he was Caucus Secretary-General for the Taiwan Provincial Consultative Council; upon learning of this matter, he made a call to the provincial government to plead my case, and only then did the Kaohsiung County Government grant my temple its registration. Altogether from beginning to end, I spent ten years for this one registration certificate.

I think it was fortunate that what I had built was a temple, so even waiting for ten years was no worry. But if I had opened a store and had to wait a decade before I could receive its registration certificate, how then would I have managed to stay in business?

Of course, there were also reasons why applying for the temple registration was so difficult. Some politicians are temperamental and biased, and for my part I basically take no notice of that; in any case, I am only a monk propagating the Dharma. Politicians have their terms of office, but there is no term of office for being a monk, so I could wait it out.

However, after having to wait ten years, the matter could not be put off any longer. This was because the Ministry of

Interior had granted me permission to conduct the Triple Platform Full Ordination Ceremony,[5] so if I did not even have the temple registration, how then was I to conduct the ordination? Fortunately, Mr. Ch'en P'o-fen lent a helping hand. It could be said that this was the first time I received assistance provided by a political figure. This is why I remember with extraordinary gratitude both Mr. Ch'en P'o-fen, as well as Mr. Kuo Szu-fen, who had served as the Director of the Taiwan Information Office and permitted me to register as a magazine publisher. They both played a crucially important role in connection with my life's work of propagating the Dharma.

With my propagating of the Dharma, I founded Fo Guang Shan, and the government did not give me a single brick or roof tile, though they did perhaps repair a road for me or provide a little subsidy. I did my utmost to purify society for the nation's sake, but in no way did I demand that the government do anything for me. In my way of thinking, are we not always saying "for the nation and for the people"? So why are we looking to the government for financial assistance all the time? We do not want the government to come and provide financial assistance. One could say that this too is something very amazing.

So many people come to Fo Guang Shan for visits and on tours, but we have not taken in any admission fees. As a rule, public buildings may apply to the government to do certain things, but we have not. On the contrary, the local village offices have constantly looked to us to do certain things for decades now; they even demand payment from us for taking away the garbage. So does saying that I am a political monk make any sense?

---

5 An ordination ritual unique to China that includes three sets of precepts: those of novice monastics, fully ordained monastics, and the bodhisattva precepts for monastics.

Paying Attention to Form: Dignified in Movement and Comportment

Over the course of my life, the ten years of monastic education trained me in having a strong Buddhist faith, and besides this, worldly industrial and commercial enterprise, political office, wealth and honor, love on a personal level, and so on held nothing I would wish for. Therefore, after I left the monastery, I would quite naturally pay close attention to my conduct and bearing. I was always encouraging myself: When eating, one must eat like a monk, and when walking, one must also walk like a monk.

In the past, once or twice every month, I would go from Ilan to Taipei to edit the magazine. Walking from the north entrance (of Leiyin Temple) to the train station, I would proceed along a mountain road. Every time I did so, there would be many people in shops on either side of the road standing in the doorways to watch. They would wave their hands and point as they spoke: "This young monk from mainland China does not walk the same way as other people do!" This is because I was telling myself all the time that I must walk well and let them see how a monastic behaves. That's right, I am a monk; so when walking I go straight ahead. I must fulfill the comportments that Buddhism describes as "standing like a pine, walking like the wind" so as to also walk into a bright future for Buddhism.

I paid close attention to presenting the image of a monk, even to the point of being resolute in my aspiration to not become a monk who "sponges off" Buddhism. Later on, not only did society apply the label of "political monk" to me, but they also said I was a "business monk" who could manage a

The Venerable Master advocates: "I am within the assembly, and within the assembly there I am" throughout his entire life. Here, he leads by example, carrying kneeling benches at Motosu Temple, a Fo Guang Shan branch temple in Japan.

Photo provided by Motosu Temple

business much better than Mr. Wang Yung-ching [1917–2008]. For many years now there have been people who always say that the most business-minded in Taiwan's management work is a certain Hsing Yun.

Frankly speaking, the reality is pitiful. I have always prided myself on being a "humble monk," and throughout my life I have never been in contact with money. Even though I have carried out many Buddhist projects, in all cases it was other people who handled their management, while I was merely a member of the team. If there were some author's compensation, some royalties, or even, as some people remark, the proceeds from the *One-Stroke Calligraphy* now, none of these has been handled by me, nor has any passed through my hands either.

In the past, I have also made donations in support of Buddhism just like the devotees, and I have donated the money from such income in its entirety to the building of Fo Guang Shan. It was not until after the age of eighty that I was able to take these royalties and author's compensation and deposit these many sums into the Bank of Taiwan in order to establish the "Hsing Yun Public Education Trust Fund." Putting the two words "Hsing Yun" at the beginning of the trust fund's name was also done to please the host of devotees. Everyone felt that doing so would make for more public trust. From then on, I did indeed become a "humble monk," "without a penny in the purse, and without a cent to one's name" as it were. One could say that I am now worthy of that name.

Not Doing What Is Non-Buddhist, Broadly Performing the Service of Propagating the Dharma

You can say that I am "a monk who does not 'sponge off' Buddhism," and you can call me a "humble monk," for in both cases I am content and willing to be so to my delight. However, today I am making a solemn, public announcement to those who care about and are connected to me: I kindly request that from now on you do not call me a "business monk" or a "political monk." None of these labels correlate with the facts. I am simply one of Buddhism's monks, common and ordinary, one who loves Buddhism.

Maybe you will say that I am a member of the KMT; that's perfectly all right. But in no way was I interested in becoming a party member at that time; rather, I would have been unable

Fo Guang Shan holding the International Triple Platform Full Ordination Ceremony. Photo by Pi Yun Lai, November 28, 2011

to promote the Buddhist teachings if I did not become one! This was some guidance given to me by the lay Buddhist Li Tzu-k'uan, senior statesman and founding member of the KMT. He said, "Venerable, your propagating of the Dharma will not be easy until you join the KMT!" That was how I conditionally became a member of the KMT in order to promote Buddhist teachings. In fact, even though I have been a party member of more than seventy years' standing, I have not made any contribution to it.

Speaking of "commercialization," throughout my own life and including all of my disciples at Fo Guang Shan, there is one fundamental principle for doing things, and that is "not doing what is non-Buddhist." As for everything related to Buddhism in any way—whether it be a losing proposition, a devotion, a sacrifice, or a service—as long as it promotes the Buddhist

teachings, then these should all be done. But to say that we are running a business is something we will not do under any circumstances.

For example, during the transmission of the Triple Platform Full Ordination Ceremony at Fo Guang Shan, more than a thousand people were in attendance for every one of the many occasions when the Model Ordination Ceremony was held; more than a thousand people were also in attendance every time there was the transmission of the five precepts[6] and the bodhisattva precepts, as well as the conducting of the Triple Platform Full Ordination Ceremony held at Buddhist centers here and abroad, including Hsi Lai Temple and Nan Tien Temple, as well as at Bodhgaya where the Buddha attained enlightenment. Then there are the many sessions of the Youth Summer Camp and Chan Seminar that have been conducted on so many occasions. No fees have been charged for any these

6 These are the fundamental principles of conduct for monastics and laity: refrain from killing, stealing, sexual misconduct, lying, and consuming alcohol and intoxicants.

activities. Besides supplying room and board, assistance is further given to impoverished young people by covering transportation costs and providing scholarships as an encouragement for them.

All the homes for the aged, preschools, mobile clinics, and so on that we operate do not charge fees either. As for the Buddhist colleges, not only do we not charge fees, we even provide students with allowances to cover their various daily needs. So how can you say we are running a business? I now would like to pose some questions to the exemplary members of society: Have I ever made any money off you? Have I ever made any deals with you? Or have I ever managed any business in cooperation with you?

Why do you concern yourself with a humble monk's Fo Guang Shan, which is operating so many institutions? These include five universities, three middle schools, elementary schools, community colleges, Chinese schools, and reading groups; as well as many kindergartens, homes for the aged, preschools, newspapers, television stations, mobile library trucks, and Buddha Museum; and there are more than a thousand monastic disciples, and so on. Where would the money for their board and daily needs come from?

Turning Nothing into Something: Obtaining Supporting Conditions from All Directions

That there can be such doubts is not bad. At Fo Guang Shan there is a separate organization structure for temple management; examples include the Executive Office, as well as the individual departments for administering the work of education, charity, culture, and Buddhist groups. These all have their methods for dealing with the devotees, and they all obtain the support and assistance of the devotees. For me, the highest principles for policy making are to "treat not having as having" and "treat emptiness as joy," because this character inspires even more people who share good affinity with these organizations. One could say that Fo Guang Shan's development is dependent upon such ideas of a "humble monk," a "monk who does not 'sponge off' Buddhism," for it is such means that have enabled the work of Buddhism's emergence into society to be accomplished. As for initiating what is called "Humanistic Buddhism," I have in fact only devoted some service to human society and nothing more.

I was happy to be present when victory was declared in the Sino-Japanese War when I was nineteen years old. The many schools and institutions relocated to the rear area under KMT control were all returning to the areas previously occupied by the Japanese, "returning to peacetime conditions." That is, the universities in each place, the institutions in each place, and so on were resuming normal operations. At that time, there were many professors living temporarily at Mount Qixia awaiting official orders from the government to reactivate their school there. A few of these professors had some contact with me, and they indicated that I could go and study at their college (probably something equivalent to a normal or teaching university today). I spoke with them and said that I did not even have the qualifications for graduation from an elementary school, so how could I be qualified to study at a college? They said it did not matter: "Our teaching team has chosen you, so you can study at the college."

When I heard these words, I too became extraordinarily delighted, I felt like this was really a gift from heaven; lucky me, I would actually be going to college. So it was in such high spirits that I went looking for my teacher and reported to him about my going to study at the college. My teacher was a straightforward person; he rebuked loudly, "Idiot, what do you mean studying at some college!"

After he had spoken, it suddenly seemed to me that I was in sympathy with him: "Right, now that I have become a monk, why would I go and study at a college?" I joined my palms together toward my teacher, and, while walking back to the monastic dormitory, I kept thinking that what my teacher had said was quite right. I muttered to myself, "Idiot, why would I go and study at a college!"

Thinking about it now, what my teacher said is really pretty good. If I had gone and studied at the college, I would have had a diploma, and with the educational qualifications for a high school, my original poor but honest life of a Buddhist would have suddenly and in one stroke gained such privileged treatment in society, including a salary, money, and various social temptations. Would I have been able to continue as a good monk?

Or it could be said that had I been just a little bit smarter and cleverer, I could indeed have become a school principal, then an education commissioner, and then head of the education department. Would I still be a monk now? Have we not seen as well how so many officials are continuously going from one position to another just like a merry-go-round? How would that be like the life I have led as a monk? It is for this reason that I am truly grateful to my admirable teacher, for he after all had the foresight to give me a lesson on how to be an upright monk: not getting myself mixed up with the mundaneness of society by simply putting on a "monkish appearance" (the

At age twenty-one, Venerable Master became the principal of Baita Elementary School.

appearance of a monk), instead of being a real monk. Therefore, my being able to become a monk who does not "sponge off" Buddhism is something, the truth be told, that my teacher fostered.

In order to not become a monk who "sponges off" Buddhism, I told myself that I had to be self-reliant. In speaking about this, people in general are unable to understand that over the course of my life and except for the term in which I served as principal of the Baita Public Elementary School for which I received some wages, I have never had any other salary. That year and a half of wages was also calculated in terms of a quantity of rice, so every month I would receive the price for three piculs of rice. However, I never inquired into it, for I left it completely up to my brother monk, Venerable Jin Guan, to manage. Later on, due to the calamity of being imprisoned, my brother monk told me that my life was spared from the firing squad precisely in exchange for that one and half years of rice I earned. I am grateful to my Dharma brother for coming to my rescue and rejoice in the decisions I myself had made earlier.

Now I can say that I have never received any salary in my entire life, and I have not had an ordinary, going-to-work type job for which one receives some income every month. This has gone on to the point where I have never taken a vacation in my entire life. Everybody today takes some sort of two-day break during the week, and additionally there are many vacations during the holidays, but whenever holidays come around, we become on the contrary even busier. It could be said that throughout my entire life, not only have there been no vacations, but I work no less than twelve hours every day; and I have never received any overtime pay either, nor have I ever possessed a desk. Sometimes it is a dinner table, or a side table, or some long strip of a board, or even my thighs; these became my desk upon which I wrote and edited my articles.

Income from the Written Word as an Offering to All Sentient Beings

During several decades or so of my residence in Ilan, the Buddhist Chanting Association would give me three hundred [Taiwan] dollars every month, though sometimes this did happen and sometimes it did not, but that did not bother me. At the beginning of Fo Guang Shan's founding, any stipend or support through donations was of course out of the question, so it seems to me that it was not until I was serving my third term as abbot that the treasury keeper (accountant) gave me one thousand [Taiwan] dollars every month. After I stepped down from that position, and as I no longer hold any post at Fo Guang Shan now, that stipend of one thousand [Taiwan] dollars is gone too. However, throughout my life I have not depended at all upon such economic resources to maintain myself. I have my own author's compensation and my own royalties, and in addition, I now have the proceeds from the *One-Stroke Calligraphy*, so I am able to remain self-sufficient.

At the Founder's Hall where I live, I have instructed the relevant persons in charge that they cannot draw upon the temple money, for we can support ourselves. Even when it comes to the cost of gas for the car and the toll fees for driving south to north and back again, these expenses are our own responsibility, and we will not draw upon temple funds. The people who have meals here are also numerous, and occasionally there are times when there is not enough rice; then we can make an application to the temple for some, but we try as much as possible to not draw upon temple resources, since those are the supplies for everyone to use in cultivating enlightenment.

Within the fifty years since the founding of Fo Guang Shan, all of the tables and chairs as well as the cushions for worshipping the Buddha used in the temple have been offered to the temple by me personally through reliance upon some income from my writings. I myself am not a consumer in society, and I am not a squanderer of the temple's assets, for I want to increase the income for Buddhism. I do not want to become a monk who "sponges off" Buddhism, so much so that I even want to make offerings to the vast numbers of sentient beings.

There are still some other things I want to say, but limited as I am by this article's length, I will not go into further details here. So please wait for the next article in this series, part three of "I am Not a Monk 'Sponging Off' Buddhism."

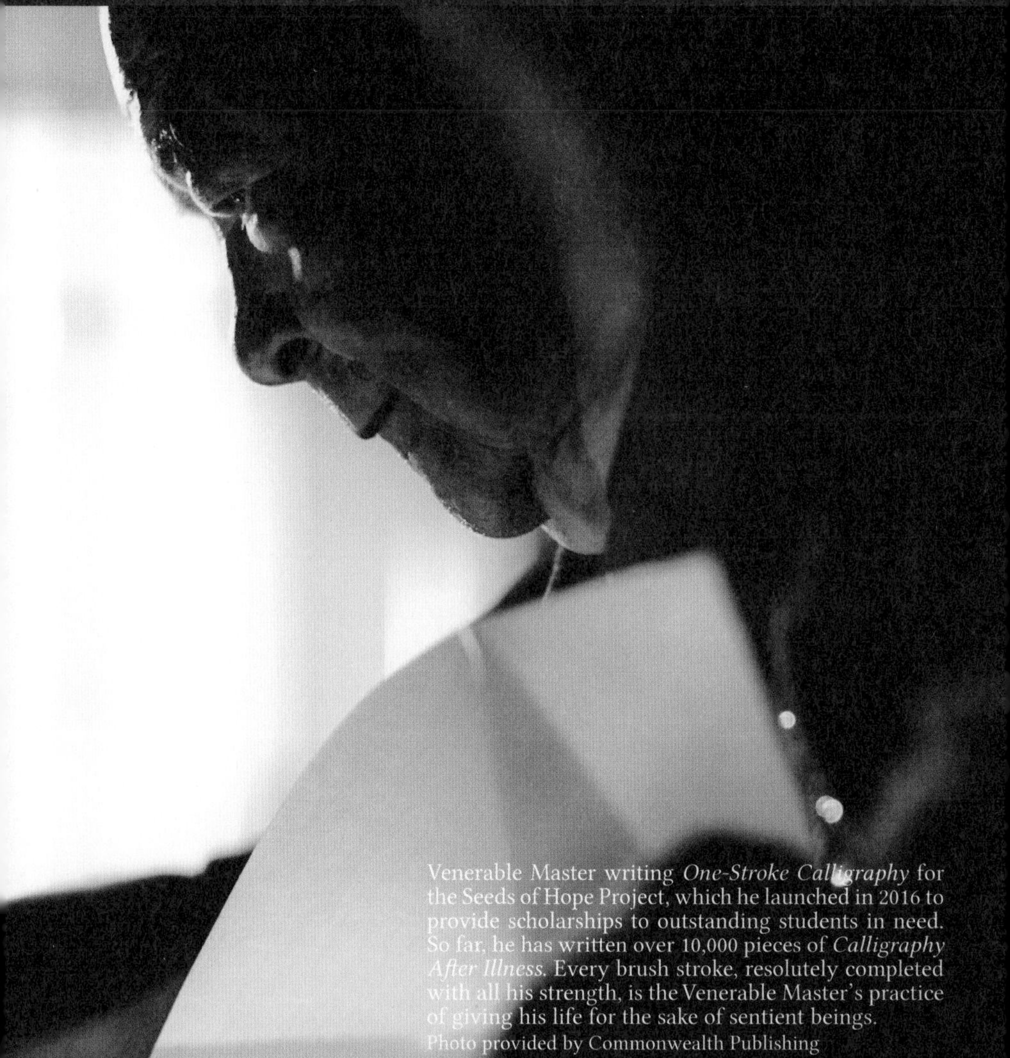

Venerable Master writing *One-Stroke Calligraphy* for the Seeds of Hope Project, which he launched in 2016 to provide scholarships to outstanding students in need. So far, he has written over 10,000 pieces of *Calligraphy After Illness.* Every brush stroke, resolutely completed with all his strength, is the Venerable Master's practice of giving his life for the sake of sentient beings.
Photo provided by Commonwealth Publishing

I Am Not a Monk "Sponging Off" Buddhism (Part III)

It is my hope that our Buddhist monks will all become monks who give support in all directions and not become monks who live off all directions. Whoever it may be, the monastic followers or the lay disciples, although we have not yet attained enlightenment, we can still broadly make affinities with others first, so as to become aspiring bodhisattvas who will ensure that "Buddhism depends upon [us]," and not have ourselves become dependent upon Buddhism.

I wrote the article "I Am Not a Monk 'Sponging Off' Buddhism" without any intentions. My only consideration at the outset was that the faith of our monastics ought to be purified: aspiration must be genuine, and patience must be strengthened. Particularly in their life of spiritual practice, monastics must have a sense of "for Buddhism," so as to develop the habit of showing care toward the devotees. They must be "strict with themselves, but lenient toward others"; they must do the work of propagating the Dharma for the benefit of sentient beings, with all their might; they must treat others in a wholesome way; and they must do good naturally and happily, and so on. In this way, they can be somewhat up to par as disciples of the Buddha.

Hence, I could not have imagined that its publication in *The Merit Times* for January 23rd and 24th would meet with such an enthusiastic response from all circles, and there would be people abroad in regions such as England and America who were reading this article. Examples include Zhang Shaowei who is studying for a PhD degree at Oxford University and Venerable Miao Xiang of London, both of whom sent back their responses; some of the staff at Dajue Temple in mainland China even had a more enthusiastic response. Furthermore, Ms. Lydia Chao, who resides in Houston and is the second daughter of Mr. Koo Chen-fu [1917–2005], also offered her strong approval, and I was so touched that I went on to write another article on "I Am Not a Monk 'Sponging Off' Buddhism."

After this article was published on January 30th and 31st, the response was even more enthusiastic. I was momentarily stirred to action, so I simply extended the article with a third installment! This is why I am talking once more about how "I Am Not a Monk 'Sponging Off' Buddhism."

I am not parading myself for being such an outstanding monk, for my own shortcomings are also numerous. What makes me different from other people regarding my own shortcomings is just that I am willing to acknowledge my own mistakes and am willing to correct them. If there are some aspects of the Buddhist work I do that are recommendable, then that is also quite normal, because that is the duty for those of us who are monks.

The reason why I have said so much here is that I only want Fo Guang Shan's disciples to know how, in their life of spiritual practice—of having few desires and being content—they must make earnest efforts "for Buddhism," must make the aspiration for enlightenment, and must propagate the Dharma for the benefit of sentient beings. Later on, I learned that Buddhism associated leaders and monastics in mainland China were able to read this article. For me, I really feel overwhelmed by this unexpected favor, which gives me the feeling that there is hope for Buddhism, that it has a future. This is why I have explained the reasons for this third installment above.

Being Faithful in Promises: Publishing the Magazine on Time

We know that in this human world, the most important thing is being able to eat; therefore, "sponging off Buddhism" is also for the sake of living and for the sake of eating. Although I have experienced times teetering on the verge of starvation, as for my not becoming a monk who "sponges off" Buddhism, it remains an article of faith over which I have never wavered.

Let me explain through an example: I have been a diabetes sufferer for fifty years already, and in my mind, this condition

Group picture at the six year anniversary of *Human Life* magazine with the publisher, Senior Monastic Dong Chu (*front row, fourth from the left*); the president, Venerable Nan Ting (*fifth from the left*); the Venerable Master, editor in chief; and colleagues. *Front row, from the left*: Li Yongmo, Zhu Jingzhou, Li Zikuan, Venerable Dong Chu, the Senior Monastic Nan Ting, the Venerable Master, and Huang-Wang Yuan-Tong. *Back row*: Zhou Xuande (*second from the left*), Venerable Miao Ran (*third from the left*) and Householder Sun-Chang Ching-yang (*first from the right*).
November, 1954

was the product of the several occasions when I experienced extreme hunger, leading to the impairment of insulin. Since no one in my family has the genes for diabetes, it should not be something that I inherited. I once talked about this idea with a doctor, but the doctor shook his head and was not too willing to accept my opinion.

I remember one fairly serious experience of hunger, which occurred when I was editing the inaugural edition of *Human Life* magazine in the fortieth year of the Republic (1951). Because of the work I was doing on editing the magazine at the time, I was lodging at Shandao Temple in Taipei. One day early in the morning after I had guiltily eaten one of their breakfasts,

I set out on foot to do proofreading at the printing house in [Taipei's] Wanhua District because I wanted to save the one [Taiwan] dollar fee for taking the public bus.

By the noon hour, the manager at the printing house said to me, "Venerable Hsing Yun, have lunch." But I thought to myself: Where was I going to go for lunch? I bore with it for a while and forgot about lunch, and I continued with the proofreading. By evening, I missed another meal the same way, and after dinner time had passed, the workers went into overtime especially for me, and bound one hundred fifty copies of *Human Life* magazine for me first. This was because I had already promised the publisher, the Senior Monastic Dong Chu, that I would be handing these over to him on time.

Into a steady fall of drizzling rain, I doggedly walked from Dali Street in Jiangzicui to Wanhua's train station. I took the train to Beitou, and then changed trains at Laobeitou for the train to Xinbeitou. The time needed to do this was not too long, it was probably sometime after 9:00 pm. From the window, I could see a light drizzle coming down, and fearing that the magazines would get wet from the rain, I took off my outer gown and wrapped these one hundred fifty copies of *Human Life* magazine up in it, and then carried the package on my shoulder. Under the dim lights of the street lamps, I walked from Xinbeitou's train station to Fa Cang Temple. I then climbed its four hundred steps, so by the time I reached the temple it should have been sometime after 10:00 pm.

Afraid of Disturbing Others, Patiently Waiting in Silence

When Venerable Dong Chu saw me bringing the magazines over, he was extraordinarily delighted. He praised me, saying,

"You are very responsible, something very rare." Average young people are always extraordinarily delighted upon hearing the praise of their seniors.

He further said to me, "There is no need for you to go back to Taipei; you can stay right here." That was my thinking as well. It was nearly 11:00 pm already, and if I were to return to Taipei, I would also find it embarrassing to disturb Shandao Temple in the middle of the night. Given that the senior monastic had told me to stay, I stayed the night.

Venerable Dong Chu then called someone in the temple to find a room for me, allowing me to stay by registering as a visiting monastic. At that time, I did not think of asking about the facilities for washing and the like, for I just wanted a place to sleep. I rose early the next day, but I could not get the door of my room to open. It turned out that they had locked it from the other side. I did not dare call out for someone to let me out either, as I was afraid of disturbing them, so I just took my time and waited there.

It was not until after 9:00 am that they came to open the door and said apologetically, "We are sorry; we forgot you were here, so we forgot to open the door." I did not take offense, for in my mind, this was a Buddhist center for female monastics, and as I was a young *bhiksu*,[1] perhaps everyone was concerned about rules in Buddhism, so I did not take any notice of it.

I went to take my leave from Venerable Dong Chu; he said, "You do not have to. I am having guests over today, and you can help out here by handling some of the reception." I thought that as this was an instruction from a senior monastic, I would agree, so I helped him out with the work of setting up the tables and chairs and preparing the rooms for the visitors.

1 In Sanskrit, "male monastic."

However, inviting guests from Taipei was no easy matter: It was not until we had waited past 1:00 pm that eight or nine guests arrived. He had originally prepared food for two tables, and as it was already 1:00 pm, I thought to myself that the meal simply would now be served. Senior Monastic Dong Chu would keep four or five guests company during the meal, and I would be keeping company with the other four or five people at a separate table during the meal on his behalf.

The Experience of Hunger: Vowing to Widely Open the Universal Gate

As I was thinking in this way, Venerable Don Chu said to me, "You're such a child; how come you're not going to the kitchen to eat?" This is the tone in which a senior monastic speaks, and he was still treating me like a child.

It was only then that I thought to myself, "I have been a principal at an elementary school; I have been a dean of academic affairs; and I have also been the abbot of Hua Zang Temple in Nanjing. I ought not to be a child anymore." But keeping company with visitors and partaking of a meal, I was still too young and not qualified. At the time, I was distracted for a moment, and I thought to myself, I am really hungry. I will go to the kitchen for something to eat.

As I passed the kitchen, I saw how the meal for the guests was just then being prepared. There was a lot of hasty disorder, and I did not know a single person there either. I really felt too embarrassed to go right in and ask for something to eat. Therefore, I went from a small lane outside of the kitchen directly down the hill and returned to Taipei.

In my memory, I felt absolutely famished. This was because I had not eaten lunch yesterday, nor had I had any diner; and I had not had any breakfast today either. So now it was already into the afternoon, and I still had not eaten anything.

In walking down those four hundred stairs, every step felt like I was treading on cotton. It seemed to me that I was walking on air, and I have no idea how I was able to go down the hill; that was the way I returned to Taipei. Perhaps everyone experiences something they cannot imagine for a while, yet I did not have any sense of resentment. I made a firm resolution at that time, for if I could find a way in the future, I would certainly feed everyone. I can become a monk who does not "sponge off" Buddhism, but I cannot fail in feeding the masses. In the future, I will certainly "widely open the Universal Gate," welcoming in the people who want to eat.

Therefore, I later on founded Pu-Men[2] Temple, Pu-Men High School, Pu-Men Kindergarten, *Universal Gate* magazine, *Universal Gate Buddhist Journal*, and so on, precisely in hopes of widely opening the Universal Gate. At my center in Taipei and in the Pilgrim's Lodge at Fo Guang Shan, I always called on the managers to prepare a couple tables' worth more of food every day. This was because at that time, the partaking of a vegetarian meal was relatively difficult, and we always offered it unconditionally: No need to ask for a visitor's name, and they could leave as soon as they finished the meal. We have maintained conditions like this for many years already. This is so much the case that at Fo Guang Shan, if there are members of the monastic community, we even have little red envelopes containing five hundred [Taiwan] dollars that we offer to them for their travel expenses.

2 In Chinese, "Universal Gate."

Camphor Grove Tea House does not have listed prices. Visitors can support Fo Guang Shan by donating as they wish.

Photo by Shi Dehua

"A monk who does not 'sponge off' Buddhism" is still something passive. I should be doing things in a more active way; that is, "making things convenient to others." It can be said that even today in the Buddhist dining hall at Fo Guang Shan, regardless of whether you know anyone or not, you can just go in, sit down, and eat during meal times; and, after you have finished your meal, you can just leave, and no one will ask you about it. Of course, that is not much of a reception, it is only some small sense of offering, which ought not to disappoint the Buddhas and bodhisattvas, as well as all the good people and guests. This is also a small measure of our vow.

Today there is a place with the most sublime scenery at the Buddha Museum called the "Camphor Grove Tea House," offering a bowl of rice or a bowl of noodles to everyone. Every day roughly several hundred people go in to have their meal. I do not allow any prices to be listed or any fees to be collected, and over the past five to six years it has indeed become a place that brings great delight to everybody!

Actions Are Implemented: Speeches at Institutions of Higher Learning for Propagating the Teachings

In order to become a monk who does not "sponge off" Buddhism, I cannot simply talk the talk and do nothing more; I must express how I am through my actions. Consequently, I must actively busy myself with the work of propagating Buddhism to a greater degree. It is just like early in the fourth decade of the Republic [the 1950s], for at that time I did not yet possess the strength to set up a university, but I did win over the Ministry of Education for registering the Guang Hua Tutoring Center I set up in Ilan. The center provided young people with an environment conducive to study, and people such as Lin Tz'u-long, Lin Ch'ing-chih, Cheng Shih-yen, Huang San-yü, and others had all once attended this tutoring center.

I also went to all the prisons in Taiwan to propagate the Dharma, and I went to every factory to propagate the teachings, but my ideal was the hope of giving a speech at the universities. I had given speeches at several universities across Taiwan already, but in my mind, I simply had to give a speech at National Taiwan University, for only that could be seen as introducing the Dharma to institutions of higher learning.

With the arrangements made by a community organization, my disciples made the preparations for the lecture, and the posters were all put up. I also took a train from Ilan to

Kōgen Mizuno, Vice President of Komazawa University in Japan, was invited by the Venerable Master to the Fo Guang Shan Institute of Chinese Buddhism to lecture on "The Fundamental Differences between Theravada Buddhism and Mahayana Buddhism."
April 6, 1978

Taipei as I hurried to attend the lecture at the university. However, as soon as I got off the train, Cheng Tz'u-wen spoke to me with an expression of dismay: "I am sorry, teacher, the school does not permit monastics to give speeches." I felt very disappointed upon hearing these words. Buddhism is also about education, so why would the university want to discriminate against Buddhism? I did learn later that it was because some public figures in the Buddhist community opposed my entering the campus. They advised the school not to allow me to give the speech, in that a monk may not enter a school.

Be that as it may, I was not discouraged in any way. A few years later, I invited Mr. Kōgen Mizuno [1901–2006] in Japan to come to Taiwan as a visiting scholar. He was an emeritus professor at Tokyo Imperial University and a scholar of global renown. He was also a monk; it is just that it is customary in Japan not to call monastics "monks," but to address them as "professor" instead. In addition, there was Mr. Mou Tsung-san [1909–1995], a famous professor doing research on Tiantai Studies;[3] and Mr. Tang Chun-i [1909–1978], who studied Confucianism;[4] among others. I invited all of them to Taiwan University to teach classes and give lectures.

Success need not be mine: isn't the ability to ensure that other accomplished monks can enter Taiwan University to lecture on the Dharma the same thing? As things turned out, I have already given lectures on many occasions at National Taiwan University, and I have even been invited to give many lectures at the University of Hong Kong, the Chinese University of Hong Kong, and the Hong Kong Polytechnic University; and those in mainland China such as Beijing University, as well as dozens of others, including the universities of Nanjing, Renmin, Fudan, Sun Yat-sen, Shanghai Jiaotong, Shandong, Zhejiang, Tongji, Hunan, and Xiamen, among others. Therefore, this concept of mine, "not sponging off Buddhism," is not merely for appearances; it also has the same meaning for my faith in mental and psychological terms.

An Initial Resolve: Love of the Teachings Makes Contributions to the Buddhist Faith

The thirty-eighth year of the Republic (1949) was the year I first arrived in Taiwan as a young monk, and when I had reached an impasse, Professor Ch'in Chiang-ch'ao of National Chung

3 The Tiantai School is one of eight schools of Chinese Buddhism; it was named after its founder, Zhiyi (智顗538–597 CE), who lived on Mount Tiantai. It is also known as the Lotus Sutra School because it derives many of its teachings from *The Lotus Sutra.*

4 A philosophy and ethical system based on the teachings of the Chinese scholar Confucius (551–479 BCE) focusing on humaneness, righteousness, etiquette, loyalty, and filial piety, along with strict adherence to social roles.

Hsing University once wanted me to participate in the work of editing *Free Youth Magazine*; which they were running. Then there was the director of Radio Taiwan International who wanted me write broadcast scripts. Additionally, there were newspapers that sought me out to become a reporter, and so on, but I politely declined them all without exception because I did not need to depend upon a career in society for my support. I am a monk of the Buddhist faith, so I ought to do my best in fulfilling my role as a monk. Therefore, even as I lived without money or prospects, I still followed my own initial resolve to not become a monk who "sponges off" Buddhism, nor become someone who is supported by society.

Therefore, I stand by my job for Buddhism, and I do so with diligence. Although I have not achieved much in the way of results, I still exert myself while engaging in the ascetic practice of and the care of the Buddhist faith, so as to become a monk who loves the Buddhist faith and who does not sponge off it. This is how I have fixed this identity of mine, which is unshakable.

Owing to my own diligence, I also formed some positive connections when I first arrived in Taiwan. For example, someone wanted to give me a house to live in, which would have allowed me to focus on writing my essays in a western-style house with a garden; and there was also someone who was even willing to bestow upon me a certain building that would serve as my base for propagating the Dharma. What kind of person am I? I dared not accept such considerable donations. I cannot draw assistance in the name of Buddhism and so become unworthy of the donations given in faith. I definitely must depend upon my own diligence in order to propagate the Dharma; therefore, I gracefully declined their kindnesses.

The Venerable Master enjoying simple living with one vegetable dish and one bowl of rice.

Success need not be achieved in a moment of haste. I can let it come slowly. In ten or twenty years, I will surely manifest something for Buddhism. Be it fetching water or carrying firewood, regardless of whether it is physical labor or mental labor, it does not matter; what matters is that I be a monastic who makes a contribution to the Buddhist faith and not become unworthy of my Buddhist training. I was nurtured by ten years of monastic education, so not until I am able to repay the kindness of the Triple Gem and the kindness of sentient beings can I be considered a monk who genuinely does not "sponge off" Buddhism. This is also the position that I have firmly maintained unchanged throughout my entire life.

I have many shortcomings, like a bad temper and a disposition that can be too direct; even craving fame, desire, ignorance, and so on can still be perceived in my intentions through introspection. Then there is jealousy in particular, for I always feel that I cannot lose to others; I do feel ashamed of this sense of competitiveness and an eagerness to win. Thinking about it now, it was truly that youthful period of intemperateness

Cardinal Paul Shan Kuo-hsi, as Chairman of the Board of Trustees of Fu Jen Catholic University, presented an Honorary Doctorate of Law to the Venerable Master. They joined palms respectfully toward each other.

Photo taken at National Dr. Sun Yat-sen Memorial Hall, Dec. 16, 2006

for which I feel ashamed and deep remorse! It is just that no matter what, this determination "not to let Buddhism down" cannot be changed.

There are quite a lot of devotees who have made a connection with me in Taiwan, and with the ceremonies for taking refuge[5] in the Triple Gem conducted both here and abroad, if you add these up, there should be several million devotees. Nevertheless, I have never maintained any special contact with any devotee. I consistently teach my disciples that as monastics, we cannot become too involved in courting worldly relationships so as to better our social standing. We must not consider how certain devotees with a high social position and great prestige are deserving of some special attention on our part.

I understand that with the mind not being fair and equitable, one is unable to become a true follower of Buddhism.

5 In "taking refuge," one seeks guidance from the Triple Gem (Buddha, Dharma, and Sangha) for spiritual cultivation and liberation from suffering; it is the first step of being a Buddhist.

Therefore, up to now, these devotees in their millions have all become my best and closest friends, but there is no special distinction as to who is close and who is distant. This is also a viewpoint with which I am able to console myself, for I feel that one's integrity as a person should be like this.

In order to fully become a monk who learns about giving from the devotees, I myself also modestly perform some good deeds on a routine basis. For example, when Cardinal Paul Shan Kuo-hsi of the Catholic Church was preparing to build Mount Beatitude,[6] although I lacked the power to do so, I still agreed to donate five million [Taiwan] dollars for his project. I did not have the means to pay him that sum all at once, so all I could do was pay in installments over five years in order to fulfill this promise. There was also a Christian pastor who once brought me a letter, indicating that help was needed in rebuilding a church, and I also supported him in the amount of one million [Taiwan] dollars as a small token of my kind regard.

Having the capacity to bestow kindnesses upon others is an indication of my richness. If one only knows about begging for alms from others, a giving that is solicited from people, then that makes for an impoverished person. Therefore, my not being a monk who "sponges off" Buddhism indicates that I am still a "humble monk of abundant riches." Even though I do not possess anything at all in reality and appearance, in terms of willpower and spirit, the whole world is entirely mine.

Once I even aspired to establish a chain of tea houses, in hopes of operating places that could offer simple vegetarian food throughout the world. This too represents my ideal for a simple fare that I would like to encourage. Although the cooking of vegetarian food is a simple skill, in this modern

6 The Mount Beatitude complex is a pastoral service center in Kaohsiung, Taiwan.

age, very few young people have the inclination for this kind of specialty. Therefore, I very much regret that this wish was never able to be realized. Even though I was unable to realize a thousand tea houses, the fact that the Buddhist restaurant, the Camphor Grove Tea House, exists now among the tea houses of Fo Guang Shan still fills me with confidence as to its feasibility, for I feel that one day I may still fulfill my dream.

Supporting Each Other: Working as One to Develop a Religious Organization

One example is the yearly "Bathing the Buddha Festival."[7] The BLIA refits a small truck into a mobile vehicle for bathing the image of the Buddha as part of the celebration. This enables the general public along the avenues and alleyways to all make a connection with the Buddha. Additionally, every year on the eighth day of the twelfth lunar month, there is the *laba* porridge[8] that is distributed by Fo Guang Shan's main monastery, affiliate temples, and each affiliate of the BLIA, so that throughout the world a total of several million bowls are served by which people can make a connection. I am thankful to my disciples who work so hard to realize this dream for the sake of Buddhism and for making a connection to it, in that they do so for the sake of my small wish and for the sake of an utterance of mine. Availing myself of this opportunity, I too want to express my deepest gratitude to my disciples. Like me, all of them want to become monastics who do not "sponge off" Buddhism as well.

7 Also known as Buddha's birthday celebration, the ritual of bathing the Buddha is done to commemorate the birth of Siddhartha Bodhisattva, the future Buddha; it is observed on the eighth day of the fourth month of the lunar calendar.

8 In Chinese, 臘八 (laba) means "12 and 8," referring to the 8th day of the 12th lunar month; it is the day of commemorating the Buddha's enlightenment by eating rice porridge.

The Venerable Master advocates "three parts guidance and seven parts friendship" and humbly considers that it is the disciples who promote the master by assisting him in propagating the Dharma throughout the world. Pictured is the Great Five Hundred, the election launched by the Venerable Master to strengthen the mutual understanding among disciples. *Front row, from the left*: Yung Pen, Yi Lai, Hsiao Pi-hsia Shigu, Ru Chang, Tzu Jung, Tzu Hui, the Venerable Master, Hsin Pei, Hui Chuan, Hui Chao, Hui Chih, Hui Jang, Hui Zhuan, and other venerables.

Photo provided by Venerable Miao Jen

Common precedent always goes that it is the master who promotes the disciple, the senior who raises up the junior, but in the case of my *One-Stroke Calligraphy*, which is not like calligraphy, it was because my disciple, Venerable Ru Chang, consistently encouraged me. Over these past decades or so, my calligraphy has been exhibited in all parts of the world. Beginning with the Malaysian National Art Gallery in 2005, it has been exhibited in more than one hundred locations, including the United Nations Office at Vienna and various universities in the United States; the National Museum of History in Taipei; the National Art Gallery in Beijing, mainland China; European national museums; and so on. Therefore, it is only now that my *One-Stroke Calligraphy* has garnered the admiration of everyone; is this not a case of the disciple promoting the master?

Another good example is Venerable Chueh Pei: she is regularly invited to give speeches, and every time, she refers to the Humanistic Buddhism that I have advocated, to my humanistic nature, to my not becoming a monk who "sponges off" Buddhism, and so on, further enhancing my connections everywhere. Is this not the achievement of a disciple promoting the master as well?

In addition, there are disciples who have successively held the position of abbot at Fo Guang Shan such as the venerables Hsin Ping, Hsin Ting, Hsin Pei, and Hsin Bao; Tzu Chuang, Tzu Hui, Tzu Jung, Yi Kong, Hui Chuan, and so on; then there are the several hundred venerables at Fo Guang Shan who specialize in propagating the Dharma and giving teachings. It could be said that no matter where they are giving their lectures, they always make their teacher the focus. Consequently, my not being a monk who "sponges off" Buddhism is the disciples promoting me, and I too join hands with them, so that master and disciple are supporting each other. This is how Fo Guang Shan has developed as a religious organization.

In saying that it is the disciples who promote the master, this is really something of an everlasting embarrassment for me. Such diligent efforts as theirs are not only a consolation for me, but among their fellow disciples, they should be taken as an honor. Therefore, I also have a moral lesson for my disciples, for not only must I myself not become a monk who "sponges off" Buddhism, I also tell all of my disciples that they must not become monastics who "sponge off" Buddhism.

Directing All Energy to Bringing Warmth to Society

As for being "a monk not 'sponging off' Buddhism," this is what I have endeavored to do in Taiwan. Coming to mainland China, I have also adhered to the same ideal. When rebuilding Yixing Dajue Temple, the seat of my lineage, I told the Buddha's Light disciples and the Fo Guang Shan administrators that they must apply all their own energy; for example, salaries from teaching, donations for external services, income from Dharma services, and so on must all be utilized for the building of temples; work should also be done to relieve suffering and distress. This is particularly true in the case of the education for young people under the Seeds of Hope Project.[9] This is the mission that everyone must undertake.

There are also more than a dozen disciples at Fo Guang Shan teaching at universities. For example, Venerable Tzu Hui is president of the board of directors for Fo Guang University and Nanhua University; Venerable Hui Chuan is president of the board of directors for Pu-Men High School; Venerable Tzu Jung has for many years held the posts of board chair for Beautiful Life Television and publisher of the *Universal Gate* magazine; Venerable Hsin Ding and Venerable Yi Kong have been the publisher and director for *The Merit Times*, respectively; while Venerable Hui Kuan is the board chair for Hsiang Yun Culture Corp.; among others.

In Buddhism, we cannot expect to gain something without working for it or be treated with certain privileges. According to my capacity as defined by the government, for example, all the members of the many ministries and commissions such as the Mongolian and Tibetan Affairs Commission and the Overseas Community Affairs Council are specially appointed officials, so they may enter or leave the airport without undergoing inspection. I do not use such privileges. Why? I do not carry any special items, nor am I so urgently engaged in official business. I queue up along with everyone else, leaving me with a clear conscience. I want to let the customs officials know that I am also an ordinary citizen, or simply that I am just a humble monk.

9 The Venerable Master Hsing Yun Public Education Trust Fund provides scholarships to help talented students from low-income families attend school and achieve success; the trust was founded with the royalties from his books and continues through charity sales of his *One-Stroke Calligraphy*.

The Sutra Repository was built through the collaboration of Fo Guang Shan's monastic disciples.
Photo by Dai Zurong

We do the same in mainland China, and the same principle applies even more so internationally. We must make some contribution to each and every one: the Buddhism of Taiwan, the Buddhism of mainland China, and Buddhism internationally, for we must be able to serve everyone. Therefore, it is because of the spirit of contribution that we have been able to expand Buddhism from Taiwan to the five continents of the world.

The Sutra Repository that was built at Fo Guang Shan was completed through the collaboration of Fo Guang Shan's monastic disciples in raising funds over many years. Not a single penny was collected from the devotees. One lay Buddhist in Hong Kong learned about this project and expressed his determination to provide two million [Taiwan] dollars in assistance. Although all the buildings at Fo Guang Shan were entirely realized by combining the joint efforts of all throughout the ten directions, for this one building, we did not accept any

donations. Later on, I requested that Venerable Tzu Hui return the funds to him along with an apology, thereby helping our Fo Guang Shan disciples to realize their own aim of making some contribution.

A Modicum of Giving Transforms Popular Attitudes

If you do not make connections and only wish to depend upon others, then how can you expect success to fall from the sky? To not be a monk who sponges off Buddhism, one must first become a monk who serves society; a monk who propagates the Dharma and benefits sentient beings; a cultural, educational, and giving monk; and a monk who brings warmth to society. This is to become a monk who makes contributions through sacrifice for Buddhism. Each and every Buddha's Light disciple must rely upon their own aspiration to form Dharma connections with the faithful benefactors throughout all directions for a positive future.

Sometimes, all we need is to apply a modicum of energy, which gives us the ability to accomplish a great undertaking. An example of this was the transformation of Buddhism in Hong Kong. In the past, monastics arriving in Hong Kong would even find taking a taxi a difficult task. People said this was because Hong Kong people like to bet on horses, and taxi drivers believed that if they took monastics with completely shaved heads as passengers, their bets on the horses would result in a complete loss; therefore, they were unwilling to take monastics as passengers. When I went to Hong Kong to

Since the founding of Fo Guang Shan, over three hundred branch temples have opened worldwide, with over thirteen hundred monastics. Every year the Fo Guang Shan Sangha Affairs Committee holds the Worldwide Monastic Seminar at the Fo Guang Shan Monastery.

The Venerable Master held Dharma lectures at the Hong Kong Coliseum for twenty years. Pictured here, the "Morality, Meditative Concentration, and Wisdom of Humanistic Buddhism" in three sessions was simultaneously broadcast throughout the world so that tens of thousands of people were nurtured by the Dharma.

December 8–10, 2006

propagate the Dharma, I did not know the way, so of course I had to take a taxi to get to my destination.

Hong Kong is not a big place, the farthest destination at most would cost around twenty dollars, but each time I would pay one hundred Hong Kong dollars. Hong Kong's taxi drivers do have the practice of accepting tips, so I said, "You don't need to give me the change."

I have been propagating the Dharma in Hong Kong for many years, and situations like this have probably occurred twenty or thirty times, so the amount I spent would not have exceeded two thousand Hong Kong dollars. One time when I was giving a speech at the Hong Kong Coliseum,

I happened to point out, "You must imagine that each and every monastic is the God of Wealth, so if your taxi is transporting a God of Wealth every day, would you worry about not getting rich?"

In the past, when a monastic would go to a store to buy something, upon seeing the monastic the clerks would always say, "The shopkeeper is not here." Their concern being that the monastic had come to ask for donations. Now when I go to a store to buy something, the clerks take it upon themselves to say, "Master, let me give you a discount." There are even those who do not want my money, for they will come straight out and say, "Master, let me make this an offering to you!"

The development of Buddhism in Hong Kong is now quite different from times past. Some Taiwanese monks told me that when they went to Hong Kong, they even encountered taxi drivers who would not charge them any fare. The giving of two or three thousand [Hong Kong] dollars has transformed the attitude of the taxi drivers toward Buddhism. So even my being this monk who does not sponge off Buddhism cannot prevent me from making some small contribution to the Buddhism of Hong Kong!

This leads me to think about how none of the Fo Guang Shan centers established abroad were built by depending upon requests for donations. For instance, the He Hua Temple in the Netherlands, London's Fo Guang Shan Temple, Australia's Nan Tien Hall, New Zealand's Fo Guang Shan Temple, New York's Fo Guang Shan Temple in the United States, Singapore's Fo Guang Shan Temple, among others, were all purchased by their own Fo Guang Shan membership, through skimping on food and being frugal. They offer these places to the devotees so that they may come and practice together, ensuring that

Chinese boys and girls abroad can have a home for their spiritual life of wisdom.

Therefore, "to give" is "to receive," and "to relinquish" is "to gain." To not sponge off Buddhism also means elevating the moral character of the monastic order and the spiritual attainments of the monastic order. By not sponging off Buddhism, your rewards are instead more abundant. Frankly speaking, Hsing Yun is a child of a poor family, someone who never received any formal education either. But isn't today's ability to propagate the Dharma across the five continents of the world something that was achieved by relying upon this trait of "not sponging off Buddhism"?

To Relinquish Is to Gain: The Dharma Is Propagated to the World's Five Continents

Naturally, there were also some devotees who saw how we set good examples by our own conduct, and they too aspired to assist in Buddhism's development in various places. Examples include Houston's Chung Mei Temple in the United States, Zu Lai Temple in Brazil, Paris's Fa Hua Chan Temple, Nan Tien Temple and Chung Tian Temple in Australia, and so on. These temples were initially formed by a local devotee relinquishing a house for that purpose, and then later on everybody contributed money or provided labor to join in planting the Dharma banner. I too have based myself on this conviction: "What comes from all directions goes toward all directions to join in realizing the undertakings of all directions; the giving of a myriad people and the relinquishing of a myriad people together create connections for a myriad people," which is to say, "Everybody does for me, and I do for everybody." What all the monastics and the devotees share in common is this "for Buddhism." First, we ourselves must become monks who do not sponge off Buddhism, and then the devotees will naturally be willing to offer their contributions as well. If each of us can share such an understanding, would there still be any worry about Buddhism's inability to undergo a renaissance?

I have been coming to Singapore for several decades now, and the devotees who have taken refuge are in the several tens of thousands. Every year they all enjoy my Dharma teachings. So now I will ask a question: Have I ever asked for a single dollar from anyone? As for the Buddhists of Singapore, their attitude for making offerings is great, but I want to give them the new understanding that I am not a monk who sponges off Buddhism. Therefore, their making offerings to Buddhism is acceptable, but I dare not permit them to make offerings to me personally.

Over the course of my association with Malaysia for nearly fifty years, except for the contribution I accepted from an old lady, Auntie Li, there was only that time when Venerable Guang Yu made a donation of twenty thousand US dollars to Fo Guang Shan. Later on, as he was rebuilding Hoeh Beng Temple, I repaid his favor with a donation of twenty thousand US dollars as well, and we kept in contact with each other. The current abbot, Venerable Chuan Wen, is a disciple of Venerable Guang Yu and also a student at Fo Guang Shan's Buddhist College. He should know about this matter.

Directors of the Malaysian Buddhist Association such as Venerable Chuk Mor and Venerable Kim Beng have both invited me to give teachings. After the teachings, I sat there as the devotees divided into four lines and queued up to make their offerings of red envelopes, a process that lasted nearly an hour.

The Venerable Master autographing books for readers.

How many red envelopes were there? I do not know, for all of it was donated to the Malaysian Buddhist College to serve as an educational fund. If there are any charitable contributions, I always turn these over to the local Buddhist group for the purpose of propagating the Dharma.

I recall how in the fifty-third year of the Republic (1963), I made my first visit to Malaysia. Venerable Hong Zong said to me, "Taiwan sent me forty-two donation request leaflets; I really do not know how I can pay them." I felt quite ashamed when I heard this. How can our Taiwan Buddhism appeal for help from others in this way? I made the vow right then and there: if we do not have enough strength on our own, then we will not be going back to Malaysia to propagate the Dharma.

Therefore, during the building of Fo Guang Shan over several decades, I never solicited donations from abroad. Why is that? I want those people who are inclined to make affinities with Buddhism, and I want those in Buddhism to make affinities with each other. I will not let the devotees think that I am a monk who "lives off all directions."

Consequently, as for Fo Guang Shan's various centers, youth groups, youth corps, and so on for propagating the Dharma in Malaysia, they will have that kind of aspiration. It could be said that this is because they have followed a monk who does not sponge off Buddhism, for I too am like other Buddhists who also generate some merit from giving, in terms of my finances, my books and writing, and my *One-Stroke Calligraphy.* When giving, the average devotee will want their name written down in commemoration. I do not even want my name recorded. What I have advocated throughout my life, that "giving should be formless, and liberating sentient beings should be egoless," was accorded a commendation given to me by Professor Chen Jun, President of Nanjing University, but saying so just makes me really ashamed, for that is my job! Why would I want anyone's praise?

Propagating Buddhism: Giving Support to Sentient Beings in All Directions

Recently I heard that the *Shin Min Daily News* in Singapore had published a collection of the "Words of Wisdom" columns that I had written in installments, which has now gone into its sixth printing. I am very grateful to Zhu Zhiwei, their Catholic vice editor in chief, for his diligent efforts. My disciples have said that as soon as a volume of *Words of Wisdom* is published, it immediately joined the charts for best-selling new books in Singapore, Malaysia, and Hong Kong every time. I have further heard that this column has already exceeded five years of publication so far, setting a record for the longest serialized column since the beginning of the newspaper.

I am grateful to a Catholic believer who has been so friendly toward me, and as a consequence, I have unconditionally told my disciples to take the whole series of "Humble Table, Wise Fare • Hsing Yun's One-Stroke Calligraphy" published recently in *The Merit Times* and send them to him. This is a small expression of my gratitude, which I offer to him for his consideration; I also recall fondly his friendliness toward Buddhism.

As for the publication of my articles, there are disciples and devotees who frequently give me their reactions. They are often going back and forth to such places as mainland China, and they often see how other people have printed pirated copies of my books and writings. I always tell them that it is not important, and not to be upset by it, for I am quite pleased. Although pirated copying is indeed wrong, the Dharma may then be propagated far and wide because of it, and those so inclined may gain benefits owing to one or two sentences of Dharma within such copies. What is wrong with that?

As for my point in writing this article, I only hope that our Buddhist monks will all become monks who give support in all directions and not become monks who live off all directions. This is what the disciples of Fo Guang Shan should know, and it is also what the devotees in Taiwan, members of BLIA, and people of the international community should know. In short, I want to let everyone know that there are many monastics in Buddhism who do not "sponge off" Buddhism, and I want everyone to be at ease in their contact with monastics who do not sponge off Buddhism. Is there still any worry about Buddhism's inability to undergo a renaissance?

The ninety-three-year-old [2019] Venerable Master encourages disciples: Before attaining Buddhahood, one should first broadly form affinities with others and become an aspiring bodhisattva. Let "Buddhism depend upon me," and therefore Buddhism will flourish.

Photo provided by Commonwealth Publishing

Whoever it may be, the monastic followers or the lay disciples, although we have not yet attained enlightenment, we can still broadly make connections with others first so as to become aspiring bodhisattvas, and not become monastics who "sponge off" Buddhism. We must also treat ourselves as one of Buddhism's devotees, and we must undertake the responsibility of "having Buddhism depend on me." This represents some token of my kind regard in my declining years.

The Progress of Faith

Insights to reverse a life of adversity—enhancing the power of faith

At Fo Guang Shan, not only are the bhiksus and bhiksunis[1] happy, Shigu and Jiaoshi[2] are also happy; the male and female students studying at the Buddhist college are happy; the old folks as well as the young children living at the monastery are happy; people who have become devotees are happy; people who serve as volunteers are happy; the young women who have become Fo Guang ladies are also happy; and even visitors who travel here are happy as well. Why? Because when the power of faith strengthens our spirit, do we still need to worry if happiness exists and grows in our hearts? All this joy comes from the practice and realization of "patience for life, patience for phenomena, and patience for the non-arising of phenomena!"

1 In Sanskrit, "female monastic."
2 Shigu (female) and jiaoshi (male) are lay disciples of the sangha who maintain a celibate life.

My Progress of Faith

I once copied out a sutra in blood by pricking myself, and once I also burned my arm as an offering. I once remained silent for a year without speaking, and once I also kept my eyes closed for three months without seeing. Later on, I would occasionally open my eyes and suddenly feel: Oh, there are still verdant mountains; there are still trees; the sky is still there; and my feelings would then return to this world. Ever since I was young, I have had such sheer enthusiasm.

Within the Buddhist faith, special attention is paid to having resolve. Having the resolve toward personal advancement belongs to the Buddhism of the human and heavenly being vehicles; it is the Buddhism of the human, mundane world. Having the resolve to renounce the world belongs to the Buddhism of the *sravaka*[3] and *pratyekabuddha*[4] vehicles; it is the Buddhism that does not crave or cling to the worldly. Integrating supramundane thinking with the resolve of the mundane world is the Buddhism of the bodhisattva path; it is also the Humanistic Buddhism that I have promoted.

Speaking of the bodhisattva path, there are altogether fifty-one stages that one must go through in a specific order; these are the ten levels of faith, the ten levels of dwelling, the ten levels of practice, the ten levels of dedicating merit, and the ten grounds; then one enters the stage of universal awakening[5] to finally reach the Buddhahood state of wondrous awakening. Those with preliminary faith whom we call "bodhisattvas of initial resolve" will pass through various forms of practice until they eventually attain Buddhahood. There are also many great bodhisattvas like Avalokitesvara Bodhisattva, who originally could have become a Buddha, but kept some "ignorance as a mark of existence" that was not yet severed. He did this in order to remain in the human world to broadly liberate sentient beings, practicing the bodhisattva path.

The process of cultivating the bodhisattva path is like beginning with kindergarten and proceeding all the way to the

3 In Sanskrit, "one who has heard." One who has been liberated from the cycle of birth and death after listening to the Buddha's teachings but does not seek to become a Buddha.

4 In Sanskrit, one who is awakened to the teaching of dependent origination by himself during the time there is no Buddha in the world.

5 Bodhisattvas at this stage have an understanding and discernment of the Dharma that is the same as that of the Buddhas; however, they are less cultivated than the Buddhas.

Avalokitesvara Bodhisattva in the Great Compassion Shrine, Fo Guang Shan.

completion of a PhD degree. My faith is also the same, and it too slowly and gradually ascended grade by grade. In what follows below, I will talk about the levels of my faith.

Wholesome and Unwholesome Karma: The Inevitable Principle of the World

Once a person arrives in this world, they are confused, ignorant, and full of curiosity during childhood, wanting to understand all that is bright and colorful in this world. However, the culture of my hometown was not all that developed during my childhood; it was just a backward area north of the Yangtze River. There were no multistoried buildings, cars, trains, and modern electric machinery, let alone any multicolored lights. The people were all engaged in farming and manual labor as their livelihood. Everybody lived and struggled in the midst of poverty. On top of this, there were successive years of war, exorbitant taxes and levies, and the rampages of bandits. Sometimes, it even felt that death was better than life; the people did not really have great knowledge of the world.

However, after a person is born, a person's inherent nature has an inclination, which may be a source of energy for faith. But I make a distinction concerning faith; that is, I should have faith in what is good and not in what is bad; I should have faith in what is wholesome and not in what is unwholesome; I should believe in what is true and not in what is false.

When I was young, I often accompanied my maternal grandmother as she frequented what Daoism calls "families of do-gooders," and my natural character became even more steadfast in the belief that there is wholesome as well as unwholesome, and good as well as bad in this world; there is heaven and there is also hell. In particular, I saw the ten courts of Yama[6] described in the *Jade Record* at a beneficent shrine. It truly was a horrible and ghastly sight, guarding people against doing evil. It was especially so when I heard my maternal grandmother singing in the Buddha Hall with her wonderful voice:

Good deeds stand tall like a green pine, while evil
deeds bloom like flowers.
It seems the pine is not as brilliant as the flowers;
When the frost comes, the pine will stand tall,
While the flowers, withered, can be seen no more.

Such a cautionary verse for the world slowly entered my heart, and I felt that wholesome and unwholesome karma is an inevitable principle of the world.

Moreover, there are many sayings and popular ditties in the beneficent shrines, such as, "In a past life I wore a pair of your shoes, so in this life I will carry you ten miles," or "You were told to practice cultivation, but you did not; so after death you'll be reborn as a brown cow pulling a yoke on your neck." Imperceptibly, these also initiated my young mind, allowing me to slowly come into contact with faith at a preliminary level.

Strangely, as to the many deities in the beneficent shrines, I could not remember their numerous names, nor did I worship them that much. However, as soon as I heard of "Mother

6 In Sanskrit, "King of the Underworld."

Guanyin,"[7] a profound sense of faith was kindled in me. Later on, I heard my mother say that when I was a month old, she had entrusted me to Avalokitesvara Bodhisattva as an adopted son. After hearing this, my feelings were further magnified by a sense of deep adoration.

Activities at Temples: Nurturing a Foundation for Faith

During my childhood, I did not have any religious sentiments, nor did I have much faith. I simply accompanied my maternal grandmother as she made the rounds at the temples. I could leave the house and played around in the temples. There were also candies and snacks that I could eat. I can only say that my childhood was spent in such an environment, which nurtured some small foundation for my religious faith.

Due to the reasons mentioned above, there were those who saw me, a small child in the Buddha Hall, and out of respect for my maternal grandmother, they naturally showed some kindness and care toward me as well. They would frequently say to me with a merry laugh, "Ah, you are quite like a 'little monk.'"

I did not know what it meant to be a "little monk" or why they called me a "little monk." Moreover, someone later on said, "Your facial expression is very auspicious," and "You have the roots of goodness." These many words of praise made me feel that becoming a "little monk" was something quite good indeed.

However, I also did not understand how one did or did not become a monk. I was just a child who wanted his dad, his mom, and his family. Being home was best, because there were

7 "Guanyin" is the Chinese name for the Sanskrit "Avalokitesvara." This bodhisattva is affectionately referred to as "mother" because of his great compassion.

people outside who could cheat you, and even children would fight amongst themselves; going back home was the safest choice of all. Therefore, except for playing some games with a few neighborhood children, I remained mostly at home, and I dared not go anywhere beyond a mile from home.

What evokes the most profound memory during this period of time, was the effort my maternal grandmother put into her spiritual practice. It goes without saying that she would burn incense in the mornings and change the offering bowls of water in the evenings, but in particular, she would sit in meditation on her bed in the middle of the night. The loud rumbling of her stomach was like the roaring of pounding waves, and sometimes I would be awakened by the sound of her stomach grumbling and growling, yet I dared not ask, "Grandma, why does your stomach make so much noise?" I was quite afraid of crossing the line with my maternal grandmother.

At that time, a child at home waits most expectantly to enjoy the holidays and celebrate the New Year, and the most joyous times were family reunions. Even bowing ceremoniously in a small hall was an experience of extraordinary excitement.

That was how I grew up until the age of eleven. That year, the Luguo Bridge Incident[8] occurred, and it was said that eighteen large temples and monasteries in Yangzhou were invaded and occupied. Some of the eminent monks fled north as refugees, hurriedly looking for a place of safety. They passed through Jiangdu, and knowing that my maternal grandmother was a devout Buddhist, they would come to her home for a meal; my maternal grandmother would be extraordinarily delighted to offer her support. I remember there was one time, a dozen or

8 July 1937; also called the Marco Polo Bridge Incident, it marks the beginning of the China's war with Japan.

so eminent monks sat in the small hall of my maternal grandmother's home. I was not afraid of them, but knowing that these many eminent monks were so prestigious, dignified, and so holy as if they were not to be intruded upon, I leaned against the doorway full of curiosity, observing them and sizing them up.

At that time, some of the eminent monks also saw me, and one said, "Little kid, you are just like a little monk. Do you want to become a monk?" I do not know where my courage came from, but I said to them, "I do." He replied, "Okay, if you want to become a monk, you must formally become the disciple of a master first. Look at us here, which one do you want to acknowledge as your master?" I simply went over to the side of one of the eminent monks in a mischievous sort of way and pointed at him, meaning that I would formally acknowledge him as my master.

He said, "Then good, we will conduct the tonsure ceremony for acknowledging the master right here today. We will let this master accept you as a little monk."

I remember in the Buddha Hall, the candles were blazing, and incense was burning in the incense burner; there were also some offerings of food, flowers and fruits for conducting the great ceremony of acknowledging the master. It was at that very moment that I suddenly asked, "What happens to me after I acknowledge the master?"

He replied, "Then you will come with us!" I had no idea where we would go, so naturally I dared not just leave with them. At that moment, there was some hesitation in my mind, so I asked, "If I go with you, will my grandma be going with me?"

He said, "She need not go." My heart sank as soon as I heard this. [I thought:] Without the protection of my grandma, where am I going with you by myself?

I asked again, "Will my mom be going with me?" He said, "She won't be going either."

I further asked about my sister who was three years older than me. At the time, she was already thirteen or fourteen years old and was a young lady. In my eyes, she had always been capable and experienced, and perhaps somewhat fierce, for no one was able to impose upon her. I said, "Can my older sister go with me?" He said once again, "She won't be going either."

As soon as I heard this, I said petulantly, "Then I won't go either."

That was how the whole ridiculous farce ended. Having finished their meal, they strode out and left. The matter of becoming a monk also vanished like mist after this, and it seemed that no one ever mentioned it again. As to how my family felt at the time, I have no idea. However, I guess perhaps they only wanted me to acknowledge a master and form positive connections with those many eminent monks; they didn't really want me to go and become a monk. Thus, after that, no one ever mentioned it again.

A Nation at War: Young and Old Are Mobilized to Resist Japan

Hostilities grew more and more intense after the Luguo Bridge Incident, and the whole country was shaken. There was a wave of anti-Japanese actions among the people, and everywhere was filled with the sentiments of making sacrifices for the nation and resisting the "Japanese devils." During the day, the adults were busy holding meetings and training in the militia, participating in the war of resistance. We children also joined in a children's brigade, singing songs, learning to read, and marching in demonstrations. Thus, during the day, I would sing along with other children; in the evening, I would join in the literacy classes. Perhaps, since we wanted to resist Japan, it was necessary to raise the educational level of the citizens. I remember that in the literacy classes, many interesting things happened. Occasionally, the teacher would call on us to read out a character. There was one time that I mispronounced one, and the entire classroom erupted into laughter. I was completely mortified and felt very embarrassed. Never again did I dare open my mouth so casually.

The children's brigade that was established would sometimes march in demonstrations and sing during the day. The lyrics that I now vaguely remember are "There is only iron; there is only blood; only iron and blood can save China." Or we would sing, "Onward, onward, China's sons and daughters, rise up to fight in the war of resistance." Of course, I did not know what it meant, I just thought it was very exciting. When compared to the neighborhood children who played games with illustrated cards or iron nails, the children's brigade was much more fun. This was particularly so in the case of my third maternal uncle, Liu Yuhua, who had become the commander of the local militia. He was an impressive and awe-inspiring figure, and even kept a pistol holstered at his waist. I had great admiration for him. At that time, I did not have any thoughts of becoming a monk; in the future, I wanted to "become a soldier, join the guerrilla forces, and resist the Japanese devils." In the minds of children like us, the so-called "Anti-Japanese Movement" of those days was nothing more than just a game.

In Dire Peril of Life and Death: Giving Rise to the Source of Energy for Faith

During a winter in December when I was eleven years old, the Japanese attacked Nanjing very swiftly. Where was Nanjing? I had no idea, but I understood that the war there was in desperate straits. The glow of fires went on for days on end, and even from my hometown a hundred miles away, I could see the red colored skies. A few of my uncles at my maternal grandmother's place were also busily preparing to flee to the rear area under KMT control. I am not detailing here their confusion, alarm, and sorrow of fleeing from home, as well as the uncertainty of "knowing there is a today, but not knowing if there will be a tomorrow." In brief, I remember it was a severe winter of heavy snow coming down in flurries, and I carried two bed sheets as we merged together into a wave of fleeing refugees withdrawing to the rear area. Where were the rear areas? Where were the front lines? I did not know; even though it was very tough, I also felt it was fun, and I sang along with everyone else with amusement: "To where are we fleeing; to where are we roaming?"

Later on, we took our chances to move forward amid the heavy fire and hail of bullets that occurred on many occasions. We kept walking among the corpses covering the ground as the Japanese pursued us. We even hid among the piles of dead bodies for fear that the Japanese would bayonet us if they saw us. It was not until such a time that I understood the need to recite the name of Mother Guanyin, believing that Mother Guanyin would come and save us. As it turns out, it is during times of life's crises that the source of energy for faith arises in its wake, and we will feel how faith is very important. It is when we have faith that we can have the peace from Mother

The Venerable Master's teachers at Mount Qixia. *From the left*: venerables Junling, Zhikai, Jueming, Rongzhai, Daben, and Hechen.

Guanyin's rescue. At that time, I had an intangible sensation that my faith was progressing a step further.

Searching for Father, Promising the Venerable to Join the Monastic Order

During that time, my father had been working away from home, but he had not returned home for a long time. Naturally, the one who was worried the most was my mother, and she made inquiries about him everywhere. Later on, she received news that my father had come back a long time ago; but why had he not come home? No one knew. Since my father had run an incense and candle store from home, and since he had many contacts with Buddhist figures owing to my maternal grandmother's connections, my mother decided to take me to a Buddhist-related area and make inquiries. It was the first month of the lunar calendar in 1938, not long after Lunar New Year had passed. My mother took me out in search of my father. Where could we go and search for my father in the sea of countless people? However, it was because of these causes and conditions that I promised to join the monastic order at Mount Qixia near Nanjing. I was really going to become a monk.

I remember that year, on the second day after the master and my mother's conversation, the first day of the second month, the tonsure ceremony was conducted; I really became a little monk. Later on, some of my seniors said that I could not be called "little monk," the term was "little *sramanera*."[9] I did not understand much at the time, and it did not matter to me whether I was called "sramanera" or "monk," but in short, I had now left home to join the monastic order. The master said he would let me study, so that I would have faith in Buddhism and become a Buddhist disciple, and that my future would certainly be better than my past. At this time, my yearning for faith took another stride forward. My master and teacher, Abbot Zhikai, especially invited a dozen or so eminent monastics and great worthies to consult over what name I should be given. Later on, there was a Venerable Rongzhai whose Buddhist learning was very profound, and he gave me the name of "Jinjue Wuche." After this, I became known by the name of "Jinjue."

After joining the monastic order, I engaged in practice and study at temples in places such as Mount Qixia, Jiaoshan, Jinshan, Baohuashan,[10] and others. Over the ten years of cloistered life in the monasteries, even though I did not gain much learning and knowledge, in regard to the growth of my faith, it truly marked a milestone. I have always had the habit of

9 In Sanskrit, a junior monk; one who has joined the monastic order but has yet to receive full ordination.

10 By the beginning of the Republic of China, the most famous ordination platform was at Mount Baohua.

Seeking intelligence and praying for wisdom, everyone prostrates to Avalokitesvara Bodhisattva.
Photo by An Xiaode

being hardworking by nature, and during this period, I asked the monastery to give me work of my own initiative. No matter what difficult practice it was, be it cooking, bringing water, carrying firewood, and so on, I did not consider it as suffering. As I saw it, it was all for the purpose of fulfilling my own faith.

Besides the difficulties of hard work and the injustices of blows and being scolded, what influenced me the most during those ten years was the year I was fifteen. The fulfillment of monastic qualifications for joining the monastic order begins with the process of seeking full ordination. First, one receives the sramanera precepts, then the bhiksu precepts, and after that the bodhisattva precepts, what is known as the Triple Platform Full Ordination Ceremony. Each and every stage must be completed one by one, and only then is one fully ordained to become a true monastic. Originally in accordance with the Buddhist rule, one qualifies for ordination only after the age of twenty. But since this was during the war period, and because of these exceptional circumstances, many teachers made it easier for me; they unanimously agreed in their discussion that I, the youngest of the group, be permitted to take full ordination along with the many other adults.

However, when I received the Triple Platform Full Ordination Ceremony, as a customary requirement, I had to have precept scars burnt by incense. Perhaps because the ordination officiants had especially high expectation for me, they burned my twelve incense scars into one, and my whole cranium sank down into a concave shape. Henceforth, I went from being a child who was not particularly stupid to suddenly undergoing a huge transformation; I drastically turned into someone with no ability to remember.

Worshipping Guanyin, Illumination of the Mind and the Enhancement of Wisdom

I remember how at that time there was a teacher who would continually strike the palm of my hand and order me to kneel in punishment. Because I could not remember and memorize, he scolded me for being stupid. Such a strict education increased the suffering of my life as a youth. One day, Venerable Juemin reprimanded me and said, "Such stupidity! You must go and worship Guanyin Bodhisattva in order to enhance your wisdom and intelligence!" These words gave rise to boundless hope in me, and I forgot all about the pain in the palm of my hand!

I had already believed in Mother Guanyin to an extraordinary degree, but it wasn't that easy to go worship Mother Guanyin in the monastery. This was because in the Buddhist college, there was no such place for an individual going to act on one's own. All I could do was furtively get up in the middle of the night and worship in the small Buddha Hall of the Buddhist College. Being devout in faith, I respectfully knelt before Guanyin Bodhisattva and worshipped her wholeheartedly. I recited this verse: "May the resolve for enlightenment be entirely made, and may lotus flowers spring forth everywhere. The mind of your disciple is dim, so I worship Guanyin, seeking intelligence and praying for wisdom. Homage to the great loving-kindness and compassion Guanyin Bodhisattva who brings liberation from tribulation through vast spiritual power."

During his youth, the Venerable Master made the vow to "have gratitude for the four kindnesses and follow the Dharma to cross over the three lower realms of existence" for all of his life.
Photo provided by Fo Guang Shan Tsung-Lin University

Some people encouraged me, "Keep on worshipping, and Guanyin Bodhisattva will lay hands on your head to give the prediction of enlightenment, or she will bless you, conferring upon you the ambrosia empowerment!" My deep belief in this was beyond any doubt, and quite inconceivably, a few months later, my memory really did improve compared to the past. Of course, I did not see the bodhisattva come and lay hands upon my head and confer the ambrosia empowerment. But wondrously, perhaps due to the bodhisattva's blessing, it was as if my mind was suddenly illuminated with the Buddha's light; not only was my memory restored, but I also felt brighter and more intelligent. As for the textbook taught by the teacher, the *Anthology of the Best in Classical Prose*, I was able to memorize very quickly simply after reading it one or two times. Ever since then, although I dare not say that I made some meteoric rise, for me schoolwork became very smooth and easy. This was a response to my seeing faith as extremely incomprehensible. Such a moment gave me a deeper grasp of Buddhist faith, and I understood a bit more about its profundity.

But during this time, I knew that the founder of Buddhism, Sakyamuni Buddha, was the Tathagata Buddha whom I had heard about when I was a child. In my mind, the Tathagata Buddha was more important and more high-ranking than Guanyin Bodhisattva. He was the founder of Buddhism, and I wanted to search for traces of the founder and seek out his bearings, so that I would be able to join with him. I vowed to make contributions through sacrifice for the sake of Buddhism and for the sake of the founder. With the addition of tender care and concern from my teacher, I felt a sense of gratitude and made a vow referred to in Buddhism as "having gratitude for the four kindnesses[11] and following the Dharma to cross over the three lower realms of existence" and vowed to uphold this vow for the rest of my life. One could also say that it was not until this stage that I slowly entered the true ranks of the faithful. Even though it could not be called a university or high school level faith, at that time, I ought to have at least occupied a certain place at the elementary school level of faith.

11 The expression of gratitude for the kindness of parents, of sentient beings, of one's country, and of the Triple Gem.

After learning about Buddhism's founder, Sakyamuni Buddha, although I was unable to completely understand his life and teachings, I had already become endowed with a profound sense of faith in him. I felt that the Buddha's principles and instructions were in keeping with the needs of ordinary people, and it is he who is "a Savior." But there were also quite a few people within Buddhism who attacked my expression, saying that one cannot describe the Buddha as "the Savior," for that is a Christian term. I thought, how can "Savior" only refer to Jesus? Can the Buddha not be "a Savior"? I was aware that my faith toward Buddhism and the Buddha was already different from that of other people; thus, I had my own affirmation.

Furthermore, after the Song dynasty [960–1279 CE] and on through the Yuan [1279–1368], Ming, Qing, and Republican eras, Buddhism was in extreme decline. Since it lacked sufficient talent, there was no one to protect and develop the enormous cultural heritage of Buddhism. There was only the appearance of some of the fourfold assembly,[12] or it was simply reduced to sutra chanting and repentance services for which these disciples depended on to earn a living. Everyone relied on Buddhism to make a living, and no one was making sacrifices for Buddhism. Thus, Buddhism became just like the other "folk" religions, which only offered people a place to pay homage and make requests for security, karmic rewards, higher office, and riches. People only bowed to the Buddha, recited the name of the Buddha, and sought after the Buddha's help; but in my way of thinking, why could they not "practice the Buddha's Way"?

12 The collective name for bhikṣus, bhiksunis, upasakas, and upasikas.

Paying Homage to the Buddha and Reciting the Buddha's Name, Vowing to Contribute by Practicing the Buddha's Way

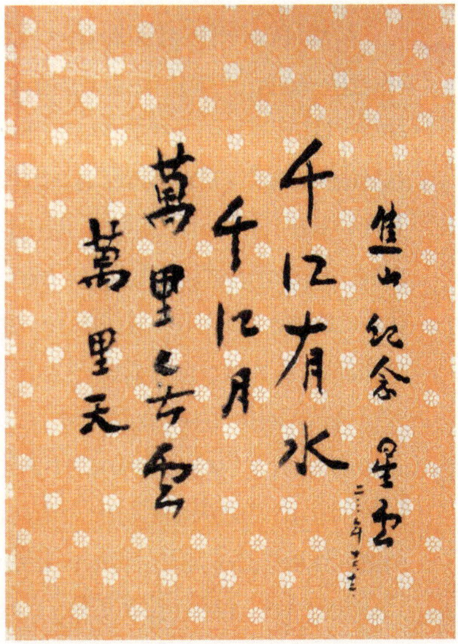

Verses of dedication written by the Venerable Master while revisiting Jiaoshan.
2000

Seeing that of the Dharma was not being propagated for the benefit of sentient beings, I could not help but make the vow: "Not only will I bow to the Buddha and recite the Buddha's name, but in the future I will practice the Buddha's Way. I will not become someone who depends upon Buddhism for a living; I will make contributions for Buddhism; I will propagate Buddhism; I will make every effort for Buddhism; even more, I will sacrifice myself as a martyr for Buddhism. I will have Buddhism depend upon me." One could say that this is the foundation of my conviction for faith.

At the same time, I also felt that the system within Buddhism had some corrupt practices, as it is commonly said that everything in the world is slowly corrupted over time. Regarding this, in my heart I also wanted some sort of reform. It was during this time that Venerable Master Taixu's three-point revolution movement entered my mind. I felt that I should not merely be a Buddhist believer, but that I would also become someone who practices the Buddha's Way.

I was still studying at Qixia and Jiaoshan, so I silently made some wishes in my heart, and did not dare tell anyone that my ambition for the future was to run a newspaper and establish a university for Buddhism. I felt that it was in this moment that I resembled a Buddhist follower and a monastic. It was not until this point that I truly entered the stage of Buddhist faith, and perhaps my faith of this period had reached the high school level.

Around the age of twenty-two, I read so much of the *Biographies of Eminent Monks*, like Master Tanwujie [ca. 420 CE] and the hardships he endured on his journey to India in search of the Dharma; like the sufferings endured by Master Faxian [d. 418–423 CE], who went by land and came back by sea; like Master Xuanzang [602–644 CE], who went by land as he traveled to India in search of the Dharma; or like the vow of the eminent monk Jianzhen from my hometown, who crossed the ocean eastward and propagated the Dharma in Japan. All of them had already streamed into my mind and so became the Buddhas and bodhisattvas I revered.

In particular, as Venerable Master Taixu was still alive and active, I wanted to see him as a leader and follow him in his undertaking of the "New Buddhism Movement." Their spirit of disregarding life for the Dharma and self-sacrificing for Buddhism was something I could not help but admire. I thought to myself, "If they can do this, I should be able to do it too. I will fight and sacrifice for Buddhism; I will go through fire and water for Buddhism; I will propagate the Dharma for the benefit of sentient beings, and practice the bodhisattva path." In all of my cultivation and vows, I felt that my faith was gradually progressing and maturing.

The Venerable Master came to Taiwan with the Monastic Relief Corps in 1949. Pictured is the Venerable Master with fellow monastics who crossed the ocean to Taiwan. *Front row, from the right*: venerables Hao Lin, Wu Yi, Sheng Hua, Kuan Yu, Yi De, and Neng Guo; *second row, from the right:* venerables Long Gen, Guo Zong, the Venerable Master, Xing Ru, and Hong Chao.

Propagating the Dharma for the Benefit of Sentient Beings, Emulating the Examples of Patriarchs through the Ages

I vowed "not to become a parasite on Buddhism, not to become a taker of Buddhism, and not to become a lazy monastic; the Buddha doesn't have to come and help me, but I will help the Buddha by propagating the Dharma for the benefit of sentient beings." It was under these circumstances that I felt I ought to leave the monastery. Also, by a wonderful turn of events, I later on served as the principal at a public elementary school for nearly two years.

After that, I felt that I must depart from the environment of those who entreat and depend on the Buddha, and that I should unite with all suffering sentient beings. Accordingly, I followed Venerable Le Guan's example by joining the Monastic Relief Corps during the war. It was in this way that I also felt how my own faith had taken another step forward and had grown more. I think that perhaps my faith at this time had entered the level of institutions of higher learning.

Regarding my faith and belief in Buddhism, besides the cultivation I received from the Dharma teachings, which transformed and refined me, I did not pay particular attention to the encouragement and compliments delivered by some good people and good deeds. On the contrary, it was some small and minor events that could be considered to have profoundly increased my belief in Buddhism.

For example, there were those who would mock the idea that someone had built a temple into something like an imposing palace and had used some rare and valuable materials in doing so. I thought to myself, no matter how opulent or magnificent, how could it possibly compare with the majestic beauty of the World of Ultimate Bliss? In building up Fo Guang Shan, there were many people who praised me for being able to construct two to three hundred temples around the world within a limited lifespan over several decades, yet I do not think there is anything incredible to it. Because this is only the way things should be: it is a joint accomplishment in reliance upon the positive affinities of all directions as well as upon the devotees; what I supplied in this was only a little power of a vow, and nothing more.

As for another example, there are those who want to build a library, so they come to me and ask for donations; there are those who want to go on a secluded retreat, so they come to me and ask for donations; there are those who want to build a temple, so they come to me and ask for donations. As a matter of fact, I myself am also building temples, and the fundraising to cover the costs is very difficult, yet I never asked for donations from anyone. If you all turn to me and ask for donations, then from where will my funds come? Those who are

The Venerable Master established the Children's Class of the Ilan Buddhist Chanting Association and conducted the Triple Gem Refuge Ceremony for the children.
August 26, 1956

more powerful and influential than me, like Venerable Dong Chu and Venerable Wu Yi, came to borrow money from me, and I still generously lent them a helping hand. Therefore, I do not care or bother too much about the many Buddhist-related matters. On the contrary, I think of it as other people helping me enhance my belief, boosting my faith among the ranks for propagating the Dharma.

Plowing and Weeding with Great Effort, Achievement through Wondrous Causes and Conditions

The word "conditions" has an extraordinarily profound as well as wonderful significance. One could say that these are the source of this human universe. But one must not abuse these "conditions." If the conditions are right for you, then the causes

The Venerable Master presiding over the Seven-Day Amitabha Chanting Retreat at the Ilan Buddhist Chanting Association: Wholeheartedly reciting Amitabha Buddha to the point of realizing the emptiness of heaven and also of earth, the emptiness of oneself and also of others.
1956

and conditions will come find you; if they are not, then even a cooked goose will still fly away.

However, I feel that charity work can be done if there is money and if there are the right causes and conditions; there is no need to insist on doing so if the money and the right causes and conditions are not in place. It all relies on causes and conditions to make arrangements for us. If you want to go on a secluded retreat, and someone comes and supports you, then you can go on a secluded retreat; why then would you go around seeking donations for it? As long as you do the plowing and weeding first, would you still worry about the harvest? If you do not first plow and weed yet still wish to bring in the harvest, then it seems like you are doing things somewhat in reverse.

I remember during the early years of the Ilan Buddhist Chanting Association. There would always be more than a thousand people participating in each year's seven-day retreat, and I treated it with a calm composure. But on one occasion, when a thousand or more children were also gathered together to recite Amitabha Buddha's name, there was one little girl less than ten years old who was carrying her little sister on her back; the little sister was perhaps one or two years old. The two sisters were sitting outdoors with their palms joined, reciting Amitabha Buddha's name there. I particularly noticed how the one- or two-year-old girl also had joined her palms together, following along in reciting Amitabha Buddha's name.

This scene suddenly touched my heart, and I found that tears were streaming down my face. I could not control myself, for I felt a burst of feelings that simultaneously combined sadness and happiness, and I was truly moved by an infinite feeling. I think at that time, the Buddha had entered my innermost being. No wonder the "Universal Gate Chapter"[13] states, "For those who should be liberated by someone in the form of a young boy or young girl, the bodhisattva will manifest in the form of a young boy or young girl and teach the Dharma to them." The way this little girl was reciting Amitabha Buddha's name was just like so many Buddhas and bodhisattvas teaching the Dharma to me, moving me and allowing my faith to mature and soar higher.

During the long periods of Amitabha Buddha's name recitation, many instances of such a spiritual response occurred. In particular, there was Mr. Zheng, an old and disabled soldier who had been paralyzed for eight years and was unable to move. He said he wished to participate in the Amitabha Buddha's name recitation, and because this kind of determination and aspiration were rare, I asked someone to help him by carrying him over to sit in a corner where he could recite Amitabha Buddha's name with us. One day, in the middle of reciting Amitabha Buddha's name during the morning chanting

13 In this chapter of *The Lotus Sutra*, the Buddha describes Avalokitesvara Bodhisattva; he has thirty-three manifestations with which to alleviate twelve kinds of danger.

service around 5:00 am, he unexpectedly stood up and walked over to bow before me; this astounded me.

At that moment, I thought that he had passed away; is this his spirit that's standing before me? But his face was radiant and he was in high spirits. Clearly, he was still a normal person! Since I was the presiding master for the seven-day retreat, I could not be afraid, so I could only calm myself and say to him, "It is good that you have made a bow, but you should go back to your seat and recite Amitabha Buddha's name." He then indeed calmly walked back, and from then on he could walk without impediment. At that time, the faith of Ilan's city residents greatly increased and word got around quickly. This gave rise to many media outlets and newspapers such as the Central News Agency vying with one another to report the story, which caused quite a sensation.

Of course, during the many years of propagating the Dharma and cultivating practice, there were also experiences of both physical and emotional exhaustion. I felt that it was not until the recitation of Amitabha Buddha's name had entered into a beneficial state within a person that it could rise to the level of faith. Therefore, I offer my own personal experience to everyone for their consideration. How can the effects of Amitabha Buddha's name recitation be accelerated? I would list the following four kinds of recitation: Joyful Recitation, Mournful Recitation, Emptiness Recitation, and Realistic Recitation. I have not relied on the formulaic kind of recitation in the past, but instead have applied my feelings, my genuineness to move Amitabha Buddha and myself. It was these feelings that I relied on for the Buddhist Chanting Association every Saturday in Ilan, and for the seven-day retreat every year; this continued for twenty-six years without any interruption.

The Resolve of the Volunteers, Support from Bodhisattva Manifestations

Ilan was where I first began treading the path of propagating the Dharma. I saw that under a blazing sun high in the sky, Zhang Rubiao and Li Zhupu built a corrugated metal shed as a temporary Buddha Hall. They received no wages for this; being a volunteer was not popular in Taiwan at that time, so their resolve on their own accord to serve sentient beings made me feel that these people were true manifestations of bodhisattvas. This also strengthened the power of my incomparable faith.

It is especially so for Lin Changqing, who was a low-level staff member at the Keelung Post Office. Solely because of his sense of identity with the people of Ilan, he would take his meager salary, which hardly covered his daily expenses, and aspire to buy a few dozen Buddhist books and a few dozen Buddhist magazines every month. He would bring these back and place them in the Tian Li Hall incense shop, distributing them free to the public. One could say that the pioneering effort in developing Ilan Buddhism was not done by me, nor was it done by the few Dharma teachers who preceded me; rather, one should say that it began with the lay Buddhist Lin Changqing. It was only owing to his resolve over the long term that resulted in Ilan Buddhism achieving widespread belief at the time.

The lay Buddhist Li Juehe helped out with the Ilan Buddhist Chanting Association for thirty years and served as its general affairs director. Initially, he did not even have a desk, but would stand in the corridor and write down people's name for them; he aspired to undertake any sundry tasks, and he never relented from these efforts. Later on, he first allowed his daughter to join the monastic order, and then his grandsons; finally, he joined the

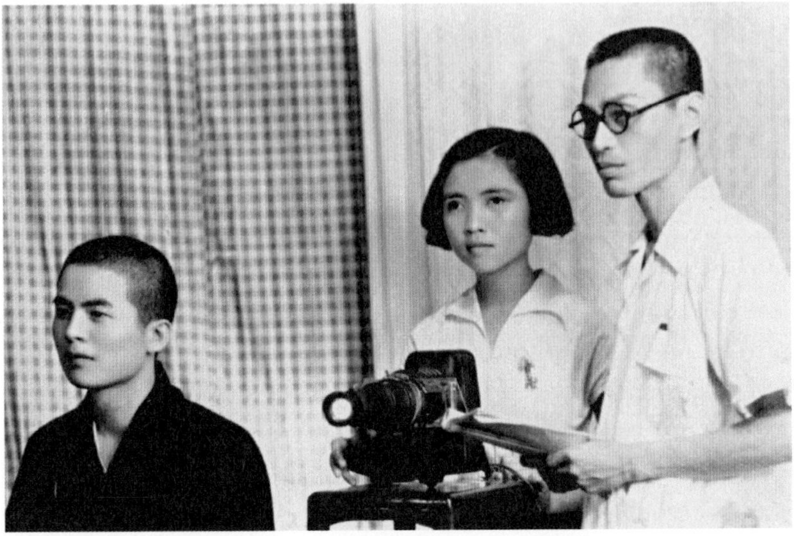

The Venerable Master was the first to use a slide projector for propagating the Dharma, ushering in the era of modern propagation of Buddhism. *From the right*: Householder Li Juehe and Miss Li Meihui.
Photo provided by the Historical Museum of Fo Guang Shan

monastic order himself. They became Venerable Tzu Chuang, Venerable Hui Lung, and Venerable Hui Chuan we have today. Can you say that this is not touching?

There was Madame Sun-Zhang Ching-yang, who once courageously debated the merits of Buddhist belief with Madame Soong Mei-ling, because the latter was anti-Buddhist. Later on, she brought many people to Ilan for the Buddhist Chanting Association's seven-day retreat. This happened many times over the course of these retreats. How could her defense of Buddhism and her courage during the period of authoritarian rule fail to make her a bodhisattva?

Around 1955, I went to a small theater in Dingshuangshi to propagate the Dharma. After my teaching, a slide projector was used to project an image of the Buddha on the screen. I asked Li Zhixin, a high school student, to read aloud a short and simple prayer before the Buddha on my behalf. I wrote its contents as follows:

> *Oh, great Compassionate Buddha! We of the Youth Group and the Youth Dharma Mission for the Ilan Buddhist Chanting Association have come to Dingshuangshi, and we pray to the Buddha that you will bless the people here with your Dharma rain, and ensure that they will honor your teachings, and that they will have secure and stable lives, be free of calamities, and enjoy auspicious peace.*

I stood beside him while he recited the prayer in this way, and I could not help that my eyes were brimming with tears; I could not control myself.

Increase the Gain for One Another, Greater and Lesser Vehicles Mentoring Each Other

Speaking of my faith, I have brought faith for the Dharma to so many people, and others have given me so many moving experiences as well; we have further benefited each other. In Buddhist history, there are teachers of the Greater Vehicle and the Lesser Vehicle mentoring each other, and there is also the perfect integration of the commonality from Buddha to Buddha and the unhindered illumination of light; even to the point that all bad deeds and bad events are also able to help in advancing our faith, as long as we understand how to transform them.

I have listened to many lectures from great worthies, and also experienced many Dharma teachings in majestic halls, but none of these have ever tugged at my heartstrings. It has always been some simple occurrence that has made me feel that my body, mind, and the universe, or rather me and the Buddha as well as Buddhism have dissolved into one. That is to say, in this kind of life for promoting the Dharma and liberating sentient beings, some boys and girls or senior volunteers all become manifestations of bodhisattvas, further ensuring that there is no retreating in my faith.

At that time, every evening there were twenty or so children who came out carrying lanterns, and along the streets and alleyways of Ilan they would spread the word for me, telling everyone to come and listen to me give teachings. I remember the words to the song:

The goal of Buddhism is to tell one the truth,
For all who believe in Buddhism will be happy and at peace.
Sing of Guanyin Bodhisattva from time to time;
Remain close to Amitabha Buddha with each and every thought.

As for those innocent and guileless children, if they are not manifestations of the Youth Sudhana or the *naga* girl,[14] then what could they be?

During the progress of my life of faith, although I don't quite praise ceremonial worship that is merely formalistic, I myself have also experienced many inconceivable states from formal ceremonial worship. For example, once when I was bowing and prostrating on the ground, compassion arose

14 As described in the "Devadatta Chapter" of *The Lotus Sutra*, the naga girl, who was barely eight years old, transformed into the body of a man and became a Buddha in the Spotless World in the south, as witnessed by members of the assembly.

from within, and I could not bear getting up. It seemed at that time as if I was already connecting with, conversing with, and confiding in the Buddha. Sometimes, in the midst of reciting Amitabha Buddha's name or paying homage to the Buddha, I would suddenly feel myself and space dissolving into one, not knowing the existence of my body, and only knowing that this spacious universe had already merged into a oneness with me.

Because I had these feelings, whether or not the Buddha had come down to show favor upon me, to take care of me, or to give me some kind of blessing, the stirring of such emotions did not bother me. However, the Buddha has indeed already occupied an important place in my heart. People say, "The Buddha is in the heart," but perhaps one still needs to ask: if someone is filled with envy, anger, resentment, comparativeness, and deviousness, such that so many complex afflictions hold an important place in their heart, then what space is there to accommodate the Buddha?

Sending Others Warmth in the Cold of Winter, Hardship Fosters Strength

Even though I am not a monk who enjoys conducting sutra chanting and repentance services, on many occasions amid Yogacara Offering Service,[15] both the chanting of the Five Buddhas and the rhythm of the Six Earthly Offerings did cause my heartstrings to pulsate with the beat. In particular, we recite in the Invocation:

15 This is a Dharma service to relieve the suffering of hungry ghosts, involving elaborate procedures. As for the specific components referred to here, the chanting of the Five Buddhas is part of setting up the boundary, the chanting of the Six Earthly Offerings follows the invitation of the Triple Gem, and the three excerpts of Invocation describe the unfortunate circumstances of hungry ghosts as they are invited to the ceremony.

Where is the general's warhorse now?
Amid the weeds and wildflowers is a land filled with sadness.

Flowers are struck with a sudden and heavy rain just as they are blooming;
The moon is covered by black clouds just when it is about to shine.

The night so long and endless, when will the sun dawn?
The frontier pass, so hidden and obscure, knows nothing of spring.

Many lines such as these made me realize that this world was really affected by suffering, emptiness, and impermanence; this enhanced my experience of human life as well.

In particular, throughout my life of faith, the time spent doing hard work was also an important supporting factor that influenced my faith. In the early days, I had to pull a handcart in order to provide the temple with daily necessities regularly. Since it was so heavy that I could not pull it, I ended up foaming at the mouth and vomiting; but in no way did I blame monastic life for being so arduous. On the contrary, I felt that I needed to redouble my efforts in making a contribution to Buddhism.

Once I was at the Yixing Dajue Temple, the seat of my lineage. In order to comply with local custom, I obeyed the orders of my senior monastics to perform the winter alms visit when the Lunar New Year was approaching in wintertime. I carried with me peace and security charms I was to distribute to the families as an equivalence of giving them a blessing. In return, the local people would present a bowl of rice to me.

That bowl of rice left an impression upon me as I ate it, something I have never forgotten. Hence, sixty years later, I returned to the rebuilt Dajue Temple at Yixing, and presented the neighboring residents within a span of ten miles with large suitcases filled with clothing, as a way to send them warmth in the cold of winter and repay them for their kindness in giving me a bowl of rice back then. That bowl of rice became something like rice shoots, growing and maturing in the rice paddy of my heart. As I see it, regardless of whether someone gives something to me or I give something to someone, the physical quantity is entirely finite; however, spiritually, there is no single amount that can possibly represent its whole meaning.

When I was a young man, I enjoyed the aged senior monastics very much, but none of my classmates liked them that much. I did not treat them like old monastics that often, but rather treated them as my own grandfather. This was because as I sat beside the old monastics, I could hear them relate how they practiced and studied as young men. Truly, it was like listening respectfully to a teaching given by a manifestation of the Buddhas or bodhisattvas.

In particular, within the Buddhist tradition, the more life became poor and simple, and the more hardship there was, the more it gave me an even stronger determination to practice the Buddha's Way, to reform Buddhism, and to repay the Buddha's kindness. This is perhaps what it means to transform grief and indignation into the power of faith. Since I was born in turmoil and grew up in adversity, being faced with glory and riches actually left me completely unmoved. Whenever there is adversity and suffering, my spirit actually responds to it more easily. Consequently, as far as suffering goes, I am very grateful for the value of suffering; suffering has given me progress, nourishment, and strength.

Faith Is Priceless, for External Objects Cannot Make One Waver

Sometimes I would also think, "Why is it that the more wronged I feel, the stronger I become? And when I experience more suffering, the more energetic I become?" Sometimes, I would also experience doubt: "Am I someone like the character of Ah Q, [who engages in self-deception when faced with defeat,] as penned by Lu Xun [1881–1936]?" I have also wondered what the real value of faith in human life is after all. Let us say I am a Buddhist working for a company with a salary of only one thousand dollars a month. Meanwhile, another company of another religion offers a salary of five thousand dollars a month. If I were to go to work at that second company, then the value of my faith would only amount to a few thousand dollars.

But I feel that faith is priceless. Suppose that because this temple is experiencing adversity, I have no faith in it and reject it, while the other temple offers a rich life, so I am attracted to it; then the value of my faith merely lies in eating, drinking, and making merry. That does not count for much in the way of value.

In particular, I also cannot allow my faith to be changed due to fear or intimidation. Perhaps because the influence I received in Buddhism is just like the social influence received by the soldiers who must sacrifice their lives in loyalty to the country, or Confucianists who must be loyal to the sovereign and devoted to the country, or people who are chivalrous and

Dharma is not seeking from outside; when you find the inherent mind, bodhi is right before you.
Photo by Zhou Yun

uphold justice. Similarly, as I am influenced by Buddhist faith, I feel that in the face of my own faith, I cannot submit to force or be tempted by wealth. I must also raise the value of my own faith, for no amount of money, no degree of affection, and no level of fame and fortune can buy my faith. Faith represents my moral quality, and it represents my life and my spirit. My faith has a value far greater than hundreds of millions dollars and has a value far greater than the number of grains of sand along the Ganges River!

Also, there are the many people who do Buddhist work and the devotees who assist in propagating Buddhism. The inspiration they have given me has also been plentiful. Examples include the lay Buddhist Yan Foon Gu of the Hong Kong Buddhist Printing Distributor, and the lay Buddhists

Zhu Jingzhou and Zhou Chunxi who established the Buddhist Sutra Printing Office in Taiwan; then there is also the lay Buddhist Zhan Liwu, who sold a large building on South Chongqing Road and donated the proceeds toward a scholarship for Buddhist youth at the junior college level. Moreover, the old lay Buddhist Li Bingnan of venerable age and eminent virtue; the lay Buddhist Dong Zhengzhi, member of the Legislative Yuan; and the lay Buddhist Cai Niansheng, who arranged the Buddhist Tripitaka[16]—they all often paid homage to us young monastics, so I cannot help but feel ashamed. We don't possess their virtue and abilities, and if we do not aspire to promote the Dharma and to liberate sentient beings, then how can we avoid disappointing these many great worthies and senior elders?

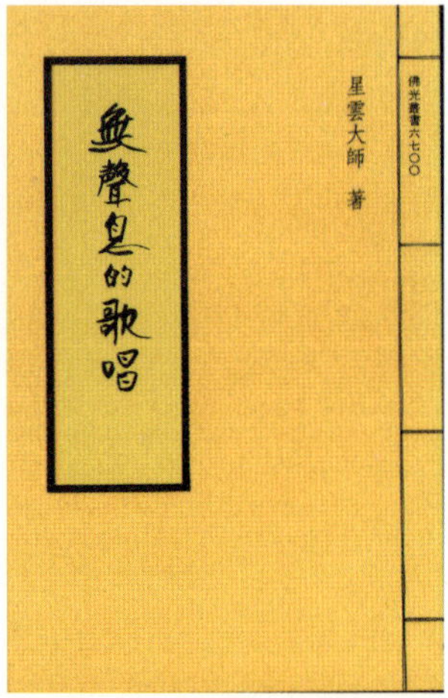

Bells, Gongs, and Wooden Fish is a collection of first-person narratives of twenty commonly seen objects of daily monastic life. Profound meanings are presented through few words, while the Dharma words reveal the Buddha's original intents.
July 1953

The lay Buddhist Wang-Zheng Falian was the wife of Wang Ping, the former vice-minister at the Ministry of the Interior. Wherever I had a new temple dedicated, she would rush over and make a donation. When I wrote *Bells, Gongs, and Wooden Fish*, she went from door to door on my behalf with volume upon volume, promoting the book to over a thousand copies or more. If I did not have that many human affinities, then how could I have made accomplishments in Buddhism? And how

16 In Sanskrit, "three baskets." The Buddhist canon divides the texts into three parts or "baskets": sutra-pitaka, or basket of discourses; the vinaya-pitaka, or basket of disciplinary texts; and the abhidharma-pitaka, or basket of treatises.

could I have developed anything in Buddhism? It was all due to the causes and conditions they gave me. This is why after she turned eighty, I brought Wang-Zheng Falian to Fo Guang Shan, where she could live out her years in good care, and she did not pass away until some years later. I was fortunate in that this allowed me to demonstrate a small token of my kind regard for her.

Auntie Li, an old woman from Kuala Lumpur in Malaysia who had her feet bound when she was young, came to visit Fo Guang Shan on one occasion. I guided her on a short tour, and although I spoke some words to her as we walked, she was Cantonese and unable to understand what I was saying, nor could I understand what she said. All I could do was make gestures and point things out as a way of telling her which way to go. However, owing to such modest causes and conditions, she would later make donations to Fo Guang Shan in the millions and millions every year. She was not a rich person, but she gave away all she had to support Buddhism.

Therefore, Fo Guang Shan is also grateful to many people who have affinities to it in this way. If there were no reliance upon the power of faith, then how could there be such good causes and good conditions?

When Devotees Make Resolve, Bodhisattvas Are in the Human World

The lay Buddhist Liu Chao-ming is one of Fo Guang Shan's benefactors. He opened a factory in Shanghai and has always hired anyone who is a member of BLIA, regardless of their capabilities. As his business developed in Shanghai, he built his own high-rise building later on, and after it was completed, he insisted on reserving a floor in the building for Fo Guang Shan, so the Dharma could be propagated there. Moreover, he set aside a car with its own driver specifically for BLIA members to use. At that time, the restriction on Buddhism in mainland China had not yet been lifted, so how could such resolve as his fail to move someone?

Furthermore, there is the lay Buddhist Chang Sheng-kai, son-in-law of Mr. Chen Mao-pang of the Taiwan Sampo Corporation. He donated his house in Brazil to serve as a temple unconditionally, all of which constitutes giving without notions. So how can one not feel touched by this?

There is the lay Buddhist Chen Shu-chu, a renowned philanthropist in the city of Taitung who was selected as one of the heroes of Asian philanthropy by *Forbes* magazine in the United States. She is a vegetable vendor at a street market who donated all her own surplus money to various charitable organizations, including Fo Guang Shan. She said, "I donated to Fo Guang Shan because Fo Guang Shan propagates the Dharma, directs cultural education, and benefits all sentient beings." What do you think? In terms of their understanding and their support, if these people are not bodhisattvas, then who is?

In truth, in my view, I feel that there are bodhisattvas everywhere throughout this human world, there are good people everywhere, there are people who support each other everywhere, helping one another as they advance along the path to the Pure Land together. Of course, I too have been to many famous monasteries and joined in the crowds of people engaged in worship. But whenever I gaze into space or look upon the ocean, it is as if I am seeing the Dharma body of the Buddhas and bodhisattvas. I also feel that even an image of the Buddha drawn on a piece of paper or an image of a bodhisattva carved out of a piece of wood are the Buddhas coming to give me confirmation and keep me company as my traveling companions.

It was not just the "half bowl of salted vegetables" that my teacher gave me in the past once when I was ill that increased the power of my vow to propagate the Dharma for the benefit of sentient beings. There were people like Venerable Guang Yu in Singapore, the lay Buddhist Sung Fu-ting in Brazil, the lay Buddhist Liao Cheng-hsiang in Thailand, and the lay Buddhist Shen Chia-chen in the United States. During the 1950s, whenever there was a publication of Buddhist texts by the Buddhist Cultural Services Office at Taipei's Sanchong District, they would send in a letter to purchase hundreds or thousands of copies and distribute them for free as a way of making affinities. They did not owe anything to Buddhism, yet they were willing to do their utmost to propagate the Dharma, to purify minds, and to increase joy and happiness in the human world. How could I not recognize them as bodhisattvas in the human world? Further, how could I not acknowledge that the Pure Land is right here in the human world?

A Crowd of a Million People, a Long-Term Response for Running a School

As I began establishing Buddhist colleges in 1965, with only a few hundred students, I already felt that the strain of such an effort was hard to bear. Since I had to provide room, board, and other things, how could I possibly have the energy to go on and run a community college? This was especially so in Taiwan; without millions and millions in funds, how could one

Fo Guang University's Million-Member Fundraising Campaign Wall of Benefactors is almost one kilometer long.
Photo by Venerable Hui Yan

establish a school? But then, I recalled the Million-Member Fundraising Campaign. With one hundred Taiwan dollars per person, and by relying upon the power of a million people, we had the spirit of a foolish man trying to move a mountain on his own and making resolve for the long term. Indeed, one million people came to me in response. In particular, there were volunteers who responded to establishing schools by means of recycling and being environmentally friendly. It gave me the strength to establish not only one university, but even a second, a third, a fourth, and a fifth, all of us working as one in the continuous building effort. I cannot help but be touched by these many bodhisattvas in the human world.

I remember there was one Dharma supporter and benefactor; she had a grandson whose body had already turned completely black, and he was on the verge of death. Nevertheless, the child was restored to life because of our fervent recitation of the "Universal Gate Chapter." There was also a middle-aged woman who had already been dressed in burial garments in

preparation for being laid into her coffin. Members of our Buddhist Youth Group, including the young Wu Suchen (the present Venerable Tzu Jung), went over to ardently conduct a chanting vigil on her behalf. Their pure and heartfelt efforts in reciting Amitabha Buddha's name made her suddenly sit up, open her mouth and say, "I'm hungry and want to eat something." Can you say that such incidents would not increase your belief in and faith toward Buddhism?

Many people increase their faith owing to the inspiration of the Buddhas and bodhisattvas. For me, it has all been because of the many bodhisattvas right in the human world; examples include BLIA members, book club readers, and young men and women. Even the children at nursery schools and child classes: they too have all become my good Dharma friends and become my good teachers. It is not that they are learning from me, rather I am maturing along with them. All of them are like living Buddhas who reinforce my belief and increase the power of my faith in Humanistic Buddhism. They also have set all example for me, directing the levels of my faith, such that my belief in myself is further refined and further elevated.

Given that I have such an understanding of teamwork, the more I undertake work for Buddhism, the more inspired my spirit becomes, and the more devoted I become to its development. I made a vow that even though human life is only several scores of years, I want to transform my limited human life into one that is equivalent to three hundred years. If I begin with my departure from the Buddhist college at the age of twenty-one and then go on up to the age of eighty, then I would have sixty years of time. If I do the work of five people in every single day, then would not five times sixty amount to three hundred? By offering this small amount of effort to the Triple Gem, *nagas*,[17] and heavenly beings, I would ensure that in the long river of history, the Dharma would be like flowing water in an unending stream as it purifies the human mind. Since it was the many bodhisattvas who inspired and enlightened me, how can I not aspire to offer my service for the sake of the mass of humanity? Thus, Humanistic Buddhism has also become the core of my faith.

Providing People with Causes and Conditions, Together We Shine Brightly

I recall the case of the historic Bhiksuni Fazhen [fl. 1149–1189 CE], who resolved to print a copy of the Tripitaka by cutting off her arm to show her determination, and then day and night she went about asking for donations. Her spirit of supporting the Dharma and defending the faith touches us deeply. I also recall Japan's Zen master Tetsugen Doko [1630–1682 CE] who suffered much hardship in raising funds for twelve years in order to print a copy of the Tripitaka. Just when he was about to prepare the woodblocks for printing, he heard that famine had struck the country, so he expended the funds donated to him for the relief of the famine victims, as he considered rescuing people the more important task. He himself began raising funds once more. Nearly ten years later, just as he could cut the woodblocks for printing, he heard once again that a famine had occurred. He then donated all the funds he had

17 In Sanskrit and Pali, "serpent" or as rendered in Chinese, "dragon." They are beings of great power and appear as protectors of the Dharma.

raised toward famine relief again without any reservation whatsoever. Later on, he slowly raised more funds over the ensuing decades, and it was not until his third attempt that the printing of the Tetsugen Tripitaka was completed. This edition of the Tripitaka, so incomparably precious, is preserved near the Manpuku Temple on Mount Obaku in Kyoto, Japan; it has come to represent the bodhisattva spirit in Japan.

As the saying goes, "The Way rises a foot, but the devil rises ten," and the devilish tribulations of the world are constantly delivering destruction, abuse, and condemnation to us, giving us various kinds of difficulties. True, there are many tribulations, but at the same time, the spirit of the bodhisattva is also radiating light in the human world, and constantly illuminating our hearts, bestowing blessings upon us, and giving us strength!

During this life of mine, I have felt a boundless reverence and admiration for those who sacrificed themselves for the faith while in the process of seeking and propagating the Dharma. An example of this is Second Chan Patriarch, Huike [487–593 CE], who cut off his arm to seek the Dharma. How can spirit such as this fail to touch our hearts? Not only has the founder of Buddhism, Sakyamuni Buddha, ensured that generations of our Buddhist disciples naturally give rise to a sense of faith, but these bodhisattvas in the human world also fostered by Humanistic Buddhism have also enhanced our conviction. In the same way, I follow their example; therefore, is it that others liberate me or that I liberate others? In fact, both cases are interrelated.

Hence, over the course of my life, I enjoy giving others causes and conditions, as everyone has also given me many causes and conditions. With these positive affinities among ourselves, we are then able to achieve many splendid and shared wishes that we share together. The compassion and belief revealed on the outside may enhance interpersonal strengths; our internal resolve can radiate light with the power of vows made by the wise. How could this advancement of faith not stride ahead and rank at the level of universities and colleges?

An Inexhaustible Treasure Awaits Everyone's Exploration

My own hidden practice over several decades is not worth discussing with outsiders. However, in my own meditation cultivation, worship, aspiration, contemplation, service, and ascetic practice, sometimes even one occasion of tears brought out by a moving experience can hold the possibility of increasing achievement on my Buddhist path of many years; one occasion of exercising patience with humiliation holds the possibility of enhancing my resolve of many years. Having a conversation with my true intrinsic nature every once in a while holds the possibility of pulling on my heartstrings; the process of meditative contemplation also holds the possibility of unearthing the infinite treasure within faith. During these several decades of my life, even though I have not attained Buddhahood or become a patriarch, can we remain completely ignorant of the Buddha's light and the Buddha's virtue, the truth of the treasure? It is not possible.

In this way, I cannot refrain from delight and glory, thanks to the great Buddha, bodhisattvas, and faith in the human world. Although I should raise my own faith to even higher levels, the height, breadth, and infinite range of faith is still something that awaits our uninterrupted ascent.

Now that I have already reached the age of ninety [2016], would you say that I have achieved awakening? I dare not say so. Would you say that I am enlightened? I do not know. Would you say that I have some sort of realization of the Dharma? That is also not something that can be fully expressed in one or two words. Would you say that I have some degree of understanding toward faith in terms of the breadth, depth, and infinitude of its meaning? It is impossible for me to say. My belief in the Dharma is boundless and endless. Space is finite; the universe is limitless; and my vow is inexhaustible. I feel that there is immeasurable treasure and limitless Dharma joy within faith, all of which is awaiting us to advance to the doctoral level and undertake more profound research. Even granted that we have already attained a PhD in faith, there is still postdoctoral research to be conducted.

Resonating with the Buddha, Practicing Humanistic Buddhism Diligently

Regarding this life of mine within the world of faith, due to my own hidden practice, I obtained many blessings from the Buddhas and bodhisattvas, which I cannot fully convey. Except for the gratitude I feel toward the Buddha's kindness, it is difficult to describe my world of faith except to say that it is inconceivable. I can only conclude this essay with the inconceivable that I have experienced, which is difficult to put into words. I offer such incense, flowers, and belief as a dedication to the Buddha and as an offering to the Buddha. We are always with the Buddha, and we are also connected to devotees in all directions, a wish of happiness to all monastic and lay believers.

I once copied out a sutra in blood by pricking myself, and I also once burned my arm as an offering. I once remained silent for a year without speaking, and once I also kept my eyes closed for three months without seeing. Later on, I would occasionally open my eyes and suddenly feel: Oh, there are still verdant mountains; there are still trees; the sky is still there; and my feelings would then return to this world. Ever since I was young, I have had such sheer enthusiasm.

I once stayed at Hsi Lai Temple in the United States for a five-month secluded retreat. I remember one morning, five or six of my Dharma friends came to see me, including Venerable Huan Sheng and Venerable Yin Hai. In the retreat quarters, I could offer one bowl of noodles for them to eat within a minute. I do not know how many times I went up and down the stairs in the retreat quarters every day, right up until my legs became swollen. The doctor warned me that I had diabetes, and that it could be quite serious, so I must not walk. It was only then that I stopped.

In mentioning these many experiences, I am not trying to advertise myself; I am just hoping that all Buddhist followers as a whole will be able to be like me, generating a strong belief in Buddhism and its practice. Even though the Buddha has not manifested physically, there is no place in space where he is absent. Therefore, regardless of whether it is an image of the Buddha drawn on paper or one carved into wood, so long as your heart is resonating with him, then the Buddha is there with you.

Hence, I also tell my disciples that we must promote faith, ascetic practice, patience, loving-kindness and compassion, service, the making of affinities, and so on. By having loving-kindness and compassion, joy, equanimity, the non-abiding states of mind, and priceless faith, we can live a completely different life and generate limitless Dharma joy as well as meditative bliss. This indeed is the goal of having faith in Humanistic Buddhism.

The Venerable Master paying homage to the Buddha in the Main Shrine, Fo Guang Shan.

Photo provided by the Historical Museum of Fo Guang Shan

Am I Really like a Monk?

Given that I have become a monk, I have placed demands upon myself. My sense of leaving the secular and focusing on the path must surpass others; my sense of self-restraint and doing for others must be strengthened. I must learn to endure disadvantage, and I must let others gain some advantage at my expense; I must learn how to be patient and how to undergo adversity. This is all as it should be.

Since joining the monastic order at a young age and over the course of my eighty years as a monk, I have constantly asked myself, "Am I really like a monk?"

Upon shaving my head and putting on my monastic robes, I was clearly aware that I had joined the monastic order and become a monk. However, I constantly examine myself: "Am I really like a monk?" At first, I examined my own mentality regarding my faith: "Do I really believe in Buddhism?"

There is no question that I already had the foundation for faith from the time I accompanied my maternal grandmother as a child. Although it was not very pure or transcendent, my faith was most certainly in Buddhism, not in some heretical doctrines.

Aspiring to Work: The Development of My Self-Education

After joining the monastic order, I further asked myself, "Am I like a monk when I talk? Am I like a monk when I walk? Are all of my actions and conduct like those of a monk?" I paid attention to my own bearing and deportment from time to time, that I must "stand like a pine and walk like the wind." In eating a meal, I must be like "a dragon swallowing pearls, a phoenix nodding its head." In speaking, I must speak "truthful and compassionate words." I must be as a monk should be.

Upon reaching adulthood, my knowledge of the world had increased, my thinking had increased, and my desires had also increased. Thus, I thought to myself, "Can I remain a vegetarian my whole life?" In being a monk, one must certainly be a vegetarian. This is not a problem in that before I had joined the monastic order, I already had the concept of vegetarianism. Furthermore, being a monk means that one should not go out into society at night, watch and listen to music and dance, or laugh merrily and joke around as people in society do. I did not think that would be difficult either because as a child I always behaved myself at home; I never got into fights with the other children, and I never scolded other people. Since I liked doing housework and acting dutifully toward my parents, I did not think it would be a problem for me to become an obedient and contented monk who honored his teachers within the Buddhist tradition. I thought, "I can be a good monk."

I also considered that in becoming a monk, one should make a resolve and be willing to undertake some hard work, such as cooking, gathering firewood, carrying water, guarding the monastery, and patrolling the dormitories at night. "Can I endure a life with so much hard work?" I asked myself. But this was not a problem either; I grew up in a poor family since childhood and was accustomed to a life full of suffering. Therefore, this kind of energy was in my intrinsic nature, and I felt that I could be still a good monk.

However, I was pigeon-toed when I walked, which was caused by my bone structure. For this reason, I wanted to correct my gait, but it really was not easy to do so. Since walking "pigeon-toed" does not look good, I became utterly resolved that I simply had to walk well. This was not something that my teachers ordered me to change either, nor did my teachers reproach me for it. But given that I had joined the monastic order, if I did not educate myself and put demands upon myself, my development would then be limited.

Furthermore, even though my negative thoughts were few in number, when it came to positive and proactive deeds, I was quite cowardly and lacked morals and courage. Of course, when people took advantage of me, I would still defend myself.

The Venerable Master at twenty years of age.

But normally, I chose to silently endure some of the illicit situations within Buddhism. It was not until much later when the cultivation of my own belief in Buddhism had been strengthened that I felt:

> *This old monk would rather fall into hell*
> *Than use the Dharma for personal favors.*

For the sake of Buddhism's prosperity, I must have the moral courage to speak out.

As far as some illicit situations within Buddhism, although I could not do much about them, I always wanted to accept full responsibility for them. However, I further thought, "Am I to say that I am absolutely right and good?" I also blamed myself. For example, although I did not eat meat, did I cherish life? Although I was unwilling to partake of eating, drinking, and making merry in this world, have I achieved anything for the cause of Buddhism? I would also blame myself, "Have I attracted too much antipathy by holding too strongly to my own position in dealing with others?"

As I slowly grew up, I further considered how a monk must have knowledge, be able to expound ideas through writing, and benefit sentient beings by propagating the Dharma. I wondered, "Am I able to do these?" When I was young, I thought about how I would found a university and run a newspaper in the future, but I knew that it was merely a dream because it was impossible to realize given my circumstances at the time. However, we must have a dream. This aspiration that I cherished in my heart remained unknown to anyone else. If I were able to realize such a dream, then I would really be a monk who propagates the Dharma for the benefit of sentient beings.

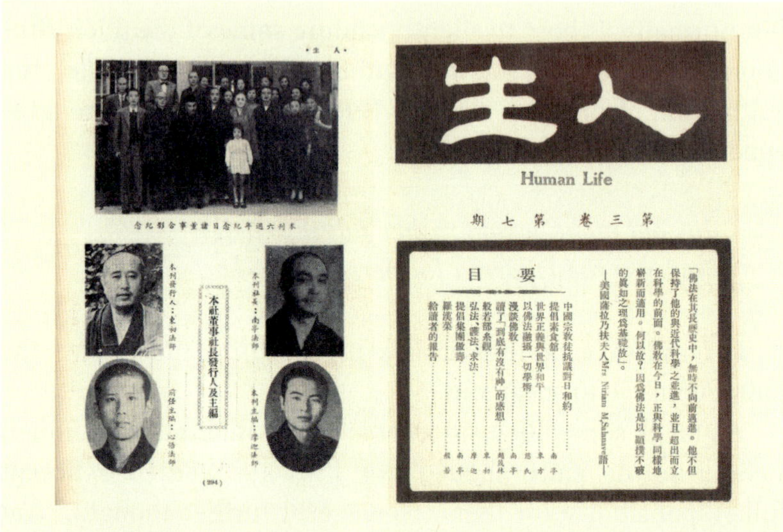

The Venerable Master was the editor in chief for *Human Life* magazine for six years under the pen name Mojia.

However, being a monk, I must be able to chant and play the various kinds of Dharma instruments. In this case, I knew of my shortcomings in these areas, but I was completely oblivious that I was tone deaf. It wasn't until I learned of it from someone else that I realized how serious things were. Since the chanting of my other classmates was especially esteemed and well received by others, as I had no sense of musical rhythm and had no voice that could carry a tune, I could not help but feel inferior at that time. My inability to be as good as those many classmates and senior schoolmates always left me feeling a measure shorter in stature compared to them.

In retrospect, I thought it didn't matter that much, as there are many ways to be a monk. As long as I am able to abide by the rules of being a monk, and to receive as well as uphold the precepts, then I may engage in cultural, educational, and charitable work. I need not remain only within the shrine conducting sutra chanting and repentance services or playing the Dharma instruments. I thought that this was not necessarily a shortcoming, for I firmly believed I could become a cultural monk, an educational monk, and a charitable monk.

Leaving the Secular for the Spiritual, Insisting upon Self-Restraint and Doing for Others

Given that I have become a monk, I have placed demands upon myself: My sense of leaving the secular and focusing on the path must surpass the resolve of others; my sense of self-restraint and doing for others must be strengthened. I must learn to endure disadvantage, and I must let others gain some advantage at my expense; I must learn how to be patient and how to undergo adversity. This is all as it should be.

Although Buddhism was very conservative at the time, I thought in the future if I had the opportunity to find a Buddhist leader, I would follow him and undertake the building, reform, and development of a new Buddhism, as well as this new Buddhism's guidance, to benefit the lives of the humanistic devotees. I thought that I should have this energy, aspiration, and resolve. I felt assured of myself that I was able to be a good monk.

Am I really like a monk? I am certain that I will be like a monk.

But later on, I saw how some monks wore their robes untidily, and felt that they were not like monks; I saw that their diets were not vegetarian, and I felt that they were not like monks; I saw that they frequently returned to their secular families, and were unable to separate themselves from

The Venerable Master leads by example: "I am within the assembly" and take formal Buddhist meals with the great assembly.

secular life, so I felt that they were not like monks. Within Buddhism, there are many people who are like monks, and there are many others who are not like monks. As long as a person wears a monastic robe, they are "monkish" (having the external appearance of a monk). Are ordinary devotees able to discern who is "monkish" and who is a "monk"? In my mind, devotees will also find it difficult to tell the difference.

If some monastics are incompetent, or even if they are mocked as "mute sheep monastics" because they are unable give teachings, it does not matter as long as they can be compassionate. The problem is that there are now people who not only lack compassion, but also harbor wrong views. We should come to some self-realization that as monks, we must have right knowledge, right view, and the heart of unwavering faith.

Especially in Buddhism, the standards of the devotees also differ in various ways. Some simply do not care whether their teacher embodies the Way or not. Such a person protects the individual but not the Dharma, protects the teacher but not the community, protects the temple but not Buddhism, and protects the incorrect but not the correct.

Nor do they distinguish between right or wrong and wholesome or unwholesome. They do not care to discern whether a monastic is a monk or simply "monkish." As long as a monastic is good to them, then it is regarded as Buddhism in their mind.

As a matter of fact, can a Buddhism like this, one that makes no distinction between right and wrong, wholesome or unwholesome, form a religious organization? Can it serve as a good interface between monastics and devotees? Can such a faith be pure and upright? I cannot help experiencing mental conflict regarding such questions, for I am thinking about how to change the "monkish" ones into real "monks."

In my mind, joining the monastic order has nothing to do with the formality of shaving the head or the donning of monastic robes at all. What is most important is that the "mind" must leave home to join the monastic order. In particular, one's faith and conviction in Buddhism, as well as one's life in the future, have to convince the larger community that one is a monk. Only in this way does one "manifest the form of a monk."

A Mind Devoid of Sentient Beings Is like an Insect on a Lion's Body

Joining the monastic order is equivalent to being reborn as a human being. One transforms anew the mundane mind and body of this world into the purified form of a monk. If one fails to understand this point, then one is not a monk, but "an insect on the lion's body." This will surely lead to the corruption of Buddhism because one neither possesses any belief nor has the value of self-affirmation.

During the time of the Buddha, there was a group of non-Buddhists who said to the Buddha, "You have seized our domain and have seized our followers. We are not going to let you off; we have come to attack you."

The Buddha spoke calmly: "I am an awakened *sramana*;[1] how would I still care about your cudgels?" Then those non-Buddhists said, "We can spread rumors about you everywhere and criticize your Dharma." The Buddha then said, "The Dharma is the truth. Your criticisms cannot do any harm to the Dharma, either."

The group of non-Buddhists threatened and intimidated the Buddha in one way or another, but the Buddha remained unmoved.

Finally, the non-Buddhists said, "In that case, we will become your disciples from now on, wear your clothes, and shave off our hair and mustaches. Nominally, we will be disciples of the Buddha, but in reality, we will engage in mundane affairs and wrongdoings contrary to the Dharma."

At that moment, the Buddha fell silent, disheartened, and then said, "If you act that way, then there is nothing I can do about it."

This is because "the insect on the lion's body still eats from the lion's flesh." The external world cannot bring down a fierce lion, but an insect on the lion's body still eats the lion's flesh, and the lion itself cannot repel it either.

Yet unexpectedly, this kind of situation has appeared today, two thousand years later. It is very common for people who have shaved off their hair and mustaches and donned monastic robes to be unaware of themselves as monks. Why? They have no faith and no Dharma; there is no Buddha in their hearts, much less sentient beings. They see joining the monastic order in the same way that some people see marriage, as a

1 In Sanskrit, a generic referent for monastics.

Monastics shoulder the tasks of Buddhism; they must go through the Triple Platform Full Ordination Ceremony to be true monastics. Pictured, in 1977, is the first time Fo Guang Shan conducted the International Triple Platform Full Ordination Ceremony, which was praised as a Model Ordination Ceremony.
Photo provided by *The Merit Times*

乙丑夏曆八月初八
正法眼藏
心平智宗受持
攝山棲霞寺佛祖源流

means of appearing to have a livelihood. They think joining the monastic order is simply a career; they have found a job that provides free room and board. They think that joining the monastic order means they can wander wherever they want, as in the saying:

The world's monasteries provide a mountain's worth of food;
The alms bowl provides a meal wherever one wants.

Yet this kind of monk who wanders around, traveling far and wide, is not the worst of it. There are some monks who live without purpose by depending upon Buddhism or making a living through sutra chanting and repentance services, coveting the offerings of the devotees; or they go from place to place asking for donations in order to fulfill their desires. They are not like monks; these are the insects on the lion's body.

As a monk, to have such conduct is even less than being a merchant, for merchants at least provide goods in exchange for money. What can these monks provide their devotees in exchange for the offerings they receive? Could one receive offerings if there were no Dharma? Could one receive offerings if there were no morality? Could one receive offerings if there were no ascetic practices and no cultivation of the Dharma? Could one receive offerings if sentient beings were absent from your heart, and you had no inclination to propagate the Dharma for the benefit of sentient beings? Today there are so many monks who make their living by depending upon Buddhism, just like parasites. In the absence of faith in Buddhism and in the absence of one's own cultivation of the practice, can there be any hope for the Dharma?

There is an expression, "There are many Buddhists and Taoists before the gates of Hell." Now all the monastic disciples of the Buddha within Buddhism as a whole ought to ask themselves, "Am I a disciple of the Buddha? Or of mara?[2] Have I come to revive Buddhism, or have I come to destroy Buddhism?"

Conduct and Mentality Must Adhere to the Dharma

Today's Chinese Buddhism has become an authentic tradition within Buddhism. As a monastic disciple, what would one know about Chinese Buddhism? Would one be able to promote and develop the Dharma in the future according to the orthodox Dharma? For example, as one joins the monastic order and comes to depend upon Buddhism, being able to receive the favor of the Buddhist tradition and being able to receive the offerings of the devotees, one must ask oneself, "Am I really like a monk?"

This question, "Am I really like a monk?" is a question that all disciples of the Buddha must constantly ask themselves every moment and must constantly consider carefully.

If one leaves the temple and then changes clothes, smokes, drinks, sings, and dances—is that being like a monk? Is going to a restaurant to drink alcohol, and eat fish and meat like a monk? Is going shopping to buy name brand items and accumulating wealth being like a monk? Is clowning around and seeking amusement as one pleases being like a monk? Is brawling and swearing being like a monk? Can one be like a monk yet not know the names of the Buddha, the meaning of the Dharma, or the mission of a monk? Can one be like a monk yet

2 Mara primarily refers to the demons to be found within the mind, that which tempts one away from one's virtues and wholesome deeds in spiritual progress.

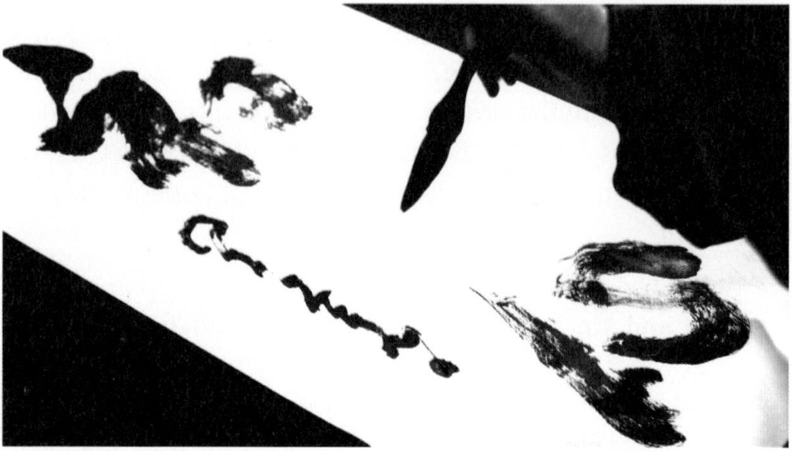

The Venerable Master always encourages young people not to forget their initial resolve, and not retreat or turn away from it; also, by remembering their initial resolve, they will have strength.

Photo provided by Commonwealth Publishing

not know the meaning of the Triple Gem, not uphold the five precepts, not faithfully practice the ten wholesome actions,[3] and not know the six perfections?[4] How can one be like a monk if the Dharma is absent from one's heart and mind?

If I can accept the leadership of the monastic community with its six points of reverent harmony[5] and dwell harmoniously with others, then I am really like a monk. If I can abide by the precepts and the monastery rules, then I am really like a monk. If I can remain a vegetarian and keep my monastic robe tidy, and uphold the three categories of pure precepts, which

3 No killing, no stealing, and no sexual misconduct; no lying, no divisive speech, no harsh speech, and no flattery; and no greed, no ill will, and no deviant views.

4 These are six qualities that bodhisattvas develop on their way to Buddhahood: giving, morality, patience, diligence, meditative concentration, and wisdom.

5 1) Harmony in view through sharing the same understanding, 2) moral harmony through sharing the same precepts, 3) economic harmony through sharing things equally, 4) mental harmony through shared happiness, 5) verbal harmony through avoiding disputes, and 6) physical harmony through living together.

are the precepts that support the observance of proper conduct, the precepts that support the practice of wholesome deeds, and the precepts that benefit sentient being then I am really like a monk. If I can faithfully carry out these three, which are also referred to as the Triple Platform Full Ordination Ceremony, then I can be like a monastic disciple of the Buddha.

Having joined the monastic order, one's physical needs are cared for by the administrators. As long as one has adequate food and clothing, knows one's place, and remains pure with few desires, then would that not be like a monk? If I can remember to bring joy to sentient beings and to add honor to the Dharma, then I would be like a monk. Or perhaps if I lack knowledge and wisdom, but I can make offerings to sentient beings as well as the Buddha by means of my physical labor, my compassion, and my sincerity, then I would be like a monk. Or if I diligently read the Buddhist canon, worship the Buddha, propagate the truth, and do the work of propagating the Dharma, not have any improper habits and wrong views, wrong thoughts, or wrong actions that violate the Dharma, then I would be like a monastic disciple of the Buddha.

Suppose today the Chinese Buddhist Association were to gather together monastics in their millions for reexamination; how many of them would be like genuine monks? With those many people who are not like monks living without purpose by depending upon Buddhism, does Buddhism still have a future? Therefore, we must now awaken all of Buddhism's monastic disciples to engage in introspection and self-examination. They can ask, "Am I really like a monk?"

If one is really like a monk, then one may not constantly go back to one's secular family; one may never again eat fish and meat; one may never again wear secular clothing; and one may not accept offerings and gifts of money from society. All one needs to do is to focus on staying in the monastery, where one worships the Buddha, cultivates the practice, and serves sentient beings according to their needs. Without the self and without notion, Buddhist activities are conducted according to the Dharma, such that the Buddhist tradition is further adorned and dignified. Even if one stays in the monastery and does not go out, offerings will still come.

Helping the Buddha Propagate the Dharma and Transform Sentient Beings: Dharma Waters Nourish the Masses

During the time of the Buddha, the bhiksus would go out with their alms bowls and beg for food, and at the same time, they would propagate the Dharma to the masses in society. Devotees gave their offerings while monastics taught the Dharma for the benefit of sentient beings; that is to say, "The gift of wealth and the gift of Dharma are equal, without any distinction." In today's Buddhism, the devotees on the whole provide offerings enthusiastically, but is our monastic order really like a monastic order? Do we deserve to receive such offerings?

One must know shame and suffering. In *The Teachings Bequeathed by the Buddha Sutra*, the Buddha constantly admonishes us that we should lay hands on our own heads, and tell ourselves, "I have already become a monk." Therefore, one must cultivate and learn the Dharma and diligently propagate Buddhism. One must know shame, as in the saying "The clothes of shame adorn one with limitless sublimity." One must be able to know suffering, for only in this way will one respect others; one must be humble, for only in this way will one be able to receive the Dharma.

If we are clamoring for riches, glory, and honor, then we can develop ourselves in career-oriented organizations, such as factories and enterprises in society; there is no need to live without purpose by depending upon Buddhism. Having received so many offerings given in faith, how should one repay people in the future? Why suffer through adversity only to realize that "Bodhisattvas dread the cause, while ordinary beings dread the effect"? If one understands how to learn the methods of cultivation for the Buddhas and bodhisattvas, one will be able to avoid such "causes" and will not act in violation of the Dharma.

Since ancient times, there have been many great exemplary worthies within Chinese Buddhism who can serve as our models to emulate, like the eminent monastics of the Chan School's "one flower opening with five petals"[6] and "Five Houses and Seven Schools."[7] Their wisdom and their enlightenment ensured that the Dharma is respected by ordinary people. As for the patriarchs of the various schools, such as Tiantai, Huayan, Faxiang, Three Treatise, and others, they used the Dharma to soothe the minds of sentient beings. So why can't we model ourselves on them? Why can't we learn from them?

Therefore, I ardently hope today that our disciples who have newly joined the monastic order will study the precepts for at least five years and engage in ascetic practice for five years; then, and only then, could they listen to the teachings and sit in meditation. They would settle in the monastery and focus on learning, and only after ten years would they be able to step outside

6 After the sixth patriarch, Huineng, the Chan School became divided into the "five houses" of Linji, Guiyang, Caodong, Yunmen, and Fayan. This period of profusion is historically known as "one flower opening with five petals."

7 During the Song dynasty, the Huanglong and Yangqi sects developed out of the Linji School; when added together with the previous five sects, they were known as the "seven schools."

the monastery's gate. Having just joined the monastic order, one cannot simply dress up in monastic robes and go around attracting attention. Even though the laws of the nation take no notice and neither do the police, karma will. It is indeed lamentable to lose one's human existence while wearing monastic robes!

"Am I really like a monk?" is not necessarily something for the daily morning and evening services. Recite this question ten times in the morning and ten times in the evening, conduct a self-examination from the heart, and bring the heart in line with this question. At the very least, one can make the aspiration of "I will act for Buddhism," for this too will assist in helping the Buddha propagate the Dharma and transform sentient beings. Only in this way will one be like a disciple of the Buddhist tradition and a monk.

I hope the disciples and devotees in the Buddhist community will be able to learn from the lay Buddhist Li Bingnan. Although he was already old and of noble character, when he saw those monks who neither abided by the rules nor observed the precepts, he would kneel down in prostration to all of them. His point was to say, "Are you really like a monk?" However, there is no need for us to pose the question in the way that the lay Buddhist Li Bingnan did; we just need to ask ourselves, "Am I really like a monk?"

I want to be like a monk. When walking, I want to walk properly; when speaking, I want to speak compassionately. I want to be able to get along with others, love all with compassion, and give people joy as well as respect. When I think about the parrot with its beakful of water [to put out the forest fire] and the many good deeds of the Buddha, giving toward sentient beings and not going against people's wishes

Buddhists should have the spirit of "Buddhism depends upon me" and shoulder the tasks of Buddhism.
Photo by Yang Guanlin

during past lifetimes, am I able to fulfill one percent of that? In our daily conduct, we must also be like the Confucianists, as in their saying "I reflect upon myself thrice daily," and engage in self-reflection. During our daily meditation practice, we must reflect upon this verse and feel a sense of shame:

> *At eighty, Chan Master Zhaozhou still set out on foot,*
> *Simply because his mind was not yet at peace.*

In the Self-Reflection of Monks, the Dharma Will Surely Flourish

I have been a monk since childhood and now I am already old and disabled. However, during my lifetime, not only have I asked myself the question "Am I really like a monk?" a billion times, I also keep to the five contemplations[8] when I eat. I do not choose between the coarse or the fine, and do not discriminate between the good and the bad. In this I am able to eat all my meals with joy and gratitude. I think that only in this way is one really like a monk. Each time I go for a walk, I imagine that there are many eyes watching me and many fingers pointing at me, so I certainly must walk in a dignified way, such that others will not look down on me. I want to walk in a poised and dignified manner like a monastic. When speaking with others, I want to be free of any coarse language or name-calling. Why? Since I am a monk, I must conduct myself in a composed manner and speak words that are kind and loving.

The months and years have passed on and on in this life as a monk for nearly eighty years, and now ninety years have passed away, all because I wanted to be someone who is like a monk. I know that my days to come are short, yet I am still asking myself, "Am I really like a monk?" Considering that I have not yet done well at being a monk in this lifetime, I vow to continue being a monk in the next lifetime. I dare not yield to the vain hope of becoming a Buddha; I just want to be a good monk.

Given the number of people who have entered the Buddhist tradition and also the high number of people who have hastily entered the ordination platform and been ordained, I address these young fellow practitioners: You must consider this question now that you have ascended the platform and been ordained. Do you think of yourself as really being like a monk? If you are not like a monk, how can the eight classes of

8 1) Assess the amount of work involved, and weigh up the origins of the food;
2) Reflect on one's own moral conduct, perfect or not, and take this offering;
3) Safeguard the mind against all error, and do not give rise to hatred or greed;
4) Regard this food as good medicine so as to treat the weakened body;
5) In order to accomplish the Way, one deserves to accept this food.

beings,[9] the heavenly beings, nagas, and other guardian spirits who protect the Dharma forgive you?

Seeing the Buddhist community around the world today, I cannot help but insist that everyone ponder this question, "Am I really like a monk?" Naturally, I dare not make this demand upon others, for I can only begin with myself. If everybody is able to engage in self-introspection regularly, then there will surely be progress and some growth in terms of one's own spiritual cultivation. If everyone is able to do this, then the Dharma will surely flourish. This is indeed something of great importance, which we have been ardently awaiting!

9 Heavenly beings, nagas, yaksas, asuras, gandharvas, garudas (golden-winged birds), kimnaras, and mahoragas.

The Venerable Master wishes—May the Buddha's light shine universally and Dharma waters flow eternally.

Photo by Venerable Hui Yan

My Reflections on Venerable Master Taixu's Fiftieth Birthday Poem

In fact, what I have enjoyed the most in my reading, and it could be said that a piece of writing that has had an important influence upon my life is the poem "Thoughts on My Fiftieth Birthday," written by Venerable Master Taixu during his visit to India when the lay Buddhist Tan Yun-shan,[1] Chairperson of the Institute of Chinese Language and Culture at Visva-Bharati University held a celebration for his fiftieth birthday.

1 1898–1983; he was a Buddhist scholar teaching in India.

Everyone celebrates their birthday on the day they were born, or it may be called a "birth celebration." In particular, all the birthdays that mark decades are especially important, such as ten, twenty, sixty, eighty, and ninety years of age. But I feel that the term "birth celebration" requires some further reflection. This is because the day we are born is the day our mothers experience suffering, so it should be called "Mother's Day of Suffering." Historically, it is impossible to calculate the great number of mothers who have experienced a difficult labor for the sake of giving birth to their sons and daughters. Therefore, for the sons and daughters who are born, is it worthy to be called a birth celebration? We should actually be commemorating a day of suffering for our mothers.

From my birth up until now, I have not been someone who enjoys celebrating birthdays, nor do I remember my ordinary birthdays. However, I can recall a few of my birthdays that marked a decade, and most of those were celebrated with the help of others, so I do have some memories that I will talk about here just for everyone's amusement.

Since my family was poor during my childhood, I had never worn any new clothes before the age of twenty. Because I had an older brother, he would of course give me the clothes he had worn and no longer wanted. Then after I had joined the monastic order, there was a Dharma brother who would also give me the clothes he had worn and no longer wanted.

New Clothes at the Age of Ten Were Burned by Mosquito-Repellent Incense and Discarded

I remember when I was ten years old, my mother finally made a set of completely new clothes for me even as we suffered from poverty. She went on to say, "Tomorrow is your tenth birthday; this set of new clothes was made especially for you."

The Venerable Master at age twenty.

Since we were poor, I knew nothing about celebrating birthdays. But now that I had a set of new clothes, I was also extremely happy. I finally had new clothes, and tomorrow I could wear them. Consequently, I placed them at the foot of my bed with the greatest of care.

We lived in the countryside, and mosquitoes during summer evenings would swarm about. One could always catch quite a few of them with a scoop of the hand at any time. At the time, there were no mosquito nets, but there was mosquito-repellent incense, which was long like a snake. Lighting it would drive the mosquitoes away so that one could sleep in peace.

Because I was young and careless, after I lit the mosquito-repellent incense, I put half of it on my clothes and went to sleep. After a period of time, the mosquito-repellent incense had burned enough that it reached my clothes. My clothes caught fire—which caused me to awaken in alarm. I quickly put the fire out, but my clothes were already ruined. This was a mistake of my own doing, so I could not blame anyone or anything else. All I could do was lament that I did not have the good fortune to wear new clothes.

Later on, upon joining the monastic order, I did not pay attention to my birthdays and basically forgot about them; I did not even remember how old I was. I only remember that year when I was twenty years old and studying at the Jiaoshan Buddhist College. My entire body was covered with festering sores, and the pain was unbearable. Taking off the clothes I was wearing was like peeling off a layer of skin even walking was very arduous.

One day at noontime, my classmates had all gone to eat at the dining hall, but since I could not properly put on my monastic robes, I just sat on the steps at the entrance and stared blankly. Suddenly a young married couple came by and saw me sitting in the courtyard. They asked me, "How old are you?" I suddenly thought, "Oh, I am twenty years old today," and that was how I answered them. But they did not hear me clearly, for they thought I said, "I am twenty years old this year." This was the day commemorating my twentieth birthday with a body festering with sores.

No Birthday Celebrations, No Feelings of Self-Importance

The year I turned thirty years old, I was already in Taiwan. The wife of General Su Li-jen [1900–1990], Madame Sun-Zhang Ching-yang, along with several like-minded friends, had established a weekly periodical called *Awakening the World.* Since they could not find anyone to do the editing, they looked to me for help.

I had written articles for magazines and had also done the editing myself, but I did not have any experience with editing a weekly periodical in the style of a newspaper. All I could do was to work hard to learn about it and see how I could edit this periodical for them. When I first started, I could not even finish the editing in a day, because I did not understand how the news was edited in newspapers, what were called lengths, special sections, and character counts; no matter how I made the calculations, they always appeared somewhat incorrect. However, those who had asked me to help knew that I was extraordinarily diligent. Later on, I was able to arrange and set the content for four pages in only half an hour.

Later on, they heard about my thirtieth birthday, marking how one "stands firm" according to Confucius. They made a special effort to lay out a table of vegetarian food for me. All the utensils, spoons, and chopsticks were made out of gold. Madame Sun's two large cases of golden tableware had never been used before, but in order to express the importance I held for her, she had the whole set brought out to celebrate my birthday. But I was not pleased at all. Why? I did not feel that

The Venerable Master at his sixtieth birthday celebration, with over one thousand devotees of the same age-group.

Photo provided by Historical Museum of Fo Guang Shan, July 22, 1992

I was that important. However, in the face of so many people senior to me, I found it difficult to turn them down, and the event passed in a baffling muddle.

My fortieth year came with the founding of Fo Guang Shan, and with all the bustling about at that time, I did not remember which day marked my fortieth birthday.

When I was fifty, Fo Guang Shan was at an important stage in the building project. I was so busy that I forgot all about birthday celebrations.

By the time I was sixty, the Pilgrim's Lodge, the Buddhist college, and the Main Shrine were all more or less completed. According to the monastic administrative system, I should have stepped down from my position at the age of fifty-eight.

At that time, due to considerable attention from various circles in Taiwan, a letter even came from the Presidential Office expressing concern. They all said that this should not be called a "stepping down," but rather a "Dharma transmission." I thought that the Presidential Office's understanding of the "Dharma transmission" was quite reasonable, and even the many editorials in the newspapers also discussed the issue of my Dharma transmission and stepping down. Most likely at that time in society, there were family businesses where one person was monopolizing their position and unwilling to step down. Therefore, the news of my stepping down in accordance with the rules and regulations aroused the serious attention from society.

Holding a Long-Life Celebration, Blessing the Elders on Their Sixtieth Year

In that year, Venerable Hsin Ping, my disciple who succeeded me as abbot, was determined to hold a sixtieth birthday celebration for me. The other disciples and devotees also repeatedly followed his lead in making this request. There was no way I could refuse in the face of so many people, so I had no choice but to say, "If you are able to find one thousand people who are sixty years of age and gather them together at Fo Guang Shan, then I will celebrate my birthday with you."

I do not know how they managed to invite them, but there were actually one thousand and three hundred individuals, all sixty years of age, who had come to Fo Guang Shan. In the past when they talked about celebrating my birthday, I always felt unhappy. But on that day, I was not upset at all, for I felt that being together with more than a thousand seniors who were also sixty years old made me feel like it was a grand affair. At the same time, I could also happily bestow blessings upon those many elders on their sixtieth year who have lived half a century.

When I was seventy years old, I was probably traveling abroad, and I do not know how I spent that birthday, either.

I was at Hsi Lai Temple in the United States the year I became eighty years old. I remember one day as I was eating rice porridge, I suddenly remembered that it was my birthday, and

The Venerable Master attending the book launch event for *Humanistic Buddhism: Holding True to the Original Intents of Buddha* held at Dajue Temple in Yixing.
Photo by Zhou Yun, Aug. 24, 2016

it was not until then that everyone remembered I had turned eighty. No one knew what would be the best thing to do; at which point I said, "It is alright! Rice porridge is also a suitable meal for old folks." This too is a kind of beautiful reflection.

This year (2016), I have reached the age of ninety. Since I dared not disturb anyone, I made a special effort of hiding myself away at Yixing Dajue Temple, the seat of my lineage. I spent a day in a quiet room for a secluded retreat, chanting sutras, sitting in meditation, pondering deeply, and contemplating silently. This was the Buddhist Mother's Day of Suffering, a parental kindness so difficult to repay. How could I hold a celebration for myself? The Buddha's kindness in particular is so vast and expansive, and there is no way I can recompense it. How dare I speak of longevity? All I could do on that day when my mother suffered strenuous hardship was to make a wish for her and pray for her.

That afternoon, since the People's Publishing House in mainland China had published a simplified character edition of my new book, *Humanistic Buddhism: Holding True to the*

Original Intents of Buddha, a publication announcement was held at Dajue Temple. More than three hundred college presidents, professors, and scholars from many education circles came. No one mentioned my birthday, so I felt very happy.

A Long Verse Expressing Thoughts as a Means for Cultivating the Mind

In my life, these so-called birthdays passed by more or less in this simple fashion, so I have written these many things related to birthdays. In fact, what I have enjoyed the most in my reading, and it could be said that a piece of writing that has had an important influence upon my life is the poem "Thoughts on My Fiftieth Birthday," written by Venerable Master Taixu during his visit to India when the lay Buddhist Tan Yun-shan, Chairperson of the Institute of Chinese Language and Culture at Visva-Bharati University, held a celebration for his fiftieth birthday.

Venerable Master Taixu.

It could be said that within the sixty volumes of Venerable Master Taixu's *Complete Works*, it is this poem that I feel the most affinity with, and it is the one that I consider the most brilliant. For the past several decades, this poem has become for me something like *The Heart Sutra.*[2] I often take it out and recite it, and I can even recite it backwards and forwards from memory. Even now, every time I read this poem, I seem to be drawing closer to Venerable Master Taixu, to the point of wishing to transform my own remaining years into the lifespan of Venerable Master Taixu, following his spirit and enhancing the power of his vow.

Now I respectfully present his poem here:

I was not born at the right time, and have one hundred worries;
This sadness and frustration have led to many mistakes.
I left home long ago, and cut all ties with my family,
What is hard to forget? Kindness unrepaid.

Every birthday[3] *reminds me of my mother;*
My maternal grandmother possessed rare virtue.
Having left home and entered the sangha, my karmic connections broadened;
Teachers, friends, and followers are as thick as bamboo.

Witnessing the decline of Buddhism that I tried to save,
Desiring to reform the monastic order, I wondered, how best to proceed.
Today the nation is devastated.
The people are abused and insulted; blood and tears flow.

---

2 This is a sutra that explains the fundamental emptiness of all phenomena; it is the most studied and recited text in the Mahayana Buddhist tradition.
3 Venerable Master Taixu's original wording was 母難 (munan), literally "Mother's Suffering," short for "Mother's Day of Suffering."

The world is oppressed by the flames of evil,
Afflicted with disasters, one upon another.
Propagating the Dharma, I walked the whole nation,
Traveling and teaching around the world;

The nation and the world are in dire straits.
I lead Buddhists to tour the Buddha's country.
All the Buddha's sons are powerful in mind and courageous,
Looking askance at wealth as if it were floating clouds.

Honest and refined, Upasaka Tan[4]
Who brings together the cultures of India and China,
Wishes me long life on this, my birthday.
My life is but a bubble on the sea;

I wish that one bubble could lift a myriad of sufferings,
That the wishes of the people and the nation be fulfilled.
That the people of the world would stop fighting and killing,
Look at one another with compassion and throw down their weapons;
That this bubble bursts on a calm sea, universally blissful and safe,
The Buddha's light shining throughout the universe.

The difference in age between Venerable Master Taixu and me is some thirty years; when he was fifty years old, I

4 i.e., Tan Yun-shan.

was probably sixteen. At the time, I already knew there was a Venerable Master Taixu who could serve as my leader. Then later on, I once listened to him give a lecture and further participated in the training class for staff members of the Chinese Buddhist Association he directed. As a consequence, all sorts of feelings well up in me whenever I read this poem. It seems that we shared a common lot in life, engendering in me a deep sense of respect toward Venerable Master Taixu, as if we shared the same life experiences.

Reforms in Defense of Buddhism Emulating the Example of Spiritual Conduct

Venerable Master Taixu joined the monastic order at a young age from a poor family, which is the same as me. He was raised by his maternal grandmother, and I also learned about Buddhism in the company of my maternal grandmother. His birth family was impoverished and humble, which is the same as me. After joining the monastic order, his teachers, friends, and classmates were as numerous as dense bamboo, and in this I am also the same as him.

Even thinking back to my own Buddhist aspirations after joining the monastic order, Venerable Master Taixu had his devotion to the defense of Buddhism, and he further had his ideas of reforming Buddhism. Although I dare not compare myself to him, I am aware of how I have endeavored to emulate him, learn from his conduct and deeds, and treat him as an exemplary model. He experienced pressure, calumny, and criticism within Buddhism because Buddhist circles were unable to accept his ideas for reforming Buddhism. Have I not also suffered the same fate as his all along? I willingly follow this great leader,

Venerable Master Taixu (*third from the right*) leading the group of Chinese Buddhist delegates to attend a Buddhist conference.

acting in accordance with his contributions through sacrifice for the sake of Buddhism. This is Venerable Master Taixu's poem, yet I feel as if it expresses my own state of mind as well.

In particular, Venerable Master Taixu hated war, and he was deeply concerned about the killing of his countrymen during the Sino-Japanese War. Not only do I share the same feeling of regret, but I even utterly detest war because during that time of war and chaos, despite my young age, there were many times I slept amid piles of the dead as I fled for my life, to avoid being discovered by the enemy who would give me a killing blow.

In his poem, he states, "My life is but a bubble on the sea; / I wish that one bubble could lift a myriad of sufferings," I too have a deep and personal experience regarding this. The life of an individual is not that important, but when it comes to

Buddhism's future, how can Venerable Master Taixu's sentiment and such aspiration be beyond my ability?

According to the observations of the historian Professor Tong Tekong [1920–2009] who was living in the USA, the religions of this world produce an important figure every five hundred years. Twenty-five hundred years ago there was Sakyamuni Buddha; two thousand years ago, there was Jesus; fifteen hundred years ago, there was Mohammed; in the 15th century there was Martin Luther. He believes that in the proceeding five hundred years of the 20th century, I should have fulfilled that role. I do not dare accept this statement, for it should be Venerable Master Taixu who represents this five-hundred-year period.

The Dedication of Mind and Body Given to Sentient Beings in the Universe

Venerable Master Taixu was not the same as ordinary members of the monastic community. Why? Because he was not acting for the sake of an individual, but for the sake of Buddhism as a whole; he did not depend upon Buddhism for a living, but let Buddhism depend upon him for its development. He did not let himself enjoy human life but made a contribution by sacrificing himself; he did not come into the world to enjoy personal relationships, but to give himself completely to Buddhism and to all sentient beings.

It was really unfortunate that Buddhism's old, middle-aged, and young would rather worship the Avalokitesvara and Ksitigarbha[5] [Bodhisattvas] on the altar table, yet they knew

5 He became a bodhisattva with his great vows for the well-being of all sentient beings: not to attain enlightenment until the hell realm is vacant.

The Venerable Master accompanying the Buddhist Visiting Group to pay homage to the Stupa for Venerable Master Taixu's relics.
September 10, 1963

nothing of venerating Venerable Master Taixu, a living bodhisattva in the human world.

If at that time, the Buddhist community could have responded to his call to reform Buddhism, then Buddhism would surely have made even greater progress. If Venerable Master Taixu could have lived a few more years, then under his leadership, Buddhism would surely have been completely transformed.

Unfortunately, no one recognized or acknowledged this bodhisattva when he was present in the world. Such a great bodhisattva who was endowed with a grand aspiration and compassion came to liberate sentient beings due to his vow, yet we saw him and failed to recognize him, not understanding the respect he was worthy of. This is not a personal loss for Venerable Master Taixu, but a loss for all Buddhist followers.

Venerable Master Taixu has passed away, so we hope that a few more Venerable Master Taixus will appear again. Let us just consider China: Does Zhejiang still have a Venerable Master Taixu? Does Jiangsu, the southwest, northwest, or northeast have a Venerable Master Taixu? Anyone can go to these many Buddhist monasteries in all directions, such as Tiantong, Yuwang, Xuedou, Jinshan, Jiaoshan, or the four great mountains with Buddhist pilgrimage sites and ask themselves, "Are we able to learn from Venerable Master Taixu?"

Venerable Master Taixu was also a human being, but his ideas and spirit are able to garner our reverence. Among all of our Buddha's disciples today, is there no one brave enough to carry on the ideals that Venerable Master Taixu left unrealized?

Historically, there were a few great masters such as Zhizhe [538–579 CE], Xuanzang, Huineng,[6] and Jianzhen. All of them demonstrated the Buddha's spirit to practice and transform the human world. But can such a nation as huge as China only produce a few such individuals? I hope that Buddhism today will see the appearance of a hundred Venerable Master Taixus. Even with only ten individuals like Master Taixu, today's Buddhism would be quite different.

Following the Bodhisattva Practice, Vowing that Buddhism Depends upon Me

I myself have no abilities, yet as far as the admiration of noble worthies, I am consciously "for Buddhism," which is a natural wish arising from faith. We have joined the monastic order, have been fed due to Buddhism and have worn clothes due to Buddhism. Can we not be like Master Taixu, sacrifice for and contribute to Buddhism together, and let Buddhism depend upon us?

I was grieving after Venerable Master Taixu passed away, but I spent time writing the article "So Vast, So Lofty," which was published in the magazine *Ocean Waves*. "So lofty" refers to how the aspirations of Venerable Master Taixu were as towering as the verdant mountains, while "so vast" refers to the

6 638–713 CE; he was the Sixth Patriarch of the Chan School.

cultivation of his aspiration that was as expansive as seas and oceans.

Today the verdant mountains are still here, and the seas and oceans flow unimpeded, but where are you, our venerable master? I cannot help but gaze off into space, for I am searching in the hope of finding someone like Master Taixu who was like verdant mountains and like the seas and the oceans, in my heart.

If Venerable Master Taixu were still living with us today, he would be one hundred and twenty-six years old. My admiration for him has existed for eighty years, so for eighty years, Venerable Master Taixu has remained in my heart. He is like a shining lamp, unextinguished and pointing the way forward in our development. He is also like a guide in close distance, leading us forward to the goal of the Buddha's light.

"Every birthday reminds me of my mother; / My maternal grandmother possessed rare virtue." My esteemed Venerable Master Taixu! I recall with gratitude that when I was fifty years old, you wrote the feelings of my entire life into your poem. I do not know how others feel when they read this poem, but for me, every word and every line are witnesses to how I have strained my heart over the course of my life. The words of Venerable Master Taixu also perfectly express the words in my mind, which have echoed again and again in my heart, always leaving me overcome with feelings. I will use "mixed feelings of joy and sadness" to describe them; how I feel is perhaps somewhat like that.

Thank you, my revered Venerable Master Taixu!

I had already become a disabled old man of more than ninety years of age when I wrote this article, and I am unable to bow down. All I can do is join my palms together toward you in order to express my sincere reverence and respect.

The Venerable Master was invited to attend the foundation stone laying ceremony and tree planting at the Taixu Temple Cultural Heritage Park. Also in attendance were the renowned author Yu Qiuyu (*first from the left*); Venerable Jieren, Abbot of Putuo Temples (*second from the left*); and Wang Guohua, President of Hong Kong Ta Kung Pao.

November 1, 2005

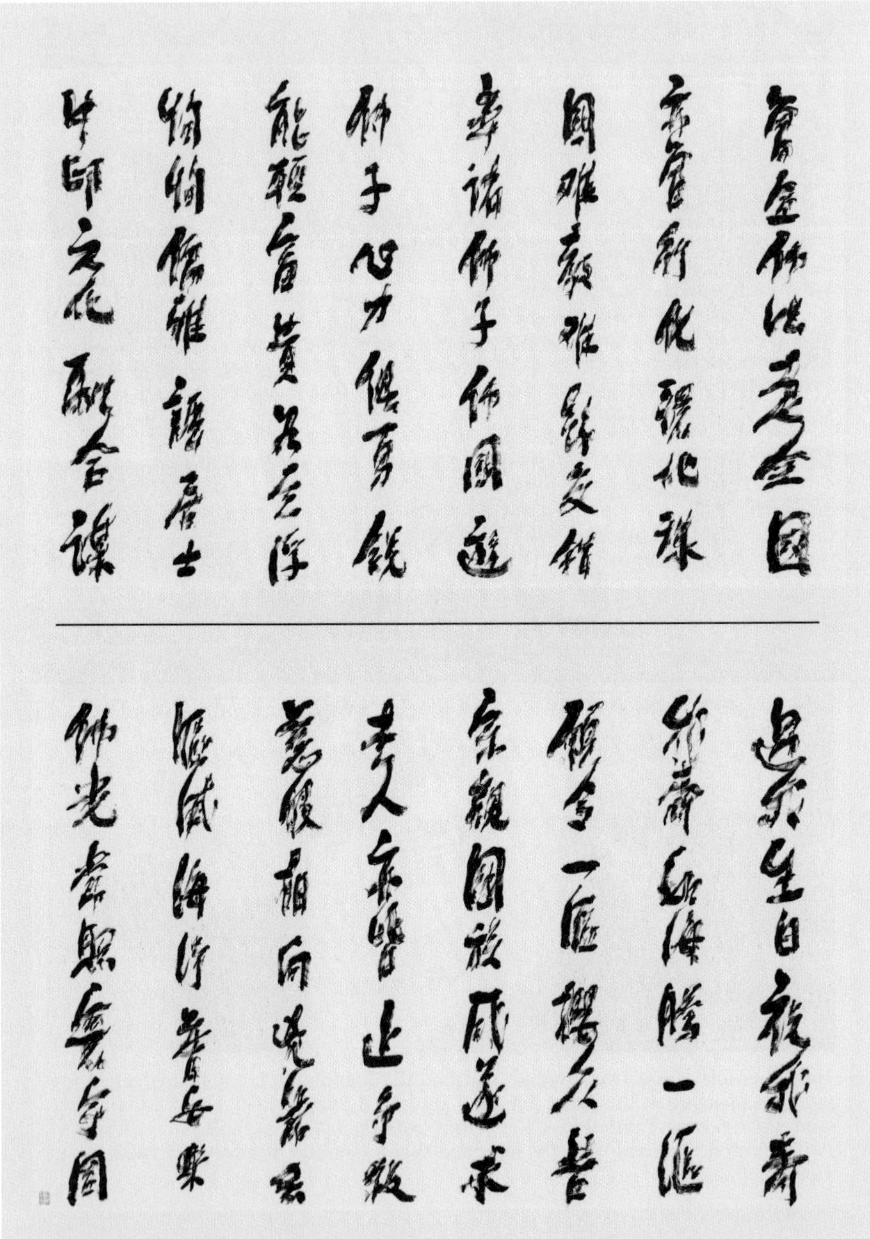

The Venerable Master's Calligraphy of "Thoughts on My Fiftieth Birthday," written by Venerable Master Taixu. Please see the translation of this poem on pages 174–175.

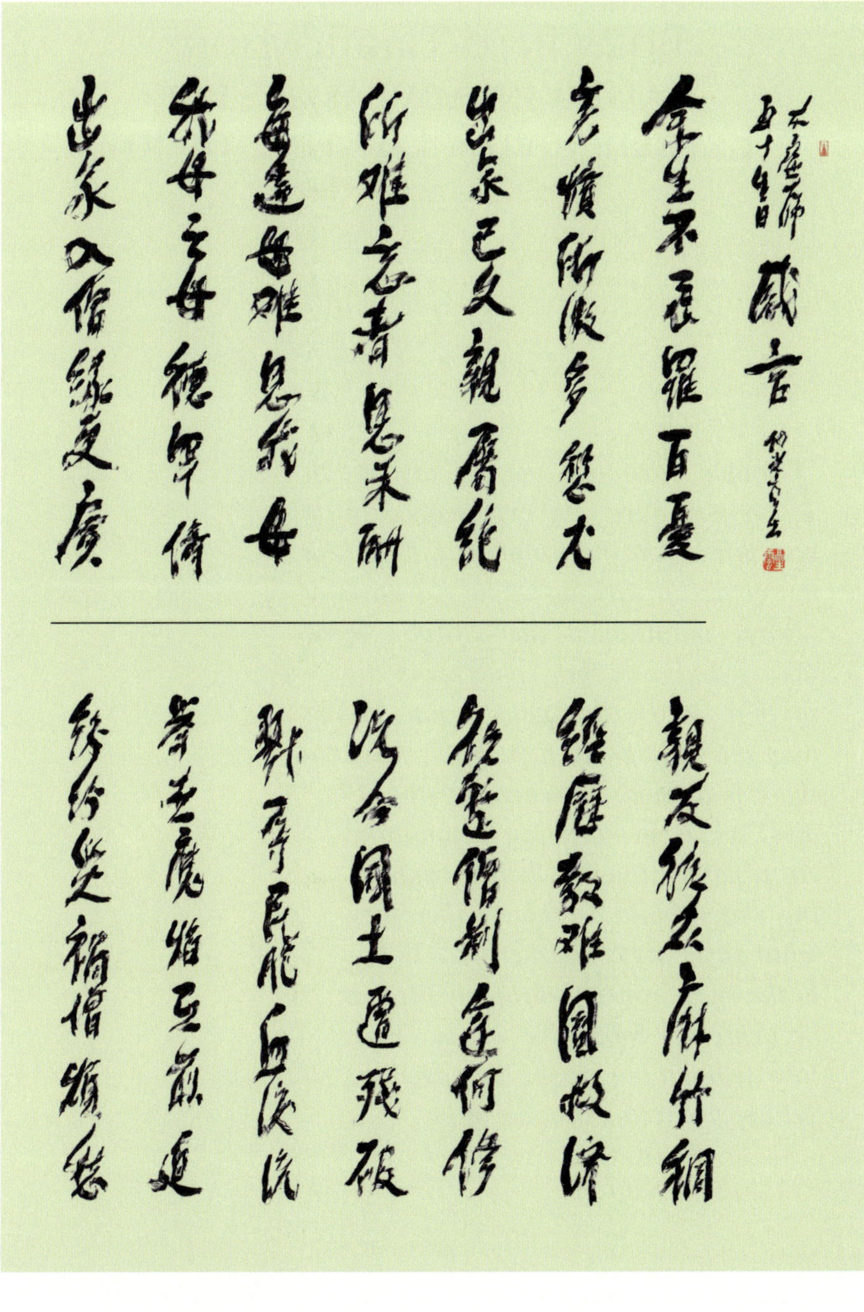

Born into Tribulation, Raised in Adversity, yet Experienced a Lifetime of Joy

People often ask me, "What adversity have you experienced in your life?" And for a moment, I cannot come up with an answer. I have always maintained the attitude of taking things as they come, as in the sayings "When the soldiers come, deploy the generals to fight back; when there is a flood, use earth to stop it" and "When encountering a mountain, cut a path through; when encountering water, build a bridge." Therefore, what adversity could there be? Today, at the age of ninety [2016], my life can be expressed by twelve words: "Born into tribulation, raised in adversity, yet experienced a lifetime of joy."

I was born in the impoverished Northern Jiangsu Province region of China in 1927. Being impoverished was actually not a serious matter. It was the unending afflictions saddled onto the poor by the country and society that were really the most strenuous. Take, for example, the Northern Expedition [1926–1928]: the warlords were conscripting soldiers and laborers everywhere, while bandits would appear at any time to rob and loot. Even if one had no possessions whatsoever, the bandits would still try to extort something of value.

Moreover, exorbitant taxes harassed the people even more; even if one possessed an acre of land, all of the harvest would be paid in its entirety to the various levels of the government. Even so, it still made it impossible to pay the various kinds of taxes and levies on revenue concocted under all sorts of pretexts. My family was originally utterly destitute, and as Li Mi [ca. 225–ca. 290 CE] stated in his "Memorial Setting Forth My Feelings," my family was declining in adult males, "externally lacking relatives close at hand and internally lacking young lads by the gate." On top of this, my father was honest, loyal, and down to earth, so his business went bankrupt. It did not matter how hard he worked at farming, it was still not enough to pay the taxes.

In addition, we had to cope with the roaming bands of refugees that came one after the other every day. They had dispersed from their hometowns in order to fill their stomachs and were called "famine dodgers." As the local people would all come out and supply them with a meal, they would strictly observe appropriate behavior and leave in a well-behaved manner after having had their fill.

The destitution brought about by poverty itself would have been enough, but once poverty-stricken neighbors even came to our home hauling a dead body, saying that my father had beaten that person to death and that we owed compensation for the life taken. Fortunately, some justice was attained in the end, and the false accusation was cleared away, allowing us to survive and prolong our feeble existence.

Next came the Sino-Japanese War that went on for eight years. Every day, the two armies would clash. By day, planes would drop bombs as machine guns strafed the skies, while artillery shells would come screaming in from all directions. By night, guerrilla bands would skirmish with the Japanese soldiers, such that when ordinary people went out they always had to carry a Japanese national flag with them. Whenever they encountered Japanese soldiers, they still had to bend down and bow, and they would not be allowed to pass until they had been searched.

Accustomed to Mental and Physical Suffering, Not Feeling Bothered

Sometimes in order to avoid being captured by the Japanese Army, I had no choice but to sleep among the piles of the dead; sometimes in order to cross the river to eke out an existence, I would carelessly fall into a hole in the ice. Even as a young child, I had already faced narrow escapes from death. Therefore, even though I later faced capture for no reason, was thrown into prison, and was even tied up at the execution ground in front of a firing squad, I did not feel the least bit afraid. Living daily amidst turmoil and upheaval, I did not know what happiness there was in human life, and in the face of death, I did not feel any pain.

The "Tangong Chapter" of the *Book of Rites* says it best: "A tyrannical government is fiercer than a tiger." Even though the imperial system of the Qing dynasty had already perished, the repercussions of the chaotic wars from the Taiping Rebellion [1850–1864] onward had not yet settled. Under these conditions of turmoil and upheaval, the people fled for their lives in droves, and I too joined the ranks of the "famine dodgers," following along as they fled in all directions to make their escape.

After joining the monastic order at the age of twelve, I was beaten and scolded every day. One could say that such a harsh and domineering education is not something ordinary people could accept. It was also because I was poor that I was subjected to discrimination by people in society. There was never a day when I did not experience depreciating looks and abrasive language. My experiences and understanding, as well as what I heard and saw, were entirely the sufferings brought about by poverty. Although I was young, I already had a thorough grasp of how difficult it was to survive during troubled times.

As a child who had never worn a set of new clothes and never even seen a school, all I heard was ridicule, mockery, or vituperation. Looking around me, there were no legal protections whatsoever in the entire society. Life seemed like a silkworm's thread, so fragile; one could still be enmeshed even if no cocoon was spun. Tell me, what dignity could possibly exist? How could this not be considered being born in tribulation? However, regarding these mental and physical sufferings, I had already grown accustomed to them for some time, and I did not mind them too much.

As I reached adulthood, the Communists' New Fourth Army was constantly clashing with the armies of the KMT. The Huangqiao Battle [October 1940], which occurred not too far from my hometown, alone resulted in the deaths of many tens of thousands of people. Whenever I was home, I would

The Venerable Master conducting the Triple Gem Refuge Ceremony at the Kaohsiung Buddhist Hall.

constantly hear the "bang" of a gunshot outside and know that someone's life was gone. Even though China's young men and women would later win ultimate victory in the Sino-Japanese War, the civil war between the Communists and the Nationalists then began. The Chinese were fighting their own people, breaking up innumerable families. Truly, this was too much to bear!

Later when I arrived in Taiwan, I was further faced with martial law, under which there was no freedom of movement. One had to ask leave through the police station every time one wanted to go out. The police even regularly came in the middle of the night to wake one up for questioning. For some unknown reason, even monastics were subjected to the calamity of imprisonment.

Suffering as an Advancing Condition, Realizing the Power for Survival

Gradually, I wished to propagate the Dharma as well as purify and transform society and human hearts, but I continually had to play hide-and-seek with the police. According to a member of the police from the Garrison Command, the documents written by those who secretly reported me were stacked more than one or two feet high; I did not know what crime I had committed nor whose wrath I had incurred. But Buddhism explains such an impoverished and destitute life as, "If the karma were not grievous, then one would not have been reborn into this Saha world." I could not help but sigh with regret, for it really meant that my karmic obstacles were deeply grievous, as I was reborn into a world such as this. Thus, I had to temper myself so as to build a Pure Land of joy in this human world.

In speaking of this, I want to express my gratitude for those many months and years of tribulation, which fostered my fearlessness toward the impermanence of life and death. As I lived in poverty and suffered hardships in life, I did not have much desire or hope for the material fame and fortune. Therefore, I often say that suffering is an advancing condition for human life. It is owing to suffering that my strength for survival was realized. This enabled me to not feel pain in the midst of difficulties, and I did not feel that I lacked anything when I was poor and destitute.

During the beginning of Fo Guang Shan, the Venerable Master personally leading disciples in clearing the ground and constructing buildings.

Thus, I went from Ilan, in the northeast corner of Taiwan, to Kaohsiung, the south. During the period of the White Terror, it was difficult to take even a single step in taking any action. But I finally had the opportunity to build a temple, set up the monastic community, and propagate the teachings. Having just completed construction on Shoushan Temple, who could have known the nearby fort command would issue an order to tear it down, saying that the five-story building I had built was too tall and would hamper military objectives.

Since society at the time was still situated in an atmosphere of turmoil, for the Buddhist centers that were connected to me, their devotees were not divided between the southerners and the northerners. They were divided into the Tainan camp, the Kaohsiung camp, and the Penghu camp, discriminating against and fighting with one another. I ruefully said, "Given that your sense of regionalism is so intense, it would be best to call for Sakyamuni Buddha return to India!"

Coming to the founding of Fo Guang Shan, since the land was initially barren and disconnected, no good use could be made of it. It was not until after untold hardships that the deep ravines were slowly filled in and made level so that buildings could be built on top of them. At that time, I had no understanding of engineering, and a rainstorm would trigger flash floods that would surge down the mountainsides in a torrent of mud and gravel, destroying my roads and buildings. With an area of several thousand square feet, the Guanyin Pool for releasing fish was washed away by these floods three times. As a portion of the berm beside Gem Bridge was about to be carried away by a torrential flood, I was forced to mobilize the disciples who had initially founded the monastery with me, and have them bring quilts and bedsheets to block the torrent from washing everything away.

The Human Mind Is Difficult to Fathom

In fathoming the human mind, countering the destructive power of nature turned out to be easy; human affairs were indeed the greater difficulty. Since the local people were not happy about a mainlander like me building a temple there, they made a pact not to sell land to a mainlander monk. In addition, since Fo Guang Shan was located in a mountainous area, forty or fifty years ago there was no need for a building permit. However, when only a few buildings had been constructed, the county government presented me with yet another conundrum. Their order required us to buy two firetrucks and provide for one hundred firefighters before we could build the temple. At that time, it was impossible for me to even buy two motorcycles; how would I have the money to buy two fire-trucks? Did I even have the spare energy to support one hundred people? This was the earliest directive of the Kaohsiung County government regarding my building of the temple.

It was only with great difficulty that the Pure Land Cave and the Pilgrim's Lodge were built. Then someone said that I had hidden a cache of two hundred rifles as well as a countless number of pistols, hand grenades, and bombs. Poor me, at the time I could not even afford two hundred sticks, so where did the two hundred rifles come from?

Since ancient times, the village and town administrative offices have welcomed the building of temples and churches in their midst, so they can assist in reassuring the heart of society and the public. But it seemed that our building the temple on a barren mountain was a large obstruction to them, and they spared no mental or physical effort in putting obstacles in our way. As Fo Guang Shan was being built and the Buddhist mission for spiritual transformation began, it aroused the suspicions of the security agencies. They kept a constant watch on my movements, for it seemed that my youthful age in itself was an offense. Some people said that the Communist Party was sponsoring my temple building efforts, while there were some who said Fo Guang Shan was where India kept in secret contact with me. There were even those who said that the Nationalist Party provided funds for my development in order to use me, and so on. All of these accusations were sheer fiction, what others had pinned on me.

Giving Rise to Moral Courage for Buddhism's Enduring Existence

Poor Fo Guang Shan, even the single application for temple registration took ten years, as the Kaohsiung County government kept to its slow pace and was unwilling to give any response. The village administrative office sent out official communications again and again, insisting that we open up a commercial avenue for development within the temple precincts (the present Bodhi Avenue beside the Pilgrim's Lodge). This would be set aside for farmers to ship in their agricultural produce. I thought it strange, as this was my private property in a mountainous area. Why were they so insistent on having me set up a commercial road?

For that reason, the local populace even surrounded the monastery with their tractors, prohibiting us from going in or out. At the time, several hundred police officers also came, but all of them stood around doing nothing. They did not stop the townspeople from creating a disturbance, nor did they let us enter or exit through the monastery gate. I could not help but feel puzzled: Did the government really want several hundred residents at Fo Guang Shan to die of starvation on the mountain?

The temple in the city was to be torn down for exceeding height restrictions; a temple built on private property in a rural area was completely surrounded, and it was insisted upon that we open a road. Tell me, was this fair?

I had never had to run to the government in my entire life, but I had run to police stations so many times; I had never had any quarrels with the people, but on many occasions, I had debated loudly with the police while standing on the roadside, just as if I were a gangster or a hooligan. In searching my conscience, for the sake of Buddhism's enduring existence and for the sake of sentient beings' life of wisdom, I truly could not be without such morality and courage!

In the past, there were the persecution of Buddhism and the expulsion of the monastic community during the three emperors Wu and the one emperor Zong,[1] the harassment of Buddhism and the burning of sutras during the Taiping Rebellion, the Eradication of Buddhism Movement launched by the Christian warlord Feng Yuxiang [1927], the Conversion of Temple Properties for the Establishment of Schools [1928] proposed by the educator Tai Shuangqiu, and the immediate burning of any temple during the Cultural Revolution period [1966–1976]. For the sake of building temples, setting up monastic communities, propagating the Dharma, and liberating sentient beings, must poor Buddhism suffer so much devastation?

The Greatest Vow: Dharma and Happiness Filling the World

The world is constantly changing. After Mr. Chiang Ching-kuo took charge of the government in Taiwan, cross-strait exchanges opened up, and the White Terror also became something of the past. In short, only when the individual lives of the people are under the protection of the law will the larger community be able to survive. There has been a general sense of chaos in society in recent years with the rampant activities of criminal groups and such incidents of murder and robbery that one hears about from time to time. Despite this, people in general are simple and honest, and their hearts are universally

1 Emperor Taiwu of Northern Wei (446–452 CE), Emperor Wu Di of Northern Zhou dynasty (574–578 CE), Emperor Wuzong of the Tang dynasty (842–846 CE), & Emperor Shizong of the Later Zhou dynasty (955–959 CE), respectively.

President Chiang Ching-kuo visiting Fo Guang Shan for the fourth time, in front of the Main Shrine in 1978.

kind. Yet even to this day, despite being under a free and democratic system, the fierce and aggressive wrangling between the two political parties in terms of their language and thinking has led to social division among the people. This causes one to lament about who should be responsible for the many causes and effects that resulted in all of this.

Although I have experienced many challenges and predicaments, I have never considered tribulations as something to be feared, nor have I ever given up hope due to the persecution I have suffered. From an early age, I have advocated for a joyful human life. It has always been my greatest vow that the Dharma and happiness will fill the world, that kindness and amicability can purify society, and that an awful environment and contentious human affairs can be transformed into a Pure Land. This would enable everyone to respect one another and to coexist in shared prosperity. I very deeply believe that "Where there is Dharma, there is a way." In my innermost being, I am still happy to serve the great mass of people.

The Children's Home and the Senior Homes that I founded were all established one by one under difficult conditions of various kinds. Over the past fifty years, the children I fostered have already married and started their careers, and their numbers must be well over eight hundred. As for the seniors at the Fo Guang Senior Home in Kaohsiung and the Senior Home in Ilan, originally it was their wish to live there so that when they passed on, monastics would recite sutras on their behalf. Later on, most of them lived there to the venerable age of a hundred, giving me the opportunity to look after them for several decades. Tell me, are these not worthy of joy?

The Achievement of Sheer Enthusiasm: Founding *The Merit Times* on April Fools' Day

Under government oppression, television stations in the past were not permitted to broadcast Buddhist programs. However, through constant struggle, has today's Taiwan not established many Buddhist television stations? Previously, non-governmental organizations were banned from running newspapers, but sixteen years ago (2000), I specifically selected April 1st, April Fools' Day, for the launching of *The Merit Times*. I thought, "When ignorance is bliss, it's foolish to be wise." I would accomplish wonderful things through sheer enthusiasm, I would have no suffering, and I would even have another instance of joy.

Several decades ago, the government restricted private schools from being established. But through unflagging efforts, there now exist Nanhua University, Fo Guang University, Pu-Men High School, Jiun Tou Elementary and Junior High School, Junyi Experimental High School, several dozen kindergartens,

The Merit Times inauguration tea reception and press conference. *From the left*: the elder Cao Zhongzhi; Chao Yi, former director-general, Government Information Office; the Venerable Master; Wu Po-hsiung; Chang-Yao Hung-Yin, Chairperson of the Board of ASE Technology Holding Co, Ltd; and Wang Bicheng, Chairman of the Board of United Daily News Group.

March 31, 2000

and more than fifty Chinese schools abroad. There are also the University of the West in Los Angeles, the United States; Guang Ming College in Manila, the Philippines; and Nan Tien Institute in Sydney, Australia. We also have fifty mobile library trucks, touring remote villages and promoting the campaign for reading. Every day, students are happily reading aloud, spreading the sound of reading throughout each region. How can this not make people happy?

In early days, Buddhist temples in Taiwan would only open their gates to welcome the public during holidays and festivals. Even so, the government suppressed Buddhism everywhere and limited the establishment of non-governmental organizations. For the past sixty years, I have been rushing about making public appeals. The Buddhist temples and monasteries built both at home and abroad already number at least two hundred or more. The several million members of the BLIA are spread across the entire globe, enthusiastically engaging in the work of propagating the Dharma for the benefit of sentient beings. Every day, the devotees and association members alone amount to thousands or tens of thousands of people. They all gather to have meals, talk about the Dharma, and cultivate the practice. How can I not be happy?

People often ask me, "What adversity have you experienced in your life?" And for a moment, I cannot come up with an answer. I have always maintained the attitude of taking things as they come, as in the sayings "When the soldiers come, deploy the generals to fight back; when there is a flood, use earth to cease it," and "When encountering a mountain, cut a path through; when encountering water, build a bridge." Therefore, what adversity could there be? Today, at the age of ninety [2016], my life can be expressed by twelve words: "Born into tribulation, raised in adversity, yet experienced a lifetime of joy."

Devotees Protecting the Dharma Is Fo Guang Shan's Support

May 16th, 2016 marks the fiftieth anniversary of Fo Guang Shan's founding, and I published this article in the *United Daily News* and *The Merit Times*. At the same time, I also published it as a series in the bimonthly *Humanistic Buddhism Journal, Arts, and Culture*. With this opportunity, I wanted to speak to the millions of devotees: "Thank you all for following such an old and disabled monk, and for giving me so many

n the 50th Anniversary of Fo Guang Shan, the Venerable Master was awarded with the Honorary octorate of Social Sciences from the Chinese University of Hong Kong at the Book Launch Ceremony or the 365 volume *Complete Works of Venerable Master Hsing Yun.* Pictured on top: The Venerable aster gave *Complete Works Collection* certificates to (*on stage, from the left*) Chen Roger C. Y., resident of National Kaohsiung First University of Science and Technology; Guu Mike Y.K., President f National Pingtung University; Lin Tsong-ming, President of Nanhua University; Yung Chaur-shin, resident of Fo Guang University; Jenny Su Huey-jen, President of National Cheng Kung University; oseph Sung Jao-Yiu, President of Chinese University of Hong Kong; Lou Yulie, professor of philosophy nd religious studies in Beijing University; Lai Yonghai, Dean of Research Institute of Chinese Culture, anjing University; Li Lian, Dean of Xuanzang Research Institute of Northwest University; Liu hangle, Chairman of the board and CEO of Phoenix Television; Koitsu Yokoyama, Professor Emeritus, epartment of Literature, Rikkyo University.

hotos by Venerable Hui Yan and Su Shaoyang, May 16, 2017

For thirty years (1977–2006), the Venerable Master has given three-day Dharma lectures at National Dr. Sun Yat-sen Memorial Hall, with a full house at every lecture.

November 1–3, 2002

good causes and good conditions. It is my hope that you can all share in this happiness along with me. Tribulation can nurture us mentally and physically, and adversity can increase our strength, but joy alone constitutes the most important treasure in human life.

Fifty years have passed in the blink of an eye, but the facts have proven that aid to Fo Guang Shan was not provided by Indian Buddhism, the Communist Party, or the Nationalist Party, but rather by Fo Guang Shan's many donors who have quietly made their contributions. Since devotees do not care about fame and rank, they have at times gathered together small amounts of money to create broad, good affinities. At times, they have employed their strength to give alms to the Triple Gem in defense of the Dharma and the monastic community; other times, they have used their wisdom to make offerings to the masses, popularize spiritual transformation, and make joint efforts in accomplishing various kinds of work to

benefit sentient beings. I can truly say that the many devotees who protect the Dharma are the most formidable support that Fo Guang Shan has.

Even if it is foreigners, friends of Buddhism, or members of political parties, their ability to provide some measure of assistance is also a good thing; it is worthy of joyous feelings. Only when everyone puts forth their joint efforts will this world become a more wonderful place. This is all the more so since we neither pervert the law by taking bribes, nor engage in under-handed, secret dealings; and we neither invade and occupy national territories, nor evade taxes and levies. Everything we do is for the sake of giving people joy. What fault is there in that?

The development of Humanistic Buddhism means promoting a human life of Dharma joy and meditative bliss. Over the past fifty years, not only has Fo Guang Shan held the Triple Gem Refuge and Five Precepts Ceremony more than a hundred times, but we have also had short-term monastic retreats and large-scale conferences of various kinds more than a hundred times. We have even had hundreds or thousands of sutra teachings, classroom lessons, street-side sermons, symposia, and forums. Is everyone not immersed in

the joy of the Dharma's truth? Although I do not collect any fees, in no way do I lack anything for having done so. On the contrary, the more I contribute, the happier I have become.

A Million Devotees, the Joy of Wonderful Affinities

The happy occasion of Fo Guang Shan's fiftieth anniversary, it also marks the sixty-eighth year since my coming to Taiwan. At the declining age of ninety [2016], I am writing this article to report on my joyous life to everyone and share my experience of happiness with everybody. How could this fail to make me happy? It is comparable to being awarded more than a dozen honorary doctorates from many universities, such as Fu Jen Catholic University, Hong Kong University, and Australia's Griffith University; also to being an honorary professor at dozens of universities, such as Beijing University, Nanjing University, Shandong University, Shanghai Jiao Tong University, Tongji University, and Zhejiang University. For a humble monk like me who was born into an impoverished family from the Northern Jiangsu Province region, who never received any formal education, and who joined the monastic order as an innocent child, have I not brought sufficient credit to my hometown?

My *One-Stroke Calligraphy* has been touring all over the world on exhibition at the invitation of many places such as the National Museum of China in Beijing and the National Art Museum of China in Beijing, as well as various provincial museums inland and so on. Countless numbers of visitors have

BLIA members from all five continents attending the Buddha's Light International Association General Conference.

Photo by Venerable Hui Yan, October 11–16, 2016

come to view and admire the exhibition, and the museums have even taken the initiative to request that the exhibitions be extended. Although my calligraphy is not good, I encourage visitors not to look at the characters but to look at my heart. I am glad that I still have somewhat of a compassionate mind that I can show to others. Indeed, everybody saw my heart as well. How can such interactions not bring me joy?

It is simply because there are several million devotees around the world that I, a humble monk, have become something like a county or a prefectural magistrate in ancient times. When attending to the county, one's meals are supported by the county, and when attending to the prefecture, one's meals are supported by the prefecture; thus, no matter where one goes, there is always food to eat, tea to drink, and carriages and boats to save one from walking. Even some of the students who attended Fo Guang Shan's College Buddhist Summer Camps in the past have already become famous doctors here and abroad. If I have some minor illness or pain, they will always give me medical care for free. Are these wonderful connections not worthy of joy?

Fo Guang Shan propagates Buddhism through culture, sports, music, and art—the Venerable Master's guidance for Fo Guang Shan over the next fifty years: the following are some highlights of activities of the "Three Acts of Goodness Sports Association."

A member of the "Children of Tathagata" soccer team presenting a soccer ball to the Venerable Master.
Photo by Venerable Hui Yan, June 18, 2016

The Taiwan High School Baseball League, Wooder Bat Division. Pu-Men High School won third plac upon competing for the first time in this league
Photo by Gao Huiping, September 22, 2016

During the 2009 High School Basketball League, the Pu-Men High School team won its very first championship.

Pu-Men High School's gymnastic team, baseball tean and women's basketball team came to Fo Guang Sha for two months of meditation training.
Photo provided by the Life News Agency

The Fourth BLIA Cup International University Basketball Tournament concluding after six days and thirty five games. University of Taipei won the women's basketball championship.
July 7, 2014

The Venerable Master giving a Dharma talk to the "Children of Tathagata" soccer team from Zu Lai Temple in Brazil.
Photo by Venerable Hui Yan, June 18, 2016

The Venerable Master doing the tip off at the start of the Three Acts of Goodness Cup basketball game. 2012

The Venerable Master at the 2016 Fo Guang Cup Basketball Tournament to encourage the Fo Guang University Basketball Team.
Photo provided by The Life News Agency

The Venerable Master giving a Dharma talk to Pu-Men High School Baseball team members at Fo Guang Shan Jin Guang Ming Temple.
November 29, 2015

Whenever the Lunar New Year comes around, many orphans who had grown up at the Children's Home return to Fo Guang Shan with their families to participate in a parade. During holidays and festivals, those who were young when they learned Buddhism from me in Ilan are now silver-haired seniors. Among them are plenty of university professors and great entrepreneurs who gladly join in and share with us the Dharma joy arising from contribution and service. As an ancient worthy once said, "Enjoying happiness alone is not as good as enjoying happiness with others." Every weekend more than a hundred teachers and principals come to Fo Guang Shan and to the Buddha Museum to serve as volunteers. How can their conduct in vowing to make a contribution not bring honor to Taiwan's educational circles as well?

The Power of Faith: Developing Happiness in the Source of the Mind

We encourage devotees to set up a Buddha shrine in their home so they can settle the mind and body into a peaceful repose; we promote the Three Acts of Goodness and A Society Filled with the Fragrance of Books; we advocate for lay volunteers to serve as teachers. We even distribute laba porridge throughout our temples around the world as a way of sharing the joy of Buddha's enlightenment. Furthermore, we have refitted small trucks to be used as mobile vehicles for bathing the image of the Buddha; they cruise around the streets and alleyways to facilitate the bathing of the Buddha and the purification of the mind by the general public. Our mobile library trucks and mentality protection mobile clinics travel to all the remote villages and to all corners of the region. Those who come along are parent volunteers who tell stories, some volunteers who perform magic tricks, cheerful drivers who do not shy away from hard work, and compassionate doctors and nurses who give friendly, free check-ups. Recipients are joyful in body and mind while those putting forth such efforts find spiritual happiness. Is this not the greatest of joys?

We have taken Buddhist Choir and Buddhist Monastic Concerts to propagate the Dharma through their performances at internationally renowned concert halls. We have also organized various kinds of sports teams for basketball, baseball, soccer, gymnastics, and roller skating, which go everywhere to compete in friendship games. In motivating society and bringing mental and physical purification through the arts and sports, and by increasing the Buddhist population, can we not experience the abundance of Dharma joy?

After visiting Fo Guang Shan and the Buddha Museum, many foreigners and government officials all say the facial expression of monastics and devotees is remarkably distinct. Everybody has smiling faces, as if every day is a New Year's celebration. Why? The reason is that the power of faith enriches our spirits. What fear is there that our hearts could fail to be a source for developing happiness? So much joy and happiness all come from the direct practice and experience of "the patience for life, the patience for phenomena, and the patience for the non-arising of phenomena!" Is this not worth of a feeling of gratification?

The Buddha once said, "I am one of the assembly," instructing his disciples that they must "integrate into the great assembly"; the Venerable Master has received boundless benefits by respectfully practicing according to his instruction.
Photo provided by Commonwealth Publishing

One of the Assembly: Monastics and Devotees Forming a Pure Land Together

We have no regionalism, no distinction between self and other, no political disagreements, and no racial barriers; nor do we take any notice of one's political allegiances. All we would like to do is to purify the human mind. We all engage in intercommunication and integration and make contributions to each other. It is the life of faith that fosters everyone's joy and happiness, and it is a life of service that brings happiness to everyone.

In addition to my gratitude for tribulation being my companion and for suffering befalling my body, both of which served to temper my courage and my determination, the pain from illness also gave my life a different sort of experience. Throughout my life, I have made a friend out of sickness, so regardless of whether it is a serious illness or a slight ailment, I have lived in peace with them as I imperceptibly strode into old age. For many years now, some of the doctors who have treated me have been Catholics or Christians, but they all have become my good friends. This has given me the experience that despite the illness, as long as I have an optimistic and diligent attitude, then the Humanistic Pure Land of joy is everywhere.

Twenty-six hundred years ago, the Buddha said, "I am one of the assembly," instructing his disciples that they must "integrate into the great assembly"; and I have received boundless benefits by pursing this idea. I give thanks to the great assembly of Fo Guang Members, for it is owing to this great assembly that the Fo Guang Shan Buddhist Order can exist; it is owing to this great assembly that there are accomplishments; it is owing to this great assembly that there is discipline; and it is owing to this great assembly that there is joy.

To every respected Fo Guang Member: Buddhism needs you, Fo Guang Shan needs you, and I need you; also, you need Fo Guang Shan. We need each other, and we need Humanistic Buddhism, for it brings a joy and happiness that has been refined through faith!

Diligent Efforts Will Not Be Wasted

Making Affinities, Engaging in Giving, and Repaying Kindness.

They were my goals in setting up the Water Drop Teahouses. It is because I "have" that I can repay kindness; if I were poor and would only accept the giving of others, how could there be a way to repay kindness? In fact, there is no need to become a wealthy person to repay kindness. We can say good words, perform service for someone, give someone a salutation or smile, or join our palms together. All of these are ways to repay kindness. Consider that what we eat, wear, and use all come from the support of society and the larger community. If one repays the kindness of a drop of water with a fountain, then it is indeed wonderful!

My Silent Revolution for Buddhism

In devoting my life to Buddhism, in order to keep Buddhism current with the advances in society, in terms of thoughts, I am always making improvements at every hour and moment; in terms of practice, I am constantly and continuously making adjustments. Even though I know that Buddhism must be reformed, innovation never comes into being in the heat of the moment. My "silent revolution" advocates that some things advance, while some things retreat; some things proceed, while some things stop. Although the results are not apparent immediately, I consistently work on them, which can slowly overcome any obstacle!

In 2016, Fo Guang Shan conducted the International Ten-Thousand-Buddhas Triple Platform Full Ordination Ceremony at Fo Guang Shan Sutra Repository.
Photo by Zhou Xuezhong

In the past, Venerable Master Yinguang [1862–1940] advanced the idea that Buddhism must get rid of "three excesses." The first is the excessive transmission of the precepts; the second is the excessive providing of temple and monastery lodgings; the third is the excessive acceptance of disciples. I agree with his proposal, but not a single one of these things was ever accomplished.

The first is the excessive transmission of the precepts. I began conducting the Triple Platform Full Ordination Ceremony in 1977, and over the ensuing thirty-odd years, I have carried out about a dozen of these. Not only have ordinations been performed in Taiwan, but they have also been performed in countries such as the United States, India, and Australia. I ask myself, "Is this an excessive transmission of the precepts?" In fact, I do so for the sake of establishing the precept banner!

The second is the excessive providing of temple and monastery lodgings. At present, Fo Guang Shan has three to five thousand beds that can provide lodging for devotees and guests. Is this the excessive providing of temple and monastery lodgings? Not at all. I only want to ensure that everyone can participate in Dharma services, so as to foster the bodhi mind!

The third is the excessive acceptance of disciples. I have more than one thousand monastic disciples and several million lay devotees. Regardless of whether they are monastics or lay disciples, they have all matured in their faith, improved their character, and increased their aspiration to serve daily. Am I excessively accepting disciples? Not at all. I am continuing the life of Buddha's wisdom!

Therefore, as for the "three excesses" raised by Venerable Master Yinguang, it would seem that all of these three do apply to me, but I feel that I am not in any way "excessive." I am very careful about transmitting the precepts; I am very cautious about providing lodgings; I am also very judicious about accepting disciples into the monastic community.

In addition, Venerable Master Taixu proposed the "three-point revolution" for the sake of Buddhism's renaissance. The first is revolution on doctrine; the second is revolution on the system, and the third is revolution on property. I too have kept the three-point revolution in mind, for I have firmly combined it with my own thinking. Moreover, I have unremittingly persevered in putting it into practice as the "silent revolution."

When it comes to "revolution," most people are afraid upon hearing the word, thinking it is about overthrowing and attacking other people. In fact, the "silent revolution" I am talking about abounds with constructive and progressive qualities, signifying the removal of corruption and the bringing about of

Buddhism advocates building happy, harmonious, and purified family relationships. Pictured is the Venerable Master officiating a double Buddhist wedding ceremony for the son and daughter of the Fo Guang Shan benefactor couple, Lai Weizheng and Li Meixiu.

Photo by Su Shaoyang

a renewal. It is a kind of reformation that everyone can happily accept without realizing it. Thus, how can advancing Buddhism's development by means of a "silent revolution" not be something quite significant?

How do I engage in silent revolution? What follows below is a brief description of my own methods and viewpoints based upon the ideal of a three-point revolution for Buddhism as advocated by Venerable Master Taixu.

First: Revolution on Doctrine

Gold Is a Poisonous Snake; Husbands and Wives Are Karmic Foes; Children Are Debt Collectors

In the past, whenever money is mentioned, some Buddhists would say, "Gold is a poisonous snake." Whenever husbands and wives are mentioned, some Buddhists would say, "If they were not foes in past lives, then they would not have gotten together." And whenever children are mentioned, some Buddhists would say, "Children are debt collectors." In fact, Buddhism does not completely negate money, for pure wealth provides the supplies needed to propagate the Dharma and cultivate enlightenment. Buddhism in no way fails to value moral principles; moreover, it actively advocates the morality of human relations. Buddhism is not critical of the emotional bonds of the family but wants to be an advocate for the building of happy, harmonious, and purified family relationships. Thus, if lay devotees are made to treat gold like a poisonous snake, husbands and wives like foes in past lives, and children like debt collectors, then what could they possess? On the contrary, this could frighten ordinary people and keep them away from Buddhism.

Therefore, the most important thing right now is for us to improve the way Buddhism propagates its teachings and ensure that everyone understands that gold is not a poisonous snake. As we cherish wealth, if we acquire it in the right way, and even use money in the right way, this ability to take money and apply it in meaningful ways is also a meritorious good deed. Moreover, in the Pure Land of Ultimate Bliss, the ground is covered with gold and the buildings are adorned with the seven kinds of precious gems such that people are glad to be reborn there, so why would Buddhism still speak of wealth as something ugly and impure?

As for the loving relationship between husband and wife, it is an important aspect among human relations. Even the Buddha himself also valued human relationships. Not only did he carry the coffin of his father and teach the Dharma to his mother,[1] but he even offered a skillful means of practice,

1 Queen Maya passed away seven days after giving birth and was reborn in Trayastrimsat Heaven (heaven of the thirty-three gods); later, the Buddha went there to explain the teachings for her.

enabling his maternal aunt, the Lady Mahaprajapati,[2] to join the monastic order and become a bhiksuni. Furthermore, there is the sevenfold assembly[3] within Buddhism. Besides the monastic bhiksus and bhiksunis who remain celibate, the lay upasakas and upasikas who receive and uphold the five precepts as well as the bodhisattva precept can live as householders. So why has this now become a situation in which lay practitioners must immediately have their husbands led away to the eastern residential halls and their wives directed to the western residential halls as soon as they register for their temple stay? Shouldn't the Buddhist tradition encourage loving husbands and wives to stay together as a loving couple? Why should the breaking up of families be considered the right thing to do? Could it be that the relationship between husband and wife is seen as something ugly and repulsive? Given that the Buddha permitted lay devotees to receive and uphold the five precepts as well as the bodhisattva precept, why must we treat them even more harshly, failing to act in accordance with the Buddha's original intent of valuing family relationships?

Furthermore, children are the pillars that uphold the nation's future, and the Buddhist sutras also relate many examples of "four small things not to be taken lightly."[4] Therefore, why must we speak of children as debt collectors? Can we say that the future of the nation and society does not depend on them to shoulder significant responsibilities? Hence, for Buddhism, the first thing we should loudly proclaim is "Value family relationships!"

---

2 She raised Siddhartha Bodhisattva after his mother's death. The bhiksuni order was established as a result of her requests to the Buddha, and she was the very first one ordained; later she attained arhatship.

3 Bhiksu, bhiksuni, sramanera, sramanerika (junior nuns), siksamana (novice nuns), upasaka, and upasika.

4 Small little sparks, small young water nagas, small young princes, small young novices.

Life Is Suffering

For the average person, it seems that after becoming a Buddhist, life then becomes suffering, because all one hears from everywhere is "life is suffering." However, Buddhism does not only speak about suffering, for it focuses even more on happiness. Don't the Buddhist sutras also speak of the Pure Land of Ultimate Bliss, the ground of joy, and the meditative state of happiness of bodhisattvas? Even more so, doesn't Maitreya Buddha[5] also favor "great joy for everybody?" Why must Buddhism talk about suffering all day long? Therefore, Buddhism should emphasize living joyfully and thinking joyfully, which bring forth a joyful life as well.

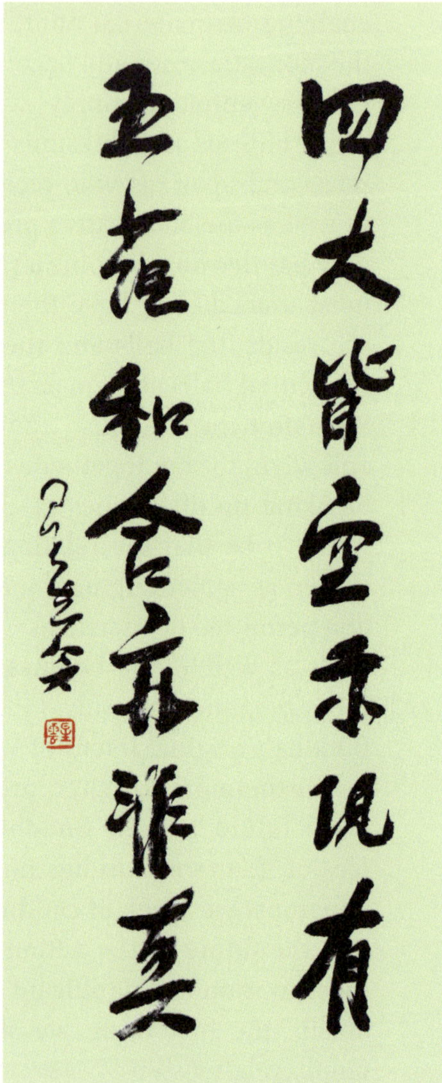

The Venerable Master's calligraphy: Please see page 221 for translation.

The Emptiness of the Four Great Elements

Buddhism teaches the emptiness of the four great elements, noting that the four essential

5 In Sanskrit, "Loving-Kindness One"; the bodhisattva of joy. He is the future Buddha of our world.

factors of earth, water, fire, and wind are not in any way eternal. However, it is too frightening for beginners to consider that the sky is empty, and so is the earth, you, and me. In my understanding of the Dharma, emptiness is established on existence. For example, a teacup cannot be filled with tea unless it is empty; a house cannot accommodate people without its empty space; people cannot live without the eyes, ears, and nose being open and empty.

In order to clarify this principle, I once composed a couplet:

The empty nature of the four great elements manifests in existence;
The combination of the five aggregates is also not real.

At the same time, this couplet also explains Buddhism's concept of the Middle Way.[6]

Impermanence

In speaking of "impermanence," Buddhism always says that the world is impermanent, and so are birth and death. This also makes the average person fearful of impermanence, as if "being petrified upon hearing a tiger." In fact, impermanence is not completely negative, for something good can turn bad, and something bad can also become good. For example, if I am foolish, I can become smart by reading; if I am poor, I can become wealthy through diligence. All that is necessary is to model ourselves on Nityodyukta[7] Bodhisattva and Gandhahastin[8]

6 This is the fundamental teaching of Sakyamuni Buddha, which guides us away from extremes—the duality of existence and non-existence or eternalism and nihilism.
7 In Sanskrit, "always diligent."
8 In Sanskrit, "never resting."

Bodhisattva in *The Amitabha Sutra*; then bad things can be corrected and tuned into something good.

Thus, since impermanence has its positive side and ensures that human life be filled with hope due to the possibility of change, then why are we still terrified of "impermanence"?

The Release of Life

Buddhism promotes the "release of life"; indeed, it is very important to release life. However, nowadays there are some Buddhists who have allowed the release of life to deteriorate into "leading living beings to death" without even realizing it, which is truly regrettable. For example, someone would celebrate a birthday by saying, "Catch some fish, so I can release lives!" Or if someone were getting married, they would say, "Catch some birds, so I can release lives!" As a consequence, there is no telling how many fish have already died in the basket before being released. Who is going to carry the unwholesome karma for this? They stubbornly insist on catching birds, breaking their families apart. They even let the birds in the cage fly about in chaos and strike the cage, such that they die before being released. For the unwholesome karma that comes of this, whose is it to bear?

Therefore, I think those who release life should focus on ecology, giving sentient beings an environment that is free from terror and that is safe with no danger. For instance, one does not go hunting in the mountains; one does not fish beside the stream; one does not abuse or mistreat animals; and one does not kill life or damage the environment. These are indeed the best ways to release life.

The Fo Guang Shan Great Welcoming Buddha.
Photo by Pi Yun Lai

Buddhism focuses upon human beings, so above the release of life, one should advocate "liberating human beings" even more. This is to give people a means of livelihood and good causes and conditions. Helping people and letting them be happy are most important in liberating lives.

The Three Acts of Goodness

For many people, once they hear that the "three kinds of karma" of body, speech, and mind can create the "three poisons" of greed, anger, and ignorance, they are terrified. In addition, in regard to the teachings of countering the three poisons by employing the "threefold training" of morality, meditative concentration, and wisdom, people tend to have difficulty following through the reasoning. Therefore, even though they study Buddhism for many years, their greed, anger, and ignorance are still not reduced.

In this regard, I wonder why Buddhism does not propagate the Dharma from an active perspective, instead of circling about on a passive level. Instead of emphasizing the three kinds of karma, it would be better to pursue the "three acts of goodness" of doing good deeds with one's body, speaking good words through one's speech, and thinking good thoughts in one's mind. In this way, one naturally does not generate unwholesome karma; in the absence of unwholesome karma, there is no greed, anger, or ignorance.

Do Not Make Amitabha Buddha Pay Kindness on Our Behalf

There is a phenomenon in Buddhism, regardless of what good deeds are done by a devotee, where people always say to them, "The bodhisattvas will bless you!" or "Amitabha Buddha will bless you!" I think this way of speaking is incorrect. Why is it that when someone supports and protects us, instead of paying our gratitude on our own, we turn the responsibility over to Amitabha Buddha and the bodhisattvas so that they can repay the kindness? All these many unfair situations in Buddhism ought to be reformed for the better.

Therefore, I built the Senior Home at Fo Guang Shan, making a special effort to reserve rooms as a way to give back to the senior monastics and great worthies people who have made contributions to the Buddhist world. Among others, those who have stayed at the Fo Guang Senior Home are Feng Yongzhen, who once served as the secretary-general for the Chinese Buddhist Association; Zhao Maolin [1903–1981], who propagated the Dharma in prisons for twenty years; Zhang Jianfen, who was renowned in educational circles as "the gifted

Fo Guang Shan conducting the "Lay Buddhist Five Precepts and Bodhisattva Precepts Ceremony." 2,500 people repented, took vows, and received the precepts with sincere, reverent minds. The spirit of the precepts is to not violate others; it is an act of kindness.

November 19, 2006

scholar from Hunan"; and Madame Sun-Chang Ching-yang, who spared no effort in protecting and sustaining Buddhism. I even keep several houses on hand at Hsi Lai Temple in the United States as well. I am thankful that the Elder Householder Zhang Shaoqi [1907–2001], who founded the weekly magazine *Awakening the World*, accepted my provision of support so that I could fulfill my wish of requiting such an elderly Buddhist follower.

Taking Refuge in the Triple Gem, Receiving the Five Precepts

Taking refuge in the Triple Gem reflects democracy and equality; receiving and upholding the five precepts reflect freedom and respect. The meaning here is extraordinary. Then, why is it that nowadays taking refuge in the Triple Gem has become solely revering a master? Why have they turned the upholding of the five precepts into the mere passive refraining from killing, stealing, engaging in sexual misconduct, lying, or consuming intoxicants?

In fact, taking refuge in the Triple Gem represents our faith in Buddhism and our willingness to take the Dharma as our guidance of life. It is not the acknowledgment that someone is the master or teacher. Taking the five precepts is putting one's faith into practice, which serves as the fundamental morality of a human being. Its essential quality lies in respecting others while not violating them. For example, no killing means not violating the lives of others, and even more, it means actively protecting life. No stealing means not violating the wealth of other people, and even more, actively respecting the property of others. No sexual misconduct means not violating the bodies of other people, and even more, actively respecting the moral integrity of others. No lying means not violating the reputation of other people, and even more, actively making the moral excellence of others known to the public. No alcohol or drugs means not impairing our sanity, thereby not harming other people; even more, it means actively respecting the physical and mental health of self and others.

As for the doctrines of Buddhism, much has been explained incorrectly or has deviated from the Buddha's intent. This is the same as the expression often used for criticism in Chinese society, "a barbarian describing the eightfold path." The eightfold path in this phrase originally referred to Buddhism's Noble Eightfold Path, the eight ways for cultivating the practice. When Buddhism was first transmitted to China, it had to pass through the Western Regions. Perhaps it was because of the people's limited ability to speak Chinese that they could not understand the Eightfold Path in depth and so could not convey the meaning clearly. Under these circumstances, in which no one understood anything, people just temporarily referred to this as "a barbarian describing the Eightfold Path." Unfortunately, the meaning of this phrase was later extended into "talking sheer nonsense," carrying with it a derogatory sense.

However, for Buddhism in the present day, not only are "barbarians" talking about the Eightfold Path, but also people around the world who have an affinity with Buddhism are also talking about the Eightfold Path. As a result, it cannot be said that distortions of the Buddhist doctrine do not exist. Here I have only listed a few preliminary explanations regarding the doctrinal problems pertaining to the nature of Humanistic Buddhism. However, I have still been able to give an explanation in depth. I hope that in the future there will be an entire book devoted to this topic, so that Venerable Master Taixu's "revolution on doctrine" can be further developed and propagated.

Second: Revolution on the System

Regarding the threefold training of morality, meditative concentration, and wisdom, Buddhists regard morality as the highest of all. Regrettably, nowadays there are some people who love to quote the phrase "The precepts already formulated by the Buddha cannot be changed; where the Buddha did not formulate precepts, no additions can be made." This makes the Buddhist teachings into something rigidly fixed. In fact, the Buddha formulated the precepts "prohibiting and permitting in accordance with the circumstances." They evolved in accordance with the time, the human heart, lifestyle, culture, and customs. If one were to insist that the precepts be immutable and unalterable, it would create too much opposition and contradiction between upholding precepts and not upholding precepts, as well as between defiance and compliance; then Buddhism would perish under the weight of inflexible interpretation of the wording of the precepts!

That the precepts cannot be changed is what people have attached for thousands of years. Observing the constitutions of every modern nation, we see that these too are regularly amended. Even the formulation of the precepts was compiled over several occasions. Therefore, why can we not revise them and compile them anew? The following are some examples:

Equality of the Fourfold Assembly

If there is no equality among members of the fourfold assembly, then it does not accord with the Dharma. When the Buddha attained enlightenment under the bodhi tree, he proclaimed, "All sentient beings in the world have the Buddha nature." Moreover, he suggested, "When members of the four castes[9] join the monastic order, they all become part of the Buddha's family," and "This Dharma is equal and universal, without better or worse." These words explain the principle of equality among sentient beings. Not only is there equality among Buddhas, but there is also equality between all sentient beings and the Buddhas. But after the Dharma began to spread, why were the bhiksus among the fourfold assembly given the first place, while the bhiksunis could not be equal to them?

9 These are classes based on hereditary social status in Indian society: Brahmin (priests), Ksatriya (ruling class), Vaisya (business and professional class), and Sudra (laborers and servants).

And why were only the monastics given priority in all matters, while the lay disciples were practically given no position or space to support the teachings and propagate the Dharma?

At the Dharma sessions where the Buddha gave his teachings, the fourfold assembly, the heavenly beings and nagas, government officials, and ordinary citizens were all crowded around. It was as in the saying "At the Lotus Assembly, there were a million human and heavenly beings." Considering such a boisterous scene; why is it that only the bhiksus are honored now, while the others are treated like the unbreakable four castes of India at the time? People who think this way really fail to live up to the Buddha's compassion and go against the Buddha's teaching of equality. Moreover, stubbornly placing devotees in a position of providing external aid for monastics makes it impossible for them to join the mainstay of the religious organization. This gives people the feeling that Buddhism is only about the monastic order, and not about the devotees. It ensures that Buddhism's development is deprived of so much power, which is deeply regrettable!

In truth, among the Buddha's monastic disciples, there were as many as several hundred great arhats[10] who were bhiksunis. However, in the Buddhist canon as compiled by the bhiksus, the names of these female members of the monastic community were categorically omitted. Of the twelve hundred and fifty great arhats, not a single female arhat was mentioned.

In view of this, in order to emphasize the idea of equality between males and female, when I built the Buddha Museum, I especially had three female arhat sculptures carved and placed among the Eighteen Arhats on both sides of the Bodhi Wisdom Concourse. These are respectively Mahaprajapati, the

10 In Sanskrit, "worthy one"; one who has attained awakening and achieved liberation.

There are three female arhats among the eighteen arhat statues at the Buddha Museum, demonstrating that there is no difference between males and females regarding enlightenment. The photo on the left is Utpalavarna Bhiksuni.

Photo by Venerable Hui Yan

first bhiksuni within the monastic community; Utpalavarna,[11] the bhiksuni foremost in supernatural powers; and Bhadra-Kapilani,[12] the bhiksuni foremost in the knowledge of past lives. These were all bhiksunis of cultivation and realization during the time of the Buddha. Additionally, in order to raise the position of bhiksunis within the Buddhist community and establish a new image for bhiksunis, so that many members of the female order can give free rein to and demonstrate their talents, Fo Guang Shan's work of compiling the Buddhist canon was led and undertaken by bhiksunis.

As for the past few thousand years, there have been lay disciples in Buddhism who protected the Dharma, devoutly believed in Buddhism, and conducted profound research in

11 In Sanskrit, "with the hue of a blue lotus."
12 In Sanskrit, "of profoundly worthy virtue."

Buddhist studies. Even considering the greatness of their cultivation and achievements, they can only be addressed as "the disciple," rather than "the teacher." I also think this phenomenon is unfair, and I feel that the Buddhism of today ought to find a way to do them justice.

Some people have said that my extreme defense of the laity will speed up the arrival of the Age of Declining Dharma[13] in which the white-robed laity occupy the seat of honor. But an overview of Fo Guang Shan since its founding shows that the fourfold assembly get along harmoniously with one another. In particular, during numerous missions of propagating the Dharma, there was no lack of energetic assistance from the laity. For example, the Water Drop Teahouses both here and abroad have been established by a group of Shigu. Moreover, since the formation of the BLIA, the system for Lay Dharma Teachers was also established, in which devotee members help Fo Guang Shan to propagate Humanistic Buddhism in various places around the world, making their contributions to society. So how can Buddhism ignore their efforts?

The Six Points of Reverent Harmony

The Buddha was a human, not a god. He never claimed that he was different from other people. He constantly reiterated, "I am one of the assembly" or "I am within the assembly." The establishment of the six points of reverent harmony by the Buddha was also a demonstration of this spirit of equality.

The six points of reverent harmony are "physical harmony through living together," which is the shared residence of the

13 Following the Buddha's nirvana, the conditions for learning the Dharma change over time; there are three ages of the Dharma: the Age of Right Dharma, the Age of Semblance Dharma, and the Age of Declining Dharma.

group; "verbal harmony through avoiding disputes," which represents praise through language; "mental harmony through shared happiness," which represents the harmony of intention; "moral harmony through sharing the same precepts," which represents the equality of the legal system; "harmony in view through sharing the same understanding," which represents the consensus of thought; and "economic harmony through sharing things equally," which represents balance within the economy.

There is such fine virtue in Buddhism and implementing it would certainly enhance the power for propagating the Dharma. However, today we have divided Buddhism into "patriarchal" and "matriarchal" Buddhism. Is this not doing a great disservice to the Buddha? Besides, the Buddha merely serves as a "mentor" to sentient beings, how can we set a "patriarchy" or a "matriarchy" above the Buddha? Do we not feel like we are offending the Buddha? Therefore, any inappropriate appellation within Buddhism ought to be reformed.

Wearing the Robe to One Side While Exposing the Right Shoulder

As instituted by the Buddha, bhiksus should put on the monastic robe by wearing it to one side and exposing the right shoulder. This is easily done in the tropics of India, but for the northern parts of China or Siberia in Russia, would it still be possible for one to survive? Therefore, shoes and clothing merely reflect a certain culture. The Buddha also said that the shaving of the hair, the dying of garments, the three monastic robes, and the alms bowl were all instituted in order to conform to the culture of the time. This being the case, why can we not allow the development of Buddhism to conform to the customs, habits, and climate of each region, and thus be given reasonable regulations? Could it be that none of these requires any reform?

The Eight Precepts of Respect

There was a devotee who originally served as an Air Force officer and was raising five children. Military pay in those early days was low, so he found it impossible to raise a family of seven. In the end, even his wife went away, leaving the family behind. There was nothing else he could do, so he sent his five small children to the Da Ci Children's Home at Fo Guang Shan, while he himself joined the monastic order.

Having joined the monastic order, one should cultivate the practice as best as one can. But one day, he came to Fo Guang Shan and complained to me, "Fo Guang Shan lacks discipline. When Venerable Tzu Hui and Venerable Tzu Jung see me, neither of them bows to me. Could it be that none of Fo Guang Shan's bhiksunis understand the eight precepts of respect?" This is because within the eight precepts of respect, there is one rule, that even an eighty-year-old bhiksuni must prostrate herself before a young bhiksu or sramanera.

I was quite astonished when I heard this and said very bluntly, "You really do not know any shame! Your sons and daughter were all raised by the Venerable Tzu Jung and Venerable Tzu Hui on your behalf, and both of these venerables have devoted their efforts to Buddhism for several decades. Considering their qualifications, record of service, spiritual practice, and contributions to Buddhism, on what basis would you have them bow to you?" As I see it, for one to be respected, the respect has to come from the bottom of other people's hearts. For someone who lacks knowledge and virtue, yet still wants others to bow before him, how can such a request even be uttered?

I think the eight precepts of respect were formulated by bhiksus, but proffered in the name of the Buddha, as a way for bhiksunis to show reverence to the bhiksus. This caused many outstanding females to be unwilling to join the monastic community due to the unreasonableness of the monastic rule. As a result, Buddhism is unjustifiably deprived of many talented individuals. In the past, Venerable Chao-hwei [b. 1957] of the Buddhist Hong Shi College once raised her opposition to the eight precepts of respect, but she still encountered strong opposition from the bhiksus, even stirring up a mighty uproar because of this. As a matter of fact, I do not talk about this matter at Fo Guang Shan, so a "silent revolution" can, on the contrary, achieve success. Nowadays, the several hundred Fo Guang Shan temples both here and abroad have all been built and completed by bhiksunis; the thousands of BLIA chapters in various parts around the world were also established by bhiksunis; there are even many learned bhiksunis who are teaching at universities. Therefore, with regard to the question of the eight precepts of respect, Buddhist circles really should no longer be swayed by personal feelings and instead give the bhiksunis a position on equal footing with the bhiksus.

The Ten Precepts of the Sramanera

There are ten precepts within the monastic rule for the sramanera. Besides no killing, no stealing, no sexual conduct, no lying, and no consuming intoxicants, there are also the precepts of no personal adornments, no partaking of music and dancing, no sleeping in a fine bed, no eating at inappropriate times, and no carrying of gold or silver. As for "no sleeping in a fine bed," given that the sramaneras are young, they really ought to learn about overcoming life's difficulties, so being more plain and simple is beneficial to enhancing their spiritual practice. With "no personal adornments," one can find contentment in a simple life and engage in a steadier spiritual practice without flaunting extravagance; this is also an advancing condition for the life of spiritual practice.

But with the way time advances today, Buddhism needs to propagate the Dharma with music, and it needs to receive the masses with dancing. If a strict adherence to "no partaking of music and dancing" is maintained, then that would make it impossible to hold some activities for propagating the Dharma, and Buddhism would gradually decline along with it. In the past, when hearing lute music, Venerable Mahakasyapa[14] felt a sense of delight and unconsciously began to move his hands and feet to the beat. Someone asked the normally solemn Mahakasyapa how he could act like that. He said, "As a matter of fact, I have not been attached to the five desires and the six sense objects for a long time now. But the sounds of the lute from Druma, king of the Kimnaras,[15] are the sounds of wisdom, the same as the sounds of the Dharma that fill one with Dharma joy as soon as they are heard, so I cannot help but begin to leap and dance."

As we can see, music and dancing are sometimes a kind of skillful means for liberating sentient beings.

---

14 One of the ten great disciples of the Buddha, he is known as foremost in austerities and is considered the first patriarch of the Indian Chan School of Buddhism.

15 One of the groups of Dharma protectors; they are skilled musicians and dancers of the heavenly realm.

Moreover, when it comes to the precept of "no carrying of gold or silver," India in ancient times did not use money. However, it is not so in modern society. For example, when taking mass transportation, one must always buy tickets with money. What should one do without carrying "gold and silver"? Perhaps some would say that having the train or bus tickets prepared in advance is good enough, but are train or bus tickets not negotiable items of value on a par with the wealth of gold or silver?

In particular, modern Buddhism regularly participates in social relief activities conducted by the government, but if this precept were strictly adhered to, then the sramaneras would be unable to do such work. So how could the bhiksus, the great worthies, of Buddhism dare commit such violations? Therefore, many precepts such as these really impede the advance of Buddhism. It is essential that Buddhism take the road toward a revival; "Humanistic Buddhism" was developed precisely for the purpose of improving conditions such as these.

No Meals After Noontime

Buddhism encourages people to engage in ascetic practice. For instance, wearing garments made of discarded cloth, carrying an alms bowl to beg for food, walking barefoot, and so on. These

The Venerable Master has more than 1,300 monastic disciples who propagate the Dharma at branch temples worldwide. Every year they return to Fo Guang Shan to attend seminars.

September 4, 2010

certainly can encourage one's resolve, but they are not necessarily applicable to every region of the world. The practice of "the eyes focusing on the nose and at the nose one contemplates the mind" is an example. In today's society, with waves of traffic all around us, if someone does not take any notice of what is on their left or right as they walk, then even if they are not struck by cars, they would definitely be knocked down by bicycles or motorcycles. So how can this not be revised?

Buddhism has consistently promoted the practice of "no meals after noontime," causing many people to believe that great merit can be gained simply by not eating after the noon hour. Consequently, no food is eaten from 12:00 noon onward, and they must wait until 6:00 am the next day before they can eat breakfast. In fact, health wise, if the digestive system does not absorb any nourishment over the course of eighteen hours, it will surely become imbalanced. In particular, without anything to be digested in the stomach and intestines, it will eventually cause rubbing along the stomach wall, resulting in what is known as a "gastric perforation."

I have seen many people who do not eat after the noon hour. During lunch time, they must forcibly hold up their stomachs as they eat many large bowls or one large plate of food after another. But in fact, Buddhism pays particular attention to the Middle Way, and it is better to be moderate when it comes to food and drink. Oftentimes there are abbots of monasteries and temples who will say, "I do not have meals after noontime; I only eat a bowl of noodles in the evening." There are also some people who say, "I do not have meals after noontime, I only drink a glass of fruit juice or a glass of milk, and that is enough for me." These prideful excuses often contribute to the appearance of a phony self without knowing it. Actually, wouldn't having normal meals while eating more lightly be just fine?

There are temples and monasteries that, due to the rule of "no meals after noontime," rather than just spending ten dollars on vegetables each day, because the resident monastics are unable to eat enough and are undernourished, have to spend much more on medicine to help keep the monastics healthy. This makes the monastics at such temples and monasteries chronically in need of medications. Here the loss truly outweighs the gain.

Long ago, Venerable Master Daosheng [355–434], one of Kumarajiva's[16] four chief disciples, could adapt to circumstances and did not rigidly adhere to fixed rules. Emperor Wen [r. 424–453 CE] of the Southern Song dynasty held a vegetarian banquet as an offering to the monastics, but the time

16 344–413 CE; one of the most prolific and influential translators in the history of Chinese Buddhism; among his translated Buddhist texts, *The Lotus Sutra*, *The Vimalakirti Sutra*, *The Diamond Sutra*, and *The Amitabha Sutra* are still widely chanted and memorized by people today.

for beginning the banquet had gone past the noon hour. No monastic dared to start eating. Emperor Wen broke the stalemate by declaring, "I see that it is precisely the noon hour!" Venerable Master Daosheng immediately followed up with the statement, "The bright sun is up in the sky, and heaven decrees that the noon hour has begun; how can it not be noontime." What he said about "heaven decrees that the noon hour has begun" means that Emperor Wen, the "son of heaven," had spoken and that it was just then noontime, and the noon hour had not passed at all. Venerable Master Daosheng took up his chopsticks at once and led the others in partaking of the meal. His helping Emperor Wen out of this predicament became a celebrated story passed down through the ages.

The Master-Disciple Relationship in Buddhism

In the Buddhist tradition, it often happens that disciples will argue, "This is my master's!" and "That is your master's!" They only know they have a master, but they do not know about protecting and supporting Buddhism. Then there are masters who say, "This is my disciple!" and "That is your disciple!" They treat their disciples as their own property, instead of encouraging them to apply their efforts to Buddhism. The breaking up of Buddhism and disciples also weakens the power of Buddhism to push forward. Although some people advocate "three parts guidance and seven parts friendship," they are unable to put it into widespread practice. The conflict between master and disciple is still something people generally disapprove of in Buddhism.

As for the Buddhist system after Buddhism was transmitted to China, because the climate, geography, faiths, and customs are quite different from India, it is difficult to abide by the earliest form of the monastic rules as formulated by the Buddha. As a consequence, before Venerable Master Taixu's advocacy of "revolution on the system," Chan Master Baizhang's [720–814 CE] expression of Buddhist reform during the Tang dynasty can be considered a true stroke of wisdom. He categorically avoided any changes to the whole monastic rule of India but instead established another completely new system of "Chan monastery rules" for China, giving Buddhism a lifeline to some small degree. Of course, a thousand years later, the "revolution on the system" advocated by Venerable Master Taixu was also done in the hope of bringing vitality to Buddhism. However, due to the deep and long-standing abuses of Buddhism, in the end, such a reform eventually failed. But the significance of his innovation still remains a contribution that cannot be erased.

Third: Revolution on Property

Of the three-point revolution as advocated by Venerable Master Taixu, the last one is "revolution on property."

When Buddhism was first transmitted to China, as soon as a temple or monastery was built, the monarch and his great ministers who were believers in Buddhism would all vie with one another to make offerings to the Triple Gem, to the point that Buddhism was amassing more and more wealth. Over time, this often attracted the envy and suspicions of society and the bureaucratic system, which eventually triggered a crisis. Even today, there are some temples and monasteries that are still harassed at every turn by some local officials because of the prosperity brought about by the offerings of incense and candles to the temple. Actually, when the monastics possess wealth, they do not shift it over for personal use, nor do they take it back to their secular families for their use. All of it is employed to propagate the Dharma, to benefit sentient beings, and to improve social welfare. So why can they not have a proper economic life? Then again, if the temples and monasteries are lacking in pure wealth, how can they undertake so many Buddhist projects and further benefit the masses?

However, currently within Buddhism, there are indeed some problems regarding the management of property that are in urgent need of reform as well. The following are examples:

1) Does Buddhist property belong to the Buddhist organization? Does it belong to the temple or monastery? Or does it belong to each individual? There ought to be some standard.
2) As to how Buddhist property is used, is that decided by the Buddhist organization? Does the abbot decide? Or does the accountant decide? There ought to be some standards.
3) There ought to be a method for the administration of the "donations" within the temple or monastery. Within society, ordinary companies and corporations all have their accounting methods for receipts and payments. Just like the rest of society, today's Buddhism also has its financial income and expenditures. Consequently, the wealth of temples and monasteries should also have a systematized method for its administration.

An overview of secular organizations shows that when they are too wealthy, they are often more easily corrupted;

when too impoverished, they more easily decline. Therefore, when moderately affluent, everyone must work hard to ensure that the organization has a surplus; when deficiencies occur, everyone should understand how to economize and save, limiting expenses in according with income. Similarly, those undertaking responsibilities for financial affairs in the Buddhist organizations must also understand how to "increase income and reduce expenditures." As to where such income sources are to be found, should the temple or monasteries rely upon the interest from property rent? Or should they rely upon buying and selling in order to increase their pure wealth? As for particular items of expenditures and their amounts, that too must be made clear and understandable.

Speaking of expenditures, the economy is required to maintain the lifelines for people's livelihoods. Temples and monasteries do indeed have some necessary expenditures and bills as well. The following are examples:

1) Water and electricity repair: All temples and monasteries have expenditures to cover the expense of water and electricity. But in addition there are problems with water and electricity that are caused by earthquakes and destructive windstorms, or long-term disrepair. All of these must have a budget for their repair.
2) Personnel expenses: In order to adapt to the developments of the times, modern temples and monasteries all require the participation of professionals in order to carry out the many activities for propagating the Dharma. This too unavoidably leads to certain expenditures for personnel expenses.

3) Books and stationery: The requirements for official correspondence and books for Buddhist research are what no temple or monastery can do without.
4) Daily food and drink: Besides attending to the food and drink for resident monastics, temples and monasteries also "widely open the Universal Gate" for the devotees, so naturally they must incur these costs.
5) Reception and making affinities: When receiving visiting devotees and VIPs, temples and monasteries will on many occasions give Buddhist souvenirs so as to form affinities with these visitors, which also involve expenditures for the purchase of these items.
6) Travel and tours: Since ancient times, monastics have mostly traveled by foot to visit good Dharma friends in the world. They do so in the hopes of seeking clarity about their confusions and realizations. For this purpose, temples and monasteries will also give some amount of support so that they may accomplish their Dharma attainments.
7) Medical treatment: In eating the five major grains and cereal crops, it is hard for people to avoid becoming sick. Since sickness must be treated, this necessarily becomes another item of expenditure.
8) Funeral arrangements: Whenever Buddhist followers pass away, temples and monasteries will conduct funeral ceremonies for them. Although there is no need for lavish services, as simplicity and solemnity are the main point, fresh flowers and fruits, offerings of food and rice, stick incense, candles, and so on are all essential items.

9) Emergency relief: For thousands of years, Buddhist temples and monasteries have eased suffering through general relief. Their performance in this area of charity work is truly no less than that of other charitable organizations. But what lies behind such spending is of course another item of expenditure.
10) Miscellaneous items: For example, there are monastic robes and monastic shoes, articles for daily use, transportation costs, various expenditures for propagating the Dharma, and so on. However, what makes Buddhism different from secular society is that as soon as there is any money, Buddhism will apply it in all directions to make broad affinities for a positive future. In having money, one must be able to use it well. Have a lot of money brings disputes, which will also increase the level of trouble. Since its founding, Fo Guang Shan has always found itself economically in the situation where "day after day is passed in difficulty, but pass they must." It is a regular occurrence for next year's budget to be spent in the current year. As a consequence, there are often people who think Fo Guang Shan has a lot of money. But in fact, Fo Guang Shan does not have money, rather it spends money, for it understands how to spend money in order to propagate the Dharma.

As for Buddhism's economic resources, during Buddhism's early period, the monastic community did not pay attention to the collecting and storing up of savings. All of the clothing, food, and necessities were supported by the system of alms giving. Monastics considered having nothing to be a point of honor. But even at that time, such a system also provoked some controversy. For example, Purna[17] advocated that the food uneaten today could be kept for tomorrow in case of civil disturbances, famine, or if something unforeseen should occur the next day; they could have some food if these should happen. Nonetheless, this proposal was vetoed by Mahakasyapa. As a consequence, Purna made a resolute decision to leave. He said, "You all carry out what you have heard from the Buddha; I will carry out what I have heard from the Buddha!" It could be said that this was the start of the schism in the Buddhist community due to financial issues.

After Buddhism was transmitted to China, the economic resources for all of China's earliest temples and monasteries were dependent upon land grants from the imperial family. A single land grant could be several thousand acres, several tens of thousands of acres, or even hundreds of thousands of acres. After gaining possession of such lands, the Buddhist monasteries instantly became huge landlords, which led them to slowly rest upon their laurels as well. They became unwilling to engage in manual labor, which impeded the development of Buddhism.

However, after the change of dynasties, it was owing to the Chinese Chan School's advocacy of "Chan practice through farming" that the fields owned by the temples and monasteries were not necessarily rented out to others for farming. Chan communities also planted their own orchards, tea plantations, and vegetable gardens, providing themselves food from their own farming efforts. They implemented the work style of "a day without work is a day without food" as advocated by Chan

17 In Sanskrit, "Fulfilled"; one of the Buddha's ten great disciples, he was known as foremost in teaching the Dharma.

Master Baizhang. It was then that the temples and monasteries were able to restore their image as spiritual transformers of society.

In recent times, Venerable Master Taixu promoted Chan practice through farming as well. Very quickly, the agrarian society was transformed into an industrial one, so he took the next step in promoting "the integration of industry and Chan." However, what was the content of "industry and Chan?" How was it to be put into practice? Venerable Master Taixu did not give any specific explanation; he only proclaimed the saying.

In modern times, what are the economic resources for Buddhist temples and monasteries in general? I will explain by listing ten examples below.

1) Dharma Service and Donations

Temples and monasteries have always relied upon donations to maintain their economic life; this is an unchanging principle. Therefore, besides the manifestations of the Buddha and bodhisattvas, the monasteries and temples must also maintain the tranquil dignity of their halls and shrines; the monastics who manage them must be virtuous and learned. It is only in this way that the donations of incense can remain abundant. An example of this is today's Mount Putuo in the Zhejiang Province of China. It cannot depend solely on the power of Guanyin Bodhisattva to ensure that everyone goes there for pilgrimages and donations. The monastic community there also has to shoulder the responsibilities of teaching and transforming the devotees.

As for having so many devotees going to Mount Putuo and offering donations, the temples and monasteries should offer these to the Chinese Buddhist Association to be distributed in all directions. These should not become the sole possession of Mount Putuo. Consequently, Venerable Master Taixu, the former President of the Chinese Buddhist Association, once listed the four great mountains of Buddhism as special key sites to be directly administered by the Chinese Buddhist Association. This means that Mount Putuo cannot be monopolized by a small number of people.

2) Buddhist Sutra Chanting and Repentance Activities

Buddhism is a religion, so naturally it cannot be separate from Buddhist sutra chanting and repentance services. In principle, for most people who believe in Buddhism, they all hope that Buddhist ceremonies can be employed to regulate their lives whenever funerals and weddings occur. In facing the needs of the devotees, however, today's Buddhism only has a particularly flourishing activity in "blessing the dead," which also makes Buddhism open to the criticism that it blesses the dead but not the living.

Buddhism is a joyful and happy religion; faith brings light, beauty, and goodness.
Photo by Zhou Yun

Of course, the merit of Buddhist services is still important. If they can be done with solemnity and a sense of propriety, then going forward they can still remain an economic lifeline upon which Buddhism's monastic order depends. However, the overly business-like activities that basically "peddle the Buddha" should be investigated thoroughly. Even in the case of a person's passing away, there are meritorious tasks, from the Buddhist activities of sutra chanting on the deceased's behalf at the time of passing, the encoffining, and the burial to the commemorative Buddhist activities for the first seven-day, the second seven-day, all the way to the seventh seven-day, the first one-hundredth-day, and the first one-year anniversary. This is quite inordinately complicated, making it impossible for the monastics to do more things, as they can only be of service to one particular donor. In such a way, what is said to be the performing of meritorious services in fact becomes more like keeping up appearances.

In short, sutra chanting and repentance services can be performed, but they must be done in accordance with the capacities of the devotees. We cannot make it difficult for the dead even after they die! In particular, in our lives, it is not only after we are dead that we need monastics to chant sutras for us. Buddhism can offer guidance for human beings throughout our birth, old age, sickness, and death. For one individual, with the celebrations from the time of birth, first full month, first full year, name conferral, adulthood, and marriage, on up to the moving into or completion of a house, it would be best if a simple ceremony of celebration and blessing could be performed on behalf of the individual. In this way, the Dharma, society, and the family can be tightly bound together.

A Sangha Offering Ceremony is held at the Fo Guang Shan Cloud Dwelling Building every year, with numerous monastics and devotees attending the celebration.
Photo by Venerable Hui Yan

3) The Four Offerings

During Buddhism's early period, the monastic community mainly received clothing, food and drink, bedding, and medicine, the four kinds of offerings, which were important economic resources for the monastic community. The willingness of the devotees to make these offerings is a good thing, for the offerings are an expression of the honor and respect of the devotees, garnered by the compassion, cultivation, and morality of the monastics. However, there have been a small number of devotees who have not made proper offerings. They would wholeheartedly provide offerings simply because a monastic treated them well, regardless of the monastic's Dharma practice. This too indirectly fosters the indolent and affinities-seeking nature of some monastics, even to the point where a temple perhaps becomes the family temple of a certain donor, making it impossible for the monastery or temple to fulfill its function of serving sentient beings.

Therefore, regarding devotees' aspiration to make offerings to monastics, I always say, "In supporting the monastics, it is making offerings for a whole year and not just a single day; in supporting the monastics, it is making offerings in all directions and not just for a single person; in supporting the monastics, it is making offerings for the future and not just for now; in supporting the monastics, it is making offerings to learn the Dharma and not just for a sense of excitement." I hope that all the devotees will be able to pay attention to all of these points.

The Venerable Master does not seek out donations, except for establishing universities. He launched the Million-Member Fundraising Campaign and the alms round procession throughout Taiwan.

Photo by Pi Yun Lai

In receiving offerings from the devotees, monastics should also reflect on whether or not they are worthy of them. In particular, the offerings should be turned over to the temple's reserves for the propagation of the Dharma to benefit sentient beings.

4) Making Affinities to Maintain a Living

"Transforming affinities" is a very beautiful expression. In the human world, if we give others good affinities, they will also give us good affinities. These affinities intertwine and accomplish one another; it is truly a beautiful thing. However, making affinities is to make wholesome affinities. Sometimes, some ignorant young monastics only push devotees to make contributions, telling the person how much the donation should be. This is truly a flaw in "making affinities." There are also monastics who purposely wait outside of Dharma services held by other temples, or they wait outside the venue of activities held by other organizations, so they can ask for donations from people. If what they are doing is on behalf of a public effort, namely "many hands make the load light," then of course asking everyone to join in charitable deeds and make a donation is permissible. But if it is for an individual's livelihood, then why would one try and make a living through transforming affinities with the alms bowl? It is no wonder that some people describe them as "living without purpose by depending upon Buddhism." It is really an unbearable and embarrassing expression!

In fact, if one could apply the time employed in asking for donations through transforming affinities toward Dharma practice, such as Chan meditation, Amitabha Buddha's name recitation, and propagating the Dharma for the benefit of sentient beings, then one would have Dharma attainments. At that point, one would not need to ask for donations, for the devotees would come forward on their own initiative to provide support and make offerings. Would not that increase one's moral prestige even more?

5) Income from Building Rentals

Temples and monasteries in the past were all very large, but the younger generations did not utilize them as meditation halls, Amitabha chanting halls, stupas and courtyards, or Buddhist colleges, nor did they know about initiating projects. As a result, buildings were no longer in use and were rented out or sold off. Moreover, some buildings were provided to other individuals as temporary housing for coffins. There were many of these bizarre instances, which have led to Buddhism's decline.

In the past, a single monastery or temple could own a parcel of land with one or two streets. However, this phenomenon has already been reduced, gradually transforming into the "urban Buddhism style." This phenomenon is also not bad, for it ensures that Buddhism is self-supporting and no longer relies upon real estate to maintain its existence. This also spares monastics from acquiring the laziness apparent in the children of the wealthy. Thus, this is something beneficial to Buddhism.

Wealth must be acquired through one's own ability, hard work, and wisdom. If one do not rely on oneself, then one is giving up one's ability to survive. Not only is this a tragedy for an individual, but it is also a failure of an organization.

6) The Arts of Painting and Calligraphy

In the past, there were some monastics who kept themselves aloof from society. They could not bear sustaining a life by asking for donations from devotees, and they were unwilling to spend their days living off the labor of others. Hence, they exerted themselves to create their own success in the areas of calligraphy and painting, so as to maintain their own living and cultivation through the income obtained from selling their works. For example, when I was at Dinghui Temple at Jiaoshan, I saw several dozen masters in hermitages along the front of the temple; they all supported the temple's expenses through painting and calligraphy. There were even quite a few monastics in the past who reached a high level of achievement in the area of painting and calligraphy. Examples include the calligraphy of Venerable Master Hongyi [1880–1942] during the early Republican period, and the paintings by the Four Great Monk Masters of the Qing dynasty: Bada Shanren [1626–1705], Shitao [1642–1707], Shixi [1612–ca. 1674], and Hongren [1610–1664], among others.

I do not have any special abilities, yet I am now able to manage the Public Education Trust Fund through the support of *One-Stroke Calligraphy*, which people are so fond of. After the devoted believers acquire my calligraphy, they all donate some money to the Public Education Trust Fund, which also ensures that our work of propagating the Dharma can attain even more assistance.

7) The Distribution of Dharma Supplies

In temples and monasteries, there is generally an office for the distribution of Dharma supplies. This ensures that Buddhist followers or people in society can conveniently obtain various kinds of Buddhist reading materials, images of Buddhas, and Dharma supplies, as well as Buddhist video and audio recordings. It is by such means that the distribution of Buddhist cultural items can be encouraged, and it also ensures that Buddhist culture attains further development. Nevertheless, Buddhist buying and selling differs from that of ordinary society because profit is not the goal. What we gain are Dharma and human affinities, thus we do not do "what is not related to Buddhism," so we do not sell souvenirs that are unrelated to Buddhism.

8) Vegetarian Meals

Taiwan has many vegetarian restaurants, which have all been opened by I-Kuan Tao devotees, providing a great convenience for vegetarians. Buddhist devotees should also think about how to engage in vegetarian food preparation so as to provide a service to vegetarians. If the temple or monastery itself cannot shoulder such a responsibility, then devotees can be invited to help manage this at the temple. Then the temple, monastery, or Buddhist association can assist in raising funds.

However, even now there is not a single standard for the preparation of Buddhist vegetarian dishes. The cooking of a single vegetable dish alone varies from person to person. It is not like western hamburgers and pizza, which always retain the same style regardless of which country around the world prepares them. Nevertheless, Taiwan's temples are quite replete with the mind of offering, and they do not worry about how much people eat. But beyond providing vegetarian meals, it would be even more ideal if they could conduct seminars that would bring in devotees to learn about Buddhism.

9) The Work of Propagating the Dharma

Temples and monasteries are not merely places to cultivate the Dharma, they could also make affinities with society's culture, education, arts, and so on by launching radio and TV stations, issuing newspapers, establishing publishing houses, founding schools at all levels, and opening art galleries. The Dharma can then be propagated by employing these various enterprises. This can also increase the income from pure wealth.

10) Sightseeing and Pilgrimages

Most temples and monasteries nowadays have instituted guest halls and pilgrim lodges to receive devotees and tourists. Not only do these ensure that the visitors can sightsee and tour around, but they also provide room and board services to them. This too can bring some increase in the resources of pure wealth for the temple or monastery. Besides room and board, if these facilities could further provide encouragement toward the Dharma and guidance related to culture and education, then in the days to come, temples and monasteries would surely become a destination for purifying the spirit.

Buddhism advocates that the acquiring of wealth should come from cultivating goodness, accumulating merits, and making broad affinities for a positive future. All income has its relationship to "causes, conditions, and effects." Hence, since the founding of Fo Guang Shan, I first instituted the method of how Buddhism should manage pure wealth. In particular, I regularly advocate for ideas to manage pure wealth, such as "Use wisdom in place of money," "Those who have power should not manage money, and those who manage money should not have power," "Do not seek donations for personal reasons," "Do not lend or borrow the monastery's finances to devotees vice versa," and "Everything goes back to the temple treasury, economic harmony through sharing equally." I always feel that Buddhism's wealth comes from all directions and goes to all directions; it is something held in common by the whole community. Not only should temples and monasteries understand how to put pure wealth to good use, but they should also have sound ideas of managing wealth. Only in this way can temples and monasteries sustain their development.

Summing it all up, in devoting my life to Buddhism, in order to keep current with the advances in society, in terms of thoughts, I am always making improvements; in terms of practice, I am constantly making adjustments. Even though I know that Buddhism must be reformed, innovation never comes into being in the heat of the moment. My "silent revolution" advocates that some things advance, while some things retreat; some things proceed, while some things stop. Although the results are not apparent immediately, I consistently work on them, which can slowly overcome any obstacle!

The spectacular fireworks celebrating the Chinese New Year Festival of Light and Peace at Fo Guang Shan Buddha Museum attracts tens of thousands of people.

2015

Only Setting the Tone and Not Becoming the Master

What Are Some Innovations I Have for Buddhism

It seemed that I had to do everything for Buddhism. For Buddhism, I have to only set the tone and not become the master, hand over my physical body to the temple and give my life to the Dharma protectors, heavenly beings and nagas, and making the aspiration to head out for Buddhism, striving to move Buddhism toward humanity and society. It seemed then that I suddenly saw people in the tens of thousands who were waving at me. I must propagate the Dharma for the benefit of sentient beings, and usher in a new set of circumstances for Buddhism.

I never received a formal education as a child, and I had not even seen a school. Before I joined the monastic order at the age of twelve, I intermittently attended some classes at a private school, but altogether it did not exceed more than two months. This was because studying at a private school meant paying four copper coins each day, for four copper coins could buy two sesame seed cakes. Often, I did not go to school for the sake of saving money.

After joining the monastic order, I lived entirely in a conservative monastery for nearly a decade. Occasionally, a teacher would come to teach a class, but that did not happen too many times. The majority of my time was spent in serving through physical labor. However, I am fortunate to have been born in this new age, in which everything must be reinvented. I know that I myself must have new thoughts and new ideas in order to reevaluate worldly values.

As for these thoughts and beliefs of mine, essentially no one demanded them of me or forced them upon me. I just naturally came to realize that in this new age, survival requires adaptation to the changing environment. Within the age-old Buddhist college, there was basically no opportunity for innovation. Thinking back on my ten years of extremely inflexible temple life, every day was simply spent lining up, bowing, kneeling, cutting firewood, carrying water, and so forth. Our discipline master did not allow us to read newspapers, use fountain pens to write characters, or read books outside the field of Buddhism. However, I was not able to understand the Buddhist classic sutras and related books, and that was how those long ten years, the years of my youth, were spent.

When I was seventeen or eighteen, I entered the Qixia Vinaya College and began my studies. I was very fortunate that my teacher sent me to the library as its administrator responsible for taking care of the books. The library had a collection of books from the library of a teacher's college. The teacher's college had been disbanded during the Sino-Japanese War. No one wanted the school's books, so we moved the books back to the temple, even though nobody wished to borrow or read them. I made use of this opportunity to read quite a few books then. At the time, I felt as if I had just been awakened from a dream to discover that the human world had such treasures.

Later on, I learned about Venerable Master Taixu, and my classmates said he was the leader of New Buddhism. In my mind, I wished for Venerable Master Taixu to be the leader of my New Buddhism. I had no idea what was meant by "New Buddhism," but I did know that Buddhism needed reform and innovation. Buddhism could not merely be in accord with the truth; more importantly, it had to be in accord with circumstances.

At the age of nineteen or twenty, I was studying at the Jiaoshan Buddhist College, and I saw Venerable Master Taixu returning to the capital after Chinese victory in the war. At the time, it seemed as if I were seeing the Buddha, and I could not help but hasten forward and join my palms together to prostrate to him. He looked at me with a smile, and responded with, "Good! Good! Good!" Then he walked past me. Even though the time was short, I was very moved and vowed at that moment to spend the rest of my life being "good." As a result, Venerable Master's disciples such as Venerable Zhifeng, Venerable Chenkong, Venerable Daxing, Professor Xue Jianyuan, and Professor Yu Yu [1909–1989] have all been my teachers, and I have taken classes from them for short periods of time. Slowly, I came to understand the orientation of New Buddhism and its goal.

At that time, my life of learning at the Jiaoshan Buddhist College had some changes, and I gave up my studies without hesitation. I made a request to my master to return to Yixing Dajue Temple, the seat of my lineage, so that I could venerate the preceding masters. But quite inconceivably and by some propitious reason also unknown to me, a friend of my teacher knew that I was returning from Nanjing and that I had also studied at the Buddhist college, so he asked me to take up the position of principal at a local public elementary school. During this time, the *Ta Kung Pao* and the *Shanghai News* newspapers became my reading materials for opening myself up to new thinking and expanding my horizons. Even though it was an elementary school, there was still a small budget for buying books, so I bought many books to read, including Hu Shizhi's [1891–1962] *The Writing of Hu Shi* and Liang Qichao's [1873–1929] the *Collected Works from the Ice-Drinker's Studio*, as well as works by Lu Xun [1881–1936], Mao Dun [1896–1981], Lao She [1899–1966], and Ba Jin [1904–2005]. This allowed me to wander through an ocean of books as my thoughts soared into the clouds. I forgot about the impoverishment of my physical circumstances, for I felt surfeited with spiritual sustenance, something even more valuable.

When I was twenty-one, the KMT was defeated again and again after the Battle of Xubang (Huaihai campaign) during the civil war. I already felt the brutality of war in Nanjing and Yixing, and my life was imperiled. Consequently, in the spring of the following year, the early spring of 1949, I travelled to Taiwan through Shanghai. I did not have anything when I first arrived in Taiwan. Besides the clothes I was wearing, the only other possession I had was my identity card and the ten silver coins with Yuan Shikai's portrait on them given to me by my master. That was how I began my life in Taiwan.

During those first two years at Chungli and Hsinchu, I read quite a few books on literature, history, and philosophy. At the same time, I gained some insights in the area of Buddhist studies. During this period, I wrote some short articles and also published a few poems, such as "The Great Buddha," "Bells, Gongs, and Wooden Fish," and "Star and Cloud."[1] Based on my experience of having read several books, I began my career of teaching and editing magazines.

I arrived in Ilan during the first lunar month of 1953. When I was in mainland China, I thought about how I would work for Buddhism in the future. I thought I would write a newspaper posted on walls along the street for publicity, distribute Buddhist fliers, give street lectures, and ensure that Buddhism would be drawn closer to the multitudes. I would do the work of propagating the Dharma in several different ways.

However, Ilan was a small and backward place, and I was significantly inadequate in economic conditions, but being there was exactly what sparked the new ideas that spurred me on, urging me to light a new kind of fire for Buddhism. Therefore, I established a Buddhist choir and organized youth groups, student associations, and children's classes. I also instituted an after-school program for the arts and a Dharma mission.

It seemed that I had to do everything for Buddhism. For Buddhism, I have to only set the tone and not become the master, hand over my physical body to the temple and give my life to the Dharma protectors, heavenly beings and nagas, and making the aspiration to head out for Buddhism, striving to move Buddhism toward humanity and society. It then seemed that I suddenly saw people in the tens of thousands who were

1 In Chinese, the Venerable Master's name, 星雲 (Hsing yun), means "Star and Cloud."

waving at me. I must propagate the Dharma for the benefit of sentient beings, and usher in a new set of circumstances for Buddhism. Even though I dared not say that I possessed any qualifications, the only thing I could rely upon was that I had aspiration and strength. The more I aspired to do for Buddhism, the more new thoughts and ideas sprang forth from my mind in an endless stream.

These innovations endured criticisms from Buddhist circles at that time, to the point where I was looked upon as a great scourge. Despite this, I had no time to think too much about it, as I was single-mindedly focused on devoting the mental and physical strength I had to Buddhism, so Buddhism would adapt to the modern world. Therefore, I made some reforms and innovations step by step. To this day, haven't Buddhist choirs, recorded discs, DVDs, TV Dharma teachings, family Dharma services, and

The Venerable Master leading the Ilan Buddhist Youth Choir records program at the radio station, using Buddhist music to propagate the Dharma.

October 17, 1954

A Discussion of Chan over A Vegetarian Meal been promoted in temples and monasteries? This piece notes a few of these items.

Music

As for singing, although I am unable to carry a tune, I know that music is a language without borders, and it is the most effective and efficient means for propagating the Dharma. When I first arrived in Ilan, I organized a choir, and did it not guide many young people to come in droves? Within the twelve divisions of the Buddhist canon, the sutras in prose style are universally applicable, while the repeated verses and verses as poems and songs are also very important. All the Buddhas have devotees in all directions singing their praises; the masses in the hundreds of thousands also hope to hear the melodious sound of this singing.

In order to use music to propagate the Dharma, I had to write lyrics and invite professionals to compose the music. In the early period, I composed many songs that were easy to sing and be passed along, such as "The West," "The Song of Dharma Propagators," "Bell Sounds," "Let's Take Refuge in the Buddha Now," "Bodhi Tree," and "The Rhythm of the Buddhist Youth." We went to sing whole-heartedly at temple courtyards, public auditoriums, and national halls. We also went to sing and chant at military camps, schools, factories, and prisons. Indeed, this was very effective.

I saw how enthusiastic the response was, so I expanded upon the influence of the singing group. During gatherings for the Buddhist Chanting Service, instead of the dedication of merit at the end of the traditional arrangement, we would use the singing of a song or a prayer; this moved everyone even further.

Fo Guang Shan Buddhist Monastic Choir performing at the world-renowned Lincoln Center in New York, a first in Buddhism.

October 19, 2001

I also invited some professional teachers to transcribe the notation for Buddhist verses into the numbered musical notation form. After we had that, everyone felt that the verses of early Buddhism could be sung quite easily. Consequently, it was no longer only passed on to others through oral instructions. With the musical notation, these Buddhist verses were quite easily learned.

Of course, the opposition from conservatives can easily be imagined. Under very difficult circumstances, I used the pure wealth from the donations of devotees to make audio tapes and even records, which expanded the scope of influence for the songs. Isn't the radio the place with the most singing? Consequently, I further promoted Buddhist songs for broadcast on the radio, enabling more people to hear them. At the time, I also created programs for the Broadcasting Corporation of China and the Ming Pen Broadcasting Company.

In short, no senior monastic came to oppose or praise this work during my time in Ilan. There were only the young people who came to sing. In my mind, these songs belonged to the youth and were for them to sing. There was no need for me to become discouraged because of different opinions. I thought I ought to offer the young people appreciation and encouragement.

"Buddhist songs soar into the clouds; Dharma sounds interrupt foolish dreams." After many Buddhist songs such as "The Song of Dharma Propagators" were broadcast on radio stations, these songs became all the rage for a time in 1953, flowing right off everyone's tongues. Venerable Xinwu, Venerable Zhuyun, Venerable Guangci, many other venerables, and the lay Buddhist Li Bingnan also followed along in making lyrics and inviting others to compose the music. Later on, there were Professor Lü Lili of National Taiwan University, Professor Wu Juche of National Taipei University of Technology, the husband-and-wife team Li Zhonghe and Xiao Huyin, and other new talents that followed. All of them joined together in response and collectively used the sound of singing to propagate the Dharma.

Besides the Buddhist hymns, I also thought about the verses of traditional Buddhism in their six-line and eight-line forms. The vocals for these are long, just like those of Beijing opera, and they are difficult to understand and not easily learned; therefore, there are very few people who can sing it. However, having been passed down the generations for more than two thousand years, there is no substitute for the splendor and sacredness of Buddhist chanting. In the past, the monastic community would only sing the Buddhist sutras and verses to the Buddha during the morning and evening chanting services in the Buddha Hall. Why couldn't we sing them to ordinary people? This way, the lives of the great multitudes can have an addition of Dharma joy, which comes from honoring the Buddha and commending the monastic community with Buddhist chanting.

Since the 1980s, Venerable Tzu Hui and Venerable Tzu Jung, who had begun their calling in the Ilan Buddhist Choir, brought the voice of Buddhist chanting to the national stage. They even took the choir on a tour of performances around the world. These venues included the Music Center and the Kodak Theater in Los Angeles, the London Royal Theatre, the Berliner Philharmoniker, the Lincoln Center in New York, the Sydney Opera House, the Queen Elizabeth Theatre in Vancouver, and many more. They encountered the multitudes of Westerners with blue eyes and high-bridged noses buying tickets to enter the theaters and then listening with rapt attention. At the end of performances, as the calls for "encore" lingered in the theater, they saw how the audience would rise up spontaneously and enthusiastically applaud for several minutes.

Finally, the ideal goal of "Buddhist songs propagating throughout a three thousandfold world system, while the Dharma is spread to a trillion lands" was truly realized.

The scope of this musical transmission slowly expanded to include Fo Guang Shan's branch temples around the world. For example, Hsi Lai Temple in Los Angeles established the Buddha's Light Youth Symphony Orchestra, the Buddha's Light Youth Stringed Orchestra was also instituted in New Jersey, and Venerable Yong Fu and Venerable Jue Yuan in Taipei had their professional Sounds of the Human World Buddhist Chinese Orchestra. Moreover, the Nanhua University in Chiayi established the Ya Yue Court Orchestra when the campus first opened for instruction. I was pleased to see this accomplishment, and further urged the school on to give it more support. Over the past dozen years of development, the ensemble has now become the one and only orchestra performing ancient Chinese court music in the world of Chinese music.

The Venerable Master attending the Sounds of the Human World event held at the National Dr. Sun Yat-sen Memorial Hall in 2003 and singing the "The Rhythm of the Buddhist Youth" with members of the Buddhist Choir of fifty years ago. *From the left*: the Venerable Master, venerables Tzu Hui, Tzu Jung, Yi Kong, and Yung Fu.

In 2003, Venerable Tzu Hui of the Fo Guang Shan Foundation for Buddhist Culture and Education took excerpts of phrases from my articles that could be turned into lyrics and edited these into a word bank, and then put out a call for musical compositions from around the world. For five to six consecutive years, the Buddhist songs were then presented in the weeklong Sounds of Human World Music: Buddhist Songs Competition at the National Dr. Sun Yat-sen Memorial Hall in Taipei. The chosen songs were suitable for the languages of various countries, such as Chinese, English, Japanese, and so forth. This made it easy for Fo Guang Shan's Buddhist choirs in various regions around the world to choose songs to perform. Therefore, every year on April 8th, the Buddha's birthday, ten thousand BLIA members from various countries around the world would sing together at the Fo Guang Shan Buddha Museum in praise of the Buddha; countless people have passed on these songs.

It is worth mentioning that in 2010, the composer Mr. Liu Chia-chang held a vocal concert for thirty thousand people at the Taipei Arena, performing the song "Sound of Cloud Lake," which he composed and I wrote. It seems that the song was quite well received. Clearly, Buddhist songs are also welcomed at performances on the modern stage. The scene at modern ceremonies for commemorating the passing of the aged or celebrating marriages has been made all that more dignified because of Buddhist music. The social mood has also been improved, but more importantly, as the human mind becomes purified, the morals of society will also naturally be elevated.

"Sound of Cloud Lake" in numbered musical notation.

Children's Classes

As Buddhist songs began to be circulated and sung, I sometimes thought to myself, "How did I think of joining the monastic order back then?" At the time, I was very young and had no understanding about what it meant to be liberated from life and death, nor did I know what the elimination of afflictions meant. Now that I think about it, I was around the age of four or five when my maternal grandmother began taking me to worship at beneficent shrines. Moreover, I have heard people say that a month after I was born, I was entrusted to Mother Guanyin as an adopted son. Thus, over the ensuing months and years as I grew up, I would see the Youth Sudhana beside Guanyin Bodhisattva and feel a deeper sense of familiarity, feeling that as children, we could also be with the Buddha.

Since I came into contact with these small but wholesome conditions during my childhood, they became ambrosia for my whole life. Later on, I saw how there were so many children that also needed meritorious causes and conditions for the future. I became aware that I ought to be of service to them and bind together a relationship between Buddhism and these children. Consequently, starting in the 1950s, in addition to starting the Tzu Ai Kindergarten, every year during the seven-day retreat held at Leiyin Temple in Ilan, I would gather the children together. Even though there were no extra rooms available, I would still hold the assembly in the small open area on the terrace and call it "Sunday School." This made it possible for these little ones to nurture a good and honest character from an early age through the stories that they heard.

At first there were only twenty or thirty kids, but after a short period of promotion, this number suddenly increased to one or two thousand. For the young people who were already studying at junior and senior high schools, student associations were organized; for the kids who were still studying at elementary schools or kindergartens, children's classes were established. When I had my hands full with other things, it so happened that the young people in the youth corps would assume the roles of teachers for the children's classes. For example, there was a teacher surnamed Lin, who has been participating in teaching the children's classes for an uninterrupted period of more than fifty or so years. That person is none other than Lin Mei-yueh, the older sister of Lin Ch'ing-chih.

I recall a pure and innocent conversation I had with many of these small ones. These memories have remained clear and distinct in my mind. I said:

> *Little friends, my family believes in Buddhism; what religion does your family believe in?*

They told me in a loud voice:

Buddhism!

I then asked:

Buddhism's founder is Sakyamuni Buddha; do you know what is the name of Buddhism's founder?

They said confidently:

Sa-kya-mu-ni-Buddha!

I further asked:

Little friends, now that you believe in Buddhism, in the future you should believe in Buddhism as well. We cannot depart from our faith in Buddhism, for we must believe in Buddhism forever and ever. Can you believe in Buddhism forever and ever?

Each of the little friends replied firmly:

We-can-believe-in-Buddhism-forever-and-ever!

Looking at the many children at that time, I thought about giving each of them a candy, but I was just so embarrassingly short of money. I could not even buy candy, let alone give each of them a piece of bread. However, even though I was impoverished materially, that could not affect the growth of the bodhi seeds. By now, some of these little kids from the children's classes have already retired from their positions as college professors or high school teachers. For example, Chang Chao served as a full-time volunteer at Fo Guang University, Lin Ch'ing-chih, the Ilan University lecturer, spent his life on prison missionary work, and Professor Cheng Shih-yen served as a former member of the Students Affairs Committee for the Ministry of Education. All of them were little kids in the children's classes back then.

Since the founding of the children's classes in Ilan, not only does every branch temple around the world have children's classes, but Venerable Tzu Jung, Venerable Chueh Pei, and others of the BLIA have also established Buddha's Light Scout Groups in various regions of the world. Moreover, they have joined the World Organization of the Scout Movement as associate members. Every year, representatives are sent to study in various regions of the world, ensuring that these children will walk into the world.

For instance, our scouts attended the first World Scout Interreligious Symposium held in Spain in 2003, during which they gained the right to host the second one; the scouts went to the 2004 Asia-Pacific Region Scout Moot in Thailand; the

The Venerable Master founded the first kindergarten in Buddhist circles, Tzu Ai Kindergarten.
July 1956

The Venerable Master says that we should love children, for they are the future of our nation. Pictured is the Venerable Master shaking hands with a child attending an outdoor learning curriculum at the Buddha Museum
June 30, 2012

scouts convened at the second World Scout Interreligious Symposium at Fo Guang Shan in 2006; and Buddha's Light Scout Groups went to the 2009 summer camp and Kanagawa Jamboree held at Motosu Temple in Japan. In addition, many scouts in the Hsi Lai Scout Group have been promoted to Eagle Scout. From what I have heard, becoming an Eagle Scout is the highest and most distinguished level of achievement for the Boy Scouts of America.

In addition, each of the affiliated temples both here and abroad holds children's summer camps every year. The little children in Taiwan all return to Fo Guang Shan for a mass rally, in which they are divided into several echelons, with thousands of people in each echelon. In 2003, Beautiful Life Television began broadcasting a series of children's educational programs, including "Happy Little Readings from the Chinese Classics," "King of the Chinese Classics," and "Searching for the Top Little Graduate." These *Chinese Classics Fun Time* programs integrate Chinese classics into young people's lives.

Starting from 2004, besides promoting sutra study classes in Taiwan, we also connected the BLIA with various organizations, including the International Classics Culture Association of Hong Kong, the Hunan College of Chinese Culture, and the Melaka Cultural Education Fund in Malaysia. For several years, they have conducted the Global Conference for the Reading of Chinese Cultural Classics in Hong Kong, Beijing, and Taipei, respectively. This conference draws the attendance of children from many areas, such as mainland China, Taiwan, Hong Kong, Indonesia, Thailand, Malaysia, Singapore, and so on. Each year, more than two thousand people have participated.

The Buddhist sutras speak of "four small things not to be taken lightly"; although children are small, they will all become pillars of the nation when they grow up. In the human world, everything is accomplished based on a single thought of ours. It was because of my single thought of the good causes and conditions in my childhood that I decided to plant many wholesome affinities broadly for the sake of today's children. In this way, we can strive to nurture Buddhism's young sprouts so that there will be people in the future who can carry on the family responsibilities of the Buddha, continuing to propagate the wisdom life of the Dharma. This will bring benefits to the human world for future generations.

Cloud and Water Mobile Clinics and Mobile Library Trucks

As early as my adolescent years, I thought about how propagating the Dharma in the modern age requires the founding of a university, a newspaper, and a radio station. In particular, Buddhism requires charity work such as medical care, senior care, orphan care, and so forth. There were also some temples in mainland China at the time that had already taken the lead in performing charitable deeds through providing free medical treatment. I made a visit to Singapore in early 1961 and saw how their free medical treatment and medical care had achieved quite a level of success. At the same time, Christianity was also flourishing in Taiwan as they founded schools and opened hospitals. They were making money off everyone, but everyone was saying how good they were. Clearly, medical care is what people need. In this case, why can't Buddhism undertake some projects that fulfill society's needs?

When I came to Kaohsiung to found Fo Guang Shan, although I was busy with building temples and propagating the Dharma, I still thought we should perform some medical care services on behalf of society. Therefore, at the beginning of Fo Guang Shan's founding, I set up a small clinic to provide Fo Guang Shan devotees and local residents with medical care for free. However, the villages and towns, such as Chishan, Liouguei, Jiaxian, Sanmin, and Taoyuan, were all situated in the mountain area. The majority of these residents were indigenous people. Because it was impossible for them to obtain good medical care, they were unable to work and make money. This was especially so given the remote mountain roads and the inconveniences of transportation, which meant that even those who were not sick became queasy with all the bumps and jolts along those roads, not to mention those who were already sick.

Therefore, I thought of a solution: Send medical care to the mountainous areas! This can allow wealthy people to contribute some pure wealth and help those who are ill obtain medical care. Then, I bought a large number of Econovans and named them Cloud and Water Mobile Clinics. I want to express my thanks to the Kaohsiung Medical University, Kaohsiung Chang Gung Memorial Hospital, and Kaohsiung Veterans General Hospital, which provided most of the assistance. Many hospital doctors and nursing staff willingly stepped up to serve as volunteers. Every morning, the mobile clinics would depart from the Fo Guang Clinic, carrying doctors, nurses, and venerables, as they went to each remote area and provided diagnosis and treatment for the local populace. These medical care vehicles were very efficient in providing medical examinations, as a single vehicle could go from point A to point B, and from one village to another, serving more than a hundred people each day.

But as we tried to promote the mobile clinics, sometimes good deeds are not that easy to do. Because the indigenous people who reside in the mountainous areas are mostly Christians, it goes without saying that the pastors there were not pleased about our promotion, and we even encountered some difficulties with the local government administration. For example, healthcare centers had been established in the mountainous areas to provide patient care to the populace, but these could not easily shoulder the entire responsibility for medical care. What's worse, when our mobile medical care vehicles arrived, almost all of these centers closed. Hence, they reported their complaints to the government, saying that we were violating medical laws. Nevertheless, the doctors in our mobile clinics were prominent doctors from various large hospitals, and our medications were all legally acquired from leading pharmaceutical companies. Moreover, we did not charge any fees for engaging in these good works, so the government found it difficult to ban us.

This led me to think about how the foundation of good works must be rooted in our concern for other people; we must not have an attitude of monopolistic trust. Even though we were doing good works, we were also making it impossible for the original healthcare centers to survive; this is also unsatisfactory. Afterward, I used some discretion in promoting the

Fifty Cloud and Water Mobile Library Trucks make rounds throughout Taiwan; each is assigned a collection of ten thousand books and carries two thousand books on every trip.

November 2, 2012

mobile clinics. I only set them up at the foot of the mountains, and I called them Buddha's Light Clinics. This provided services on a small scale to people in the mountain or those who visited there, as well as the populace of the Dashu area. Besides the professional doctors and nursing staff, the responsibility for the clinics was turned over to Venerable Miao Seng, who had once served as head nurse at a Christian hospital.

Since the concept of the Cloud and Water Mobile Clinics was unworkable, I transformed them into Cloud and Water Mobile Libraries. The consideration here was that the children and local populace in the remote areas could not easily find reading materials beyond the school curriculum, so I put forward the idea of "I buy the books; you read the books," and sent the books to these remote areas. Every day, the book-mobiles driven by volunteers would carry loads of books, both classical and modern, as well as those sought after by the children, and bring them to villages and schools in turn so that everyone could borrow them.

Each truck was assigned accompanying volunteers who would tell stories in a vivid manner. Sometimes there would be musically inclined volunteers who could play an *erhu*[2] song or a harmonica tune for everyone. Even now there are fifty book mobiles that create broad and good affinities in various areas; these have also garnered widespread welcome and positive responses. When the Dashu Fruit Festival comes around, the book mobiles are even enlisted to carry juicy Jade Purse lychees to be shared with the local teachers and students.

I started publishing *The Merit Times* mainly to encourage everyone to read the newspaper and to subscribe to the newspaper. However, some people said that although they had the money, they were too busy working to have time to read the newspaper. Hence, I initiated the "I subscribe to the newspaper; you read the newspaper," which also garnered a positive response from many people. Even today, ten or twenty thousand free copies of the newspaper are distributed to various schools, offices, and organizations. Even inmates in prison can obtain spiritual comfort from this.

As early as thirty or so years ago, Pu-Men Temple in Taipei promoted the "widely open the Universal Gate" campaign. In those days, it was quite inconvenient for a vegetarian to enjoy a vegetarian meal. Hence, Pu-Men Temple launched "I buy the rice and cook it, and you have a meal," inviting everyone to

2 A two-stringed bowed musical instrument.

come and have a meal for free. This promotion was also an exciting success. Later on, Fo Guang Shan's Taipei Vihara located beside the Songshan Station witnessed a steady stream of visitors coming and going. Therefore, I launched "porridge instead of tea," in which "peace and safety porridge" was offered daily without charge. When people came, I offered them a bowl of porridge as a substitute for a cup of tea. Some people needed to quench their thirst while others needed to relieve their hunger. For vegetarians, this was a skillful act of kindness.

As the saying goes, "Repay the kindness of a drop of water with a fountain." Therefore, I established the Water Drop Teahouses because I wanted to realize the idea of four kindnesses mentioned in the Dharma. Among these, the kindness of parents, the kindness of one's country, and the kindness of the Triple Gem are all easily understood. However, what is the kindness of sentient beings? How can one be grateful to the numerous and diverse sentient beings?

Among the numerous and diverse sentient beings, there are the various professions of scholars, farmers, artisans, and merchants. It is only because of them that we can exist in this world. And because these scholars, farmers, artisans, and merchants occasionally have some needs, I can also make affinities with them. However, this idea is not easily put into practice. Regardless, if it is a bowl of porridge or a bowl of rice, these things must be paid for; even a cup of tea or

The Venerable Master launched "porridge instead of tea," in which laba porridge, renamed "peace and safety porridge," is offered daily for free.

Photo provided by Gandha Samudra Culture Company

glass of water cannot be provided without monetary payment. Therefore, the Water Drop Teahouses in every area still charge appropriate fees in order to cover personnel and material costs.

Despite this, I have not been discouraged at all. Currently, in the Fo Guang Shan Buddha Museum, I have set up the Camphor Grove Tea House. When someone comes and wants a bowl of noodles or a bowl of rice, it doesn't matter if they pay or not. The same also holds true for Fo Guang Shan's Devotees Building. As long as someone is willing to come, we will offer them a bowl of peace and safety porridge. If they have money, they can place it in the donation box; if it is inconvenient for them, they can stride away without a second thought or any concern. There is also Fo Guang Tea in every reception hall at Fo Guang Shan; the Dragon Pavilion and Fo Guang Avenue also have tea serving pavilions set up. These areas embrace those who are tired of walking and thirsty, welcoming them to sit down, have some Fo Guang Tea, rest their feet, and enjoy the scenery for a while. All of this brings together the good intentions of the many devotees and serves as an offering of joy.

In Fo Guang Shan's Pilgrim's Lodge and the Cloud Dwelling Building's dining hall, there are hundreds to thousands of people having meals at the same time. Whether someone is a long-term guest or a passing traveler, once the wooden block is sounded, they can sit down and have a meal. After their meal, they can leave and are able to wander about. If someone is so inclined and would like to make affinities with others by doing something in return, there are many halls at Fo Guang Shan where one can make donations toward lamp oil and incense as an expression of their joy.

"Making affinities, engaging in giving, and repaying kindness" were my goals in setting up the Water Drop Teahouses.

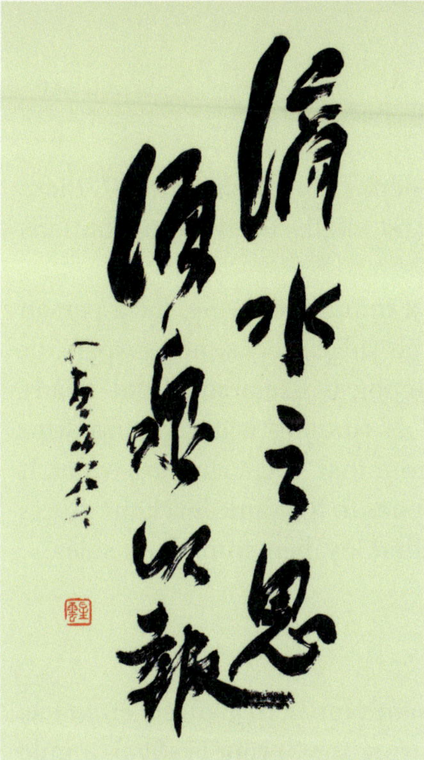

The Venerable Master's calligraphy: "Repay the kindness of a drop of water with a fountain."

If I "have," I can repay kindness, but if I am poor, I can only accept the giving of others; how can there be a way to repay kindness? In fact, repaying debts of gratitude is not only for the wealthy. We can say good words, perform service for someone, or give someone a greeting, a smile, or palms joined together in greeting; all of these methods are ways to repay kindness. What we eat, wear, and use all come from the support of society and the larger community. Considering this, how wonderful is it to repay the kindness of a drop of water with a fountain?

"Some liquor for a rich person is a year's worth of grain for a poor person." The wealthy spend extravagantly and squander their wealth, while the impoverished can hardly stay warm or be fed with their bowl of porridge or rice. I think about my hometown in Northern Jiangsu Province during my childhood; everyone had a strenuous life, where a single meal was difficult to come by. In the present day, "the well-fed should understand the hunger of the starving." I can have so much because of the contributions from all directions. Therefore, within the language of past Buddhist monasteries, there were often the expressions "goods from all directions," "sentient beings of all directions," and "community goods from all directions." These are ways to express gratitude and thanks for the contributions coming from all directions.

Therefore, we should have a mind of offering. Each person can give clothing, tea, lamps, porridge, books, newspapers, or medical care for Buddhism. Giving is like a small but steady stream. It is the fountainhead of running water, giving drips and drops of water to people from that sweet running water. It can equalize society's rich and poor to the same level; the givers are blessed, and the recipients find joy, benefiting both sides.

Festival of Light and Peace

I grew up in the barren and poor Northern Jiangsu Province. I remember that every year during the Spring Festival, a mile from my hometown, the temple to the local village god would hang up lanterns. In that time of darkness without lights, being able to hang up a lantern was already an extraordinary lantern festival. As evening drew near, the people in the village would happily say to the young and old in tow, "The lanterns are up! Let's go see the lanterns!" Thinking about it now, these were only a few simple lanterns and nothing more, but they brought joy and hope to everyone.

Therefore, during the Spring Festival, besides ensuring that the public can come to Fo Guang Shan to pay homage to the Buddha, I also arrange for the Festival of Light and Peace to be set out for everyone to view and enjoy. This allows everyone to light a lantern in a prayer for blessings.

In Buddhism, the lamp represents light, which mainly refers to how we can illuminate the lamp of our own mind. Back then, I already thought about how the public could light a

Fo Guang Shan Festival of Light and Peace.
Photo by Zheng Tiaoyi

lamp to be offered before the Buddha, serving as a symbol of illuminating the lamp of their own mind. It was unfortunate that the temple where I first resided did not have a place to display offering lamps. Even if one were to light a lamp, one would not know where to put it as an offering.

After Fo Guang Shan was built, we began to promote the lighting of Peace and Safety Lanterns. Everyone could light a lamp of their mind before the Buddha and then hang a red-colored lantern up along the corridor. The beauty of a single lamp would allow the believer to interact with the Buddha in the light of its glow.

I told the devotees at Fo Guang Shan's Light Offering Dharma Service, "Today, it is you who are illuminating the entire world; it is you who are giving warmth to the world; and it is you who are dispelling the darkness. With your lighting of a lamp here, the Buddha can see everyone's intentions to make an offering. The visitors who have come from various parts of the world will also see your lights and receive your merits. It is exactly as the Chan School states: 'A room shrouded in darkness for a thousand years is instantly illuminated by a single lamp.'" By illuminating the lamp of the mind, a person's entire life can brighten.

During the early years, we did not publicize the idea of lighting lamps to outsiders. However, over the course of a few decades, various temples, no matter large or small, from south to north, have all instituted facilities for Peace and Safety Lanterns and Buddha Lamps. Clearly, regardless of whether it is the spirits, the Buddha, or the people, everyone needs light, and everyone needs to illuminate the lamp of the mind.

For the past forty or fifty years, Fo Guang Shan has gone from Peace Lantern offerings to the Festival of Light and Peace, with ornamental flowers and rock gardens. Gradually, this has also influenced the whole of Taiwan. Currently, from north to south, each of the county governments holds a lantern festival every year in turn, and each time there are tens of thousands

In 2002, Fo Guang Shan pioneered an electrical monorail lantern display with the theme "Heavenly Horses Soaring through the Sky," which integrated the Dharma and folk arts, attracting over ten thousand people every day.

January 2 to March 13, 2002

The theme lantern for Fo Guang Shan Chinese New Year Lantern Festival, "Golden Rooster Announcing Joyous News," is eight meters tall; perched atop the highest location of the flower and art exhibit section with a bird's-eye view of everything, it wishes happy new year to all in seven languages, saying "o-mi-tuo-fo."

February 9 to March 9, 2005

or even more than a million people who turn out to view and enjoy it. In 2005, I remember that Mr. Ma Ying-jeou, who was serving as Taipei's mayor, borrowed from Fo Guang Shan the lantern featuring the theme of the year, "The Rooster Crows at Spring's Dawn." The theme lantern was the *Great Rooster* lantern, which could speak in seven different languages. He requested that the *Great Rooster* lantern take up an official place at the Taipei Lantern Festival, in order to unite everyone's celebration of the lantern festival. I heard that the *Great Rooster* lantern appearance at the event was quite well received. During the Spring Festival of 2011, our *Novice Monks of the Three Acts of Goodness* was repositioned to Kaohsiung to participate in that city's lantern festival; this too drew in quite a few members of the public to take photos with them as souvenirs.

Fo Guang Shan Abbot Hsin Bao leading the assembly to make the first incense offering for the beginning of Chinese New Year.
Photo by Liu Yunyun, February 5, 2019

The scene of the Non-Duality Gate Light Sculpture during the 2019 Fo Guang Shan New Year Festival of Light and Peace.
Photo by Zhuang Meizhao, February 5, 2019

The Three Acts of Goodness Carnival float of the Fo Guang Shan Da Ci Children's Home.
Photo by Liang Qingzhi, February 4, 2019

8,888 painted lanterns of colla
rative efforts hanging high on
sides of the Great Path to Budd
hood of the Buddha Muse
Photo by Yang Ruibao, February 5, 2

Fireworks at the Buddha Museum. Photo by Cai Rongfeng

The lantern display for the 2019 theme "Always Well-rounded and Auspicious" is based on the *Journey to the West*. Photo by Zhuang Mei Zhao

People from Xingtian village of Dashu township participating in the Light Shines on the Universe Prayer Ceremony and Lantern Parade.
Photo by Chen Shuting, February 18, 2019

2019 Chinese New Year "One-Stroke Calligraphy—A Meeting of Dharma" at the Fo Guang Shan Sutra Repository.
Photo provided by Li Chenzhen

Lamps represent light; it is only when there is light in the human world that there can be truth, goodness, and beauty. Each person must illuminate the lamp of the mind. From the illumination of the lamp within the mind, extending to the universal illumination of the Buddha's light, and further to the public recognition of the general welfare of society, is this not all the result of us lighting lamps for society's sake?

Pearls of Wisdom: Prayers for Engaged Living

The previous discussion of lighting lamps is about how lighting the lamp of one's own mind is accomplished by means of the Buddha's light. If one wants to have a mind-to-mind connection with the Buddha in the most direct manner, it is through prayers. For the brightness and wonderfulness of Buddhism to integrate with daily life, deeply enter the mind of each individual, and become a part of their lives, I composed some prayers for the multitudes, making it possible for everyone to vow and say one's prayers at any time. These vows and prayers can direct loving-kindness toward the people, each and every occupation in society, so that one feels a sense of oneness of self and all sentient beings.

As disciples of the Buddha, we all wish to tell the Buddha things that weigh upon our minds. It is just like how we exchange letters and phone calls with good friends so as to express our fellowship and concern. Therefore, how can I make a mind-to-mind connection with the founder of my faith, the Buddha? I worship, reflect, praise, and revere. However, during the many occasions of prayer, there still remains much to be said, and we would like to let the Buddha hear the voice of our minds.

In the past when Buddhists spoke to the Buddha, they mostly made requests to the Buddha: "May the Buddha bestow peace and security upon me and bring me happiness; may the Buddha ensure that I am healthy and that my business flourishes." However, these requests very rarely expressed any concern for society or any other people. Of the many hymns of praise in Buddhism, there are "In particular, we pray for world peace, and that the earth long endures" or "In particular, we pray that the people are healthy and happy, enjoying a long and blessed life." Nevertheless, these are merely what the assembly recited and do not reflect individual practice. In retrospect, my own prayers to the Buddha were slowly refined in faith over and over again.

I remember when I was around the age of twenty, I prayed devoutly like most people, asking for the Buddha's blessing and the bestowal of compassion, wisdom, courage, and strength. In my mind, I felt that this was a matter of course. By the age of thirty, I suddenly felt that I was being too selfish, asking for this or that from the Buddha every day, and all of this was for gaining wisdom, peace, and security for myself. I ought to pray for my teachers, parents, and friends, wishing that all of them could enjoy happiness, peace, and security. I wanted to make progress and no longer seek anything for myself but pray for those related to me as family and friends.

The Venerable Master composed and recited the one hundred prayers of *Pearls of Wisdom: Prayers for Engaged Living*.
Photo provided by Huang Meihua Shigu

Slowly, when I was around forty years old, I saw things from a completely different angle, and felt that what I had been doing was still not right. To only pray for my own parents, brothers, and sisters, as well as my devotees was surely too narrow and limited; I should expand further. Therefore, I changed and started wishing that the Buddha would bring peace to the world, bring strength and prosperity to the nation, bring peace and happiness to society, and bring the causes and conditions for liberation to sentient beings. Each time after I completed offering my prayers, I felt joy in my heart, and I felt that I had ascended to newer heights in terms of my own practice.

At the age of fifty, I again felt that my prayers were incomplete. How could it be that I am always appealing to the Buddha to help others gain happiness, peace, and security. What am I doing then? Why can't I learn from the Buddha and serve all sentient beings in the world, relieve their affliction and sorrow, and bring peace and happiness to them?

Hence, when I turned sixty, I felt that I ought to follow the example of the Buddhas and bodhisattvas by taking on the sufferings of others and being able to do that which is difficult.

Therefore, I declared to the Buddha, "Oh, great compassionate Buddha! Let me bear the tribulations of the sentient beings in the world and help them enjoy peace and happiness. Let me put the Buddha's great loving-kindness and compassion into practice and learn from the Buddha's beneficial teachings of joy."

This time I felt that my prayers had improved, so out of aspiration, I wrote one hundred prayers to be titled *Pearls of Wisdom: Prayers for Engaged Living*. I believe that making a vow is not a slogan, but rather it is a kind of cultivation and practical application. I hoped that when reciting the prayers, everyone would be able to refine their faith and enhance their compassion and morality. In this way, one will be able to interact with the Buddhas and bodhisattvas and appreciate the needs of society as a whole.

Over the course of composing the *Pearls of Wisdom: Prayers for Engaged Living*, I thought about the parents of everyone in the world. Hence, I prayed for the parents:

Oh, great compassionate Buddha!
Since we emerged from the womb,
Our parents have raised and educated us,
Our relatives have supported us;
We have received so much from them,
But seldom repay their kindness. . . .
If we have honor, we wish to share it with them;
If we have wealth, we wish them also to be free from need.

I thought about the painstaking work sanitation workers do in society, so I wanted to pray for them:

Oh, great and compassionate Buddha!
We are deeply thankful for our sanitation engineers.
They arise earlier than the sun itself;
They are more accurate than the clock itself;
They ready themselves for battle with dirt and refuse;
Their work brings cleanliness to our lives. . . .
We pray for your support and blessings.
As sanitation engineers clean the streets,
May they sweep away the dust of their afflictions,

Cultivate bodhi in their minds,
And wash away their karmic hindrances accumulated throughout time.

Even for the pregnant women who are about to give birth, what emotions are they experiencing? Hence, I spoke to the Buddha on their behalf as well:

Oh, great and compassionate Buddha!
A mother-to-be naturally will have emotions;
Swayed by considerations of gain and loss
And worries about the gender of their children.
We pray that you give them courage without fear.
We pray that you give them confidence without dread.

In this manner, although they are like the intercessions and prayers made to God by Christians and Catholics, our prayers are not merely about expressing thanks. We must also model ourselves on the Buddha's loving-kindness and compassion and show our care for all sentient beings of the world.

Early on in Buddhism, temples and monasteries already had a wenshu report, which records the merits of the devotees attending a Dharma service. The presiding monastic would read out loudly to the Buddha on behalf of the devotees. For example, "So-and-so has made an offering of so much incense and flowers and has chanted so many sutras and mantras, which is truly reported; I hereby beseech the bestowing of forgiveness, in the hope that the Buddha would know about it."

However, this kind of dedication is still a bit too focused on material gain to a greater or lesser degree. Since Buddhism emphasizes no notion and no self, if prayers can be made for great loving-kindness, great wisdom, great compassion, and great vows on behalf of the multitudes, society, the nation, and the world, then the masses would feel so compelled and inspired by this that everyone would pray for others instead of only doing this for themselves. This way, the prospects for world peace would be certain.

Art Galleries

Speaking of art galleries, over the course of my life as a wandering monastic, I have traveled around the whole world. In terms of architecture, I have visited the Parthenon in Athens, Greece; Italy's Colosseum and the Leaning Tower of Pisa; India's Taj Mahal; Cambodia's Angkor Wat; the Shwedagon Pagoda in Rangoon, Burma; and the pyramids of Cairo, Egypt. Among the scenic wonders of nature, I have seen the magnificence of Niagara Falls in Canada, enjoyed the natural beauty of Brazil's Amazon River, and personally experienced nature's sublime handiwork at the Grand Canyon in the United States.

In particular, there is the Buddhist art of various regions around the world, such as the Ajanta Caves in India, the cave paintings of Dunhuang, the Buddha images of the Yungang and Longmen grottoes, and the rock carvings on Mount Baoding in Dazu. The majestic mountains and rivers, along with the impressive buildings, enhance the graceful bearing of the Buddhas and bodhisattvas; the beautiful images of loving-kindness and compassion left a deep impression in my heart.

The beauty of the world needs to be exalted; the great multitudes also need aesthetic knowledge in their everyday lives.

Therefore, with the opportunity to build a temple, I hope to lead the way to the fine arts of Buddhism. There is no need to use language to introduce them for people can use their eyes to appreciate them; the pleasing sounds to the ear can also let visitors experience the compassionate embrace of the Dharma. Therefore, when Fo Guang Shan was first founded, I built the Pure Land Cave and the Buddhist Cultural Museum, hoping that goodness, beauty, and joy would fill the human world. Over the past decades, we have painstakingly collected many cultural artifacts; it is difficult to account fully the thought and care that was put into this.

I remember it was around 1971 when I accompanied a group to Japan to conduct a religious exchange. I only had one thousand yen with me, which was the cost for a single lunch. By chance I saw a cultural artifact, a carved wooden *ruyi* symbol of good luck from mainland China that had somehow made its way to Japan. I endured my hunger and bought the ruyi, which I brought back to Taiwan. Later on, there were several

A photo collage of Fo Guang Yuan Art Gallery branches around the world. *Top, left to right*: Museum of Buddhist Treasures, Main Art Gallery, Buddha Museum Exhibition Hall, Kaohsiung Art Gallery, Tainan Art Gallery, Pingtung Art Gallery, Changhua Art Gallery, Taichung Art Gallery, and Taipei Art Gallery. *Bottom, left to right*: Ilan Art Gallery, Hsi Lai Art Gallery, Melbourne Art Gallery, IBA New Zealand Art Gallery, IBT New Zealand Art Gallery, Jiaying Huiguan Art Gallery, Paris Art Gallery, and Dong Zen Art Gallery.

times when I traveled and saw images of the Buddha carved in stone that had turned up abroad. I really could not bear it, so I again decided to save up money and bring these Buddha images back. In the early years, I once carried a Buddha image on the plane with me by placing it on my lap due to the plane's checked baggage limitation. I arrived back at the Taiwan airport after enduring several hours of flight, and my legs were both numb. I even suffered the ridicule of my fellow Buddhists, who said I was an itinerant trader running a business. However, I did not try to defend myself because I knew that I was collecting important Buddhist cultural art.

I once invited the painter Mr. Li Zijian, who was living in the United States, to go on a one-year retreat so that he could concentrate on painting a series of works called *Humanity and Love*. Upon request, I also invited the art specialist Mr. Gao Ertai to paint one hundred pictures for *Chan Art, Chan Heart*.

When the famous Dunhuang painter Mr. He Shan held an exhibition of his Dunhuang paintings, I also collected a hundred of his famous paintings. A first-class artist of mainland China, Shi Guoliang, had some interactions with me over paintings, and because of this, he eventually joined the Fo Guang Shan Buddhist Monastic Order and became one of my disciples, with the Dharma name of Hui Chan. Another example is He Daitian's *Old House* series, with each painting being worth five thousand US dollars; I also bought one hundred of them for fifty thousand US dollars. As for the cartoons of Hong Kong's Ah Chong and the paintings of Taiwan's many artists that were donated to Fo Guang Shan for charity auctions, I could not bear parting with them because once these art works are sold, they will not come back again. All I could do was skimp and save so as to preserve them for the future.

What has left me fairly regretful is Chang Dai-chien's large painting, *Lotus Flowers*, which he presented to me as a gift. At the time, I was raising funds to establish the campus for Fo Guang University, and I had no alternative but to sell it to Mr. Hsu You-yang of the Far Eastern Group during a charity auction. Even though the painting bears the inscription that it was presented to me as a gift by Chang Dai-chien, now it is a part of someone else's collection, and all I can do is vainly sigh to no avail.

From the beginning, I have always hoped that Buddhism could be integrated with culture, education, and art. Therefore, I have also run twenty-three art galleries around the world. These cannot compare to Dunhuang, Longmen, and the Yungang grottoes, but seeing today's world, Buddhism must build a beautiful world that welcomes everyone to come to Fo Guang Shan. We do not only focus on the buildings, for we must also

The great master of Chinese painting Chang Dai-chien visited Fo Guang Shan and gave the Venerable Master the lotus painting *One Flower, One World.*
March 14, 1978

have many that house the collections of Buddha, for example, sculptures and paintings and other types of humanity's most precious treasures. As long as later generations can carefully safeguard these cultural relics of history, their value in terms of beauty and the appreciation of that beauty is something to which no amount of money can compare.

In order to provide a spiritual space for people, we were the first to innovate with the establishment of exhibition halls in temples. For example, there are the art galleries attached to the Taipei Vihara, Lanyang Temple, Nanping Temple, Nantai Temple, and so forth. I dare not say that these collections are the result of my painstaking labors, but they are rather an expression of my sincere fidelity in making offerings to the Buddhas throughout all directions, and in forming affinities with the people. As for the other temples abroad, such as Hsi Lai Temple in Los Angeles, Nan Tien Temple in Sydney, Chung Tian Temple in Brisbane, Malaysia's Dong Zen Temple, and others, it is our hope that through art we can beautify the human heart, society, and the world, ensuring that beauty can permeate the whole world.

Fo Guang Shan's topography is not merely a mountain, for it also includes many multifunctional halls, classrooms, and conference rooms. It also has "three galleries and one cave," which include the exhibition gallery, cultural gallery, Historical Museum, and the Pure Land Cave. The Fo Guang Shan Buddha Museum has eight exhibition areas, forty-eight Underground Palaces, and fifty-six Open Palaces. I did not receive much education in my life, and I do not have much creativity; I have only thought about offering my heartfelt devotion to Buddhism and expanding it to all directions. This can allow the splendor of Buddhist art to transcend space, time, and the gaps between self and other as a way of elaborating the Dharma's "oneness of self and other." That indeed would mean a limitless expansion of our kind regard.

A Food Fair

I have spoken about spiritual sustenance, now I want to turn to something that most directly relates to the people's welfare, and that is eating.

When I first arrived in Taiwan and wandered around various areas, I saw that when temples managed Dharma services, they would all set up tables for having meals. If a temple set out sixty or one hundred tables, then one would know the number of attendees at the Dharma service. However, I did not have such a large space for many tables, nor could I cover such costs for setting up tables. All I could do was promote "a little giving and a slight offering." In this, I ensured that the holding of

Dharma services and the pure wealth of devotees could last as long as possible, becoming a small but steady stream.

Fo Guang Shan hosting a vegetarian food fair, featuring a 100-meter-long vegetarian sushi for visitors to enjoy, which promotes vegetarianism and encourages a kind heart to protect lives.

December 1987

With meticulous planning and careful budgeting, I established a food fair to resolve the issue of eating. Hence, over the past forty to fifty years since the founding of Fo Guang Shan, most meals are taken using the dining hall, and up to a thousand people can have a meal there. However, if there are more than ten thousand people, the meals can be provided in the format of a food fair. This is just like how the Japanese started eating boxed meals, which was extremely important for the development of their culture. There is no need to expend too much time on eating, just a single boxed meal, simple and fast, and the problem of having a meal can be quickly resolved.

Fo Guang Shan was established in 1967, and by 1968, the buildings for the Buddhist College were completed. Originally, the plan was for five hundred people to come. However, better than I expected, within a short time, fifty thousand people attended. In a single moment, providing meals became a problem that needed an urgent resolution. All we could do was disperse people as much as possible to many areas so that they could have their meals there.

The Buddha Museum Inauguration Ceremony.
Debember 25, 2011

The same situation happened in 1992 when the groundbreaking ceremony was held for Nan Tien Temple in Australia. Preparations had originally been made for only three hundred people to attend, but by the time the ceremony began, the number of devotees had already reached more than five thousand.

Later on, I realized that the best solution for this problem was to host a food fair. If each booth prepared to serve two hundred people, then a fair could provide meals for twenty thousand people. Even if fifty thousand people attended, I could still make do and be able to handle them. Sure enough, the experiment at Fo Guang Shan was a success, and everyone happily enjoyed their meals. What I meant by having a food fair is to have everyone gather together in a park. On one hand, people can stroll around to enjoy the scenery; on the other hand, they can freely enjoy food and beverages. This way, people can also circulate about and interact with one another.

This is also like the "Universal Offering" promoted by Buddhism in the past. These assemblies would usually gather

people together in the several thousands to the several tens of thousands, while the people working in the kitchens would be overwhelmed by the dizzying pace of their work. However, if I set up a single booth, I could provide one thousand portions of bread, and by setting up a single small station, I could provide cold noodles that do not require any cooking. Therefore, when there wasn't enough room for people to have their meals during the various activities held at Fo Guang Shan, the format of a food fair became extremely useful.

It is comparable to the ceremony marking the inauguration of instruction for the Nanhua University campus in 1996, which made use of the format of a food fair to resolve the problem of supplying meals to those attending the event. I recall that Madame Lien Fang-yu, the wife of the vice-president at the time, also attended. She went around the food fair and visited every booth, enjoying the event along with everyone else. At the celebration of the tenth anniversary of Fo Guang University's founding (2011), a food fair was held, and even President Ma Ying-jeou came out to attend the food fair and participate in a fried rice noodle contest with the students; it was a thoroughly happy time.

Yet another example was the national holiday celebrating the Buddha's Birthday in 2009. The BLIA held a bathing of the Buddha ceremony along Ketagalan Boulevard in front of the Presidential Office Building for the first time. With a gathering of more than ten thousand people, how should people have their meals? I designed a four-color Buddha's Birthday Meal, which combined spinach, turmeric, red yeast dye, and white rice to make the four colors and then paired them with different fillings. This was easy and convenient, as well as nutritious and environmentally friendly. I placed an order with the caterers, making it easy for both sides to effortlessly resolve the issue of eating. In addition, I further arranged the Buddha's Birthday cakes and Buddha's Birthday buns to complement the meals, celebrating the Buddha's Birthday together with people numbering in the tens of thousands. This annual event has continued for eight years, becoming a page of Fo Guang Shan's history that is worth commemorating.

When gathered at these assemblies, Buddhists would all chant, "Homage to the Bodhisattvas gathering like clouds coming from all directions." With people coming and going in and out of the food fair, it is really like "a gathering of clouds from all directions." Buddhism also advocates "the joy of meditation as sustenance," so isn't the people assembled in joy during a food fair in perfect agreement with the Buddha's intent here?

When the Fo Guang Shan Buddha Museum was completed, everyone asked me, "Where are the dining rooms?" I have dining rooms, but the dining room is not solely for providing food. The dining rooms here are very spacious, so people can gather and form bonds of fellowship, and even lectures and so forth can be conducted. My idea here is that the partaking of meals can take place in the corridors, under the trees, beside the hills, and also on the lawns. As long as one takes a simple portion of food or a boxed meal, they can sit down wherever they prefer and enjoy it with their family, friends, or classmates. Hence, I asked the person who was responsible for preparing event invitations for the Fo Guang Shan Buddha Museum's completion to clearly state, "Given the large numbers of people attending, we are unable to provide banquet arrangements, and we will only be offering simple meals. We hope everyone understands."

The Chinese are a nation of people who take eating seriously, but sometimes they are too wasteful when it comes to eating. People sitting at a table full of dishes will stop eating when only one third has been consumed; the remaining two thirds are entirely wasted. If various social gatherings in society could employ boxed meals and food fairs to encourage simple meal-taking, then the lifestyle, financial ability, physical ability, and intellectual ability of the nation could be elevated. "Eating" encompasses much wisdom; therefore, if views and opinions are exchanged with each other, physical power, financial power, and vow-making power will surely be enhanced. In this regard, why cast this aside and not do it?

Concluding Remarks

In seeking survival and development, humanity has always undergone change when all means are exhausted, finding that change once enacted leads to a solution. Buddhism stresses established practices and ceremonial rites, but this also illustrates how the Dharma is not a fixed Dharma, for one Dharma is all Dharma, and all Dharma is one Dharma. The Dharma, the true Dharma, cannot be changed, but that is not necessarily so for the worldly way of doing things.

In advocating Humanistic Buddhism, I have become a proponent of democracy for Buddhism. I have conducted Fo Guang Family Gatherings in order to care for the parents of the disciples; on behalf of middle-aged and young women, I have provided opportunities for short-term monastics retreats; I established the Srimala Women's College and even Urban Buddhist Colleges, the Men's Volunteer Clubs, Women's Dharma Clubs, Weekend Chanting Services, Dharma Services for Repaying Kindness, Buddhist Family Visits, and so forth. In order to promote equality among the fourfold assembly, I included three female arhats among the eighteen arhats installed at the Fo Guang Shan Buddha Museum; doing so ensures that everyone sees the noble appearance of feminine wisdom and compassion in this world since ancient times. All of this is done for the sake of ensuring peace in the human world and the continuance of fairness and justice, which serves as some small token of my contribution and nothing more.

Another example is the Three Acts of Goodness Sports Association established in 2009, which has already organized basketball, baseball, and soccer teams. Every year, the Buddha's Light Cup invites sports teams from various countries around the world to come and join the competition. Besides raising Taiwan's visibility, the hope is that the outstanding athletes fostered by the program will also be able to put the Three Acts of Goodness into practice: "Do good deeds, speak good words, think good thoughts." Besides displaying the athletic spirit of positive completion on the playing field, these also highlight Buddhism's international spirit of peace and friendship, spreading the Three Acts of Goodness Campaign throughout the world.

The Venerable Master attending the 6th Fo Guang Cup International College Basketball Invitational Tournament held by the Three Acts of Goodness Sports Association. He encourages the players to make friends through the sport and foster international friendships. *Front row, from the left*: venerables Yung Kuang, Tzu Jung, and Tzu Hui; the Venerable Master; venerables Hui Ping, Hsin Bao, and Yi Lai; and the Fo Guang Shan benefactors from the five continents.

Photo by Pi Yun Lai, August 16, 2016

Another example is the holding of the When Buddha Meets the Gods Event. Due to the completion of the Buddha Museum, there is even more space available. Therefore, I had the idea that every year on December 25th, everyone could come to the Buddha Museum to celebrate the birth of Jesus and bring their statues of deities from various other religions and sects. Since these deities have also always blessed and protected sentient beings in a quiet way, we specifically selected this day to foster fellowship. Every year on this day, more than three to four thousand deities are invited from here and abroad, including the participation of representatives from the eight major religions such as Protestantism, Catholicism, Islam, Judaism, Taoism, Confucianism, and so forth. Not only are all four sides

The Venerable Master joining his palms in respect to the deities at Guanyin Shine, wishing that all religious organizations unite.
Photo by Venerable Hui Hao, December 25, 2013

2,000 deity statues together in the Buddha Museum to foster fellowship. The Venerable Master is tying a gold medal around one of the deity statues.
Photo by Liang Qingzhi, December 25, 2013

When Buddha Meets the Gods set the world record twice for the greatest number of shrines, temples, and churches around the world to participate in a global multi-religious reunion and was awarded two World Record Certificates by the World Record Association. Pictured *above*: the 2016 world record certificate award photo. Pictured *to the right*: Wang Jin-pyng, president of the Association of Chinese Traditional Religions (*on the left*), receiving the certificate, witnessed by Fo Guang Shan Abbot Hsin Bao (*on the right*).
Photo above by Pi Yun Lai, December 25, 2016;
photo on the right by Qiu Qianhai, December 25, 2018

BLIA enthusiastically supporting the When Buddha Meets the Gods Event.
Photo by Venerable Hui Yan, December 25, 2013

In 2011, the Venerable Master launched the When Buddha Meets the Gods Event in the spirit of "embracing similarities and celebrating differences" to promote interfaith and interracial dialogue. The event has become an internationally distinguished religious gathering that embraces Buddhism, Catholicism, Islam, Judaism, Daoism, Confucianism, Christianity, and folk religions. Photo: more than 100 religious parade troupes, over 500 temples and churches, thousands of deity statues, and more than 50,000 devotees assembling at the Buddha Museum. Photo by Pi Yun Lai, December 25, 2015

Group photo of religious representatives from across the strait attending the When Buddha Meets the Gods Event. Photo by Zhuang Mei Zhao, December 25, 2013

A group photo of the Venerable Master with the great assembly attending the When Buddha Meets the Gods Event. Photo by Zhuang Mei Zhao, December 25, 2018

When Buddha Meets the Gods Event at Fo Guang Shan Buddha Museum. December 25, 2018

Chinese New Year's Messages written by the Venerable Master for the years 2008–2019.

of the Main Hall of the Buddha Museum fully occupied, but arrangements have been extended to the Main Shrine where the altar before the Buddha is completely occupied by the deities as distinguished guests. Moreover, the people who have invited these deities to come forward also number in the tens of thousands. This is a very special celebration.

There is also the Bodhi Family Blessing Ceremony held every year on New Year's Day, which includes newly married couples or those who hope to bring new energy into their marriage. They can come and participate in the ceremony for increasing blessings, so as to improve their relationship. On average, there are several hundred couples in attendance at each of the ceremonies. I think, after a couple marries, they ought not to see things through their own eyes, but rather they ought to see with the heart and with love. Although the world is constantly changing, since they have fallen in love and married, their initial love cannot be changed! If they integrate the Dharma into life and become a bodhi couple, then they can further enhance the quality of their marriage.

Furthermore, at the Buddha Museum, there is the entire "Benefactors Wall: A Thousand Temples, A Million People." There are also the walls of multicolored ceramic tiles

manufactured by Meinung Yao[3] and installed at the Cloud Dwelling Building and the Tathagata Shrine. These are all the Benefactors Wall, listing details of the sponsors. They once greatly amazed an artist from Paris, for the most beautiful, the most natural and people-oriented art is all on the surface of these walls. At the same time, this also illustrates how Fo Guang Shan has gathered together people from various countries around the world, as well as kind efforts of support by the various temples and monasteries of Taiwan. It is by such efforts that we have the internationally oriented Fo Guang Shan of today.

There is also the Spring Festival couplet that is eagerly awaited by everyone each year. These are good wishes for the New Year that I write out in Chinese calligraphy. The main hope here is to bring a renewal to the inherent morality of Chinese culture, ensuring everyone awaiting the time of the Spring Festival will be encouraged by the words and phrases written on the red paper. For more than twenty years, these have been widely printed and distributed by my disciples. Currently more than several million copies have already been issued throughout the world. Nowadays, not only has the writing of Spring Festival couplets come into vogue among the various Buddhist temples and monasteries, but various government departments and organizations also print and

3 Meinung Yao Studio created by Chu Pan-hsiung who's work has become synonymous with the public ceramic relief mural projects he creates.

The Venerable Master has loved reading throughout his life. He reads, writes, and publishes books, thinking that reading can open our minds and broaden our visions. Pictured is the Venerable Master attending the National Reading Expo held by Venerable Chueh Pei (*front row, on the far right*), the executive director of the Humanistic Buddhist Reading Association. Fo Guang Shan elder venerables Tzu Hui (*to the right of Venerable Master*), Tzu Jung (*second right*), Yi Kong (*third right*), and Professor Chai Songlin, editor in chief of *The Merit Times* (*to the left of Venerable Master*), all attended the event.
April 16, 2011

distribute their own Spring Festival couplets, presenting them as gifts to the public. In this way, isn't the Chinese culture slowly being propagated to the five continents as well?

As for other aspects of Dharma propagation, teachings, education, and culture, there are examples such as the grand Dharma teaching assemblies at national auditoriums or the compilation of various book series, such as the *Fo Guang Tripitaka* and the *Fo Guang Encyclopedia.* These in turn have promoted the establishment of several thousand Humanistic Buddhism Reading Clubs. Thinking back to all these separate but far from

isolated cases, the impetus for every single one of them has its own causes and conditions, but what matters is that these came about because of a core idea: "May all sentient beings be free from suffering and not seek happiness only for themselves." The creativity we have comes precisely from this concern.

Over Buddhism's twenty-six hundred years, the Dharma has spread from India to China, and from the Buddha to the patriarchs and great worthies, while its original treasure remains immeasurable and unlimited. What I have been able to do is to carry these many aspects of wisdom and skillful means forward so that it "progresses with the times." Sentient beings have eighty-four thousand afflictions. However, the practices that are "the correct medicine for the illness" are not just limited to eighty-four thousand kinds.

My Realization Concerning Humanistic Buddhism

Within the faith of Humanistic Buddhism, there is no opposition between time and space, nor is there any worry about life and death. What we seek to attain in passive terms is the absence of fear, confusion, and degradation, as well as the inability to become broken; in active terms, life can become happier, more peaceful, more tranquil, freer, and more liberated.

人間佛教

As for Humanistic Buddhism's development up to now, there are some who do not understand Humanistic Buddhism and who therefore have some doubts about it. Here, I will list some concerns that have been raised regarding Humanistic Buddhism:

1) Humanistic Buddhism is vulgar, worldly, and of humans; it does not reach the highest state of Buddhahood.

2) Humanistic Buddhism attaches importance to worldly activities; these activities have nothing to do with learning Buddhism.

3) Humanistic Buddhism has no spiritual cultivation; at most, it is all about how individuals conduct themselves in society. This bears no relationship to such possibilities for transcendence, elevation, and becoming a Buddha through learning Buddhism.

4) Humanistic Buddhism is oriented toward the laity, being without the sacredness of the life of the monastic community or enlightenment through ascetic practice.

5) What is the heritage of Humanistic Buddhism and what does it impart? There is no sense of anyone having attained accomplishment in cultivation, and because no one knows, it is not easily propagated.

6) The propagation of Humanistic Buddhism is inadequate, and no one has formulated its system. There

are only proclamations that are in fragments, one-sided, and lacking in organization. This makes it impossible for anyone to gain complete understanding.

7) Humanistic Buddhism has not become widespread, and it has not entered the core teachings of Buddhism; it lacks the support of many helping hands. If the teachings of only a certain school are taught or proposals of a certain school are made, then these will not be easily accepted by the larger community.

8) Humanistic Buddhism has no path of liberation and no state of realization. Traditional Buddhism cannot easily accept it.

The above are criticisms of Humanistic Buddhism. Moreover, there are many other perceived problems including tradition versus modernism, the laity versus the monastic order, monasticism versus society, the original versus the recent, spiritual cultivation versus activism, and so on. None of these generally lend themselves to being understood by the people. As a consequence, there is a need to further strengthen the popularization of Humanistic Buddhism.

There was a time when Buddhism retreated to secluded practice and lost the Buddhist spirit of engaging in the world. Buddhism retreated to the forest and mountain and lost its service toward the devotees. Buddhism retreated to mystic talks and lost the practical application of Buddhism's undertakings. Buddhism retreated into giving passive teachings and lost its true meaning of active improvement. Now I hope to recover the genuine meaning of Buddhism's original intent.

The twenty points listed below pertain to what Humanistic Buddhism means.

1) Our Humanistic Buddhism must elevate us and affirm us, in that we possess the wisdom and excellent qualities of the Buddha by acknowledging that "I am a Buddha." This kind of self-elevation is precisely the spirit of Humanistic Buddhism. This is not giving ourselves over to the control of religious authority, rather, we assume responsibility for everything concerning ourselves. This is just as stated in *The Connected Discourses*: "Rely on yourself, rely on the Dharma, and rely on nothing else." This is our faith in Humanistic Buddhism.

2) The spirit of Humanistic Buddhism encourages us to integrate others into ourselves. There is no opposition among us. We and others are not two, therefore all sentient beings are one; everything in this world is related to us. We believe that the Middle Way and dependent origination, which the Buddha is enlightened to, is the truth of Humanistic Buddhism; and that truth, which we have inherited and now impart, is the faith of Humanistic Buddhism.

3) Faith is something complex and multifaceted. However, in terms of its meaning, Humanistic Buddhism is able to unify these many complexities because the source of our Buddha nature can accomplish everything. Despite the differing levels of faith and multiplicity of its categorization, Humanistic Buddhism

can fulfill all religious teachings. This is the magnanimity of Humanistic Buddhism, which can also serve as the faith of all humanity.

4) The faith of Humanistic Buddhism holds that life is eternal, as it cannot die. Those who believe this can attain liberation, but those who don't believe this will not perish either. It is comparable to a clock that tells time, which is circular in shape and not a straight line. In a straight line, one proceeds from birth to death, and then there is nothing. But a clock is circular in shape, so after twelve o'clock, it starts from one o'clock again as usual, circling about forever. It is also comparable to the four seasons of spring, summer, autumn, and winter; or how material things have their formation, abiding, destruction, and void; how mental thoughts have their arising, abiding, change, and extinction; and how the physical body has its aging, sickness, death, and rebirth. It is because of death that there can be birth, so there can then be a future and hope.

Hence, I feel that Buddhism's view of the cycle of birth and death is one of a limitless future. From now on, Humanistic Buddhism does not emphasize the "six realms of existence." In appearance, there should not be a rigid boundary separating the sacred from the secular. Since everybody is inherently a Buddha, why is it necessary to divide them into so many categories? We call it "cycling through the ten Dharma realms." This then is what Humanistic Buddhism advocates.

5) There is no mistaking that everybody has the Buddha nature. This is like how a seed may grow when the right conditions are met; by developing the Buddha nature, one can become a Buddha. However, if there is no energy to develop the Buddha nature, it becomes a "deformed seed," and nothing can be done about that. It is equivalent to what the sutras say about an *icchantika*[1] being unable to attain Buddhahood.

Evolution in the natural world means the survival of the fittest, so as for the so-called "burned and ruined seeds," we also cannot deny that there will be a small number who will naturally be eliminated. A deformed seed does not have the genes for life and does not have the power of karma for life. It is already dying away, and there is nothing that can be done. Under normal circumstances, life is eternal, but that is not to say there are no exceptions. Life in terms of time is limitless and undying; for life in the theory of evolution, the survival of the fittest is something quite normal.

6) Every person has the Buddha nature, but there are distinct differences in terms of faith. Take for example, the refinement of faith, the transcendence of faith, the elevation of faith, and the expansion of faith. Of course, faith is something sacred, but faith does have its higher and lower levels. As to how the faith of each individual transcends depends on the

1 In Sanskrit, "destroying roots of goodness" or "burnt seeds of goodness"; one who has completely cut off the roots of goodness and is unable to become a Buddha.

degree of energy in one's faith. It is just as in the case of a microphone: its fidelity and functionality are what determine the differences in value. If the energy of your faith is insufficient, then transcendence is not possible. This too is a natural phenomenon.

7) We believe that humanity can become higher, better, and greater; it can transcend ordinary reality. The name for this can be "arhat," "bodhisattva," or "Buddha"; nothing is fixed, for these are all simply names only. However, human nature is far-reaching, life is limitless, and faith has its gradations. Humanistic Buddhism holds that faith can determine all possible directions for the future of human life, and that it can lead one to the eternal state of no birth and no death.

8) Human society is complex. Everyone is an individual, but we are born from conditions. Nothing is able to exist apart from these many conditions. Within this universe, everyone depends on others for existence. However, the state of the ordinary individual and the state of the noble ones are different; ordinary people still have the distinction between self and other.

The human world cannot be one of world peace. World peace is only an ideal, just like the Buddha and mara; the Buddha's world and mara's world are eternally separate. Therefore, liberation can only be sought for oneself and cannot be imposed upon others. The external world cannot be peaceful, but the world within oneself can be peaceful. This is equivalent to Ksitigarbha Bodhisattva's vow, "As long as the hells are not empty, I shall not become a Buddha." The hells cannot be emptied, but the power of Ksitigarbha Bodhisattva's vow is vast. The hells in his mind can be emptied, and he will certainly attain Buddhahood.

9) As we see it, life is based upon the individual, but these many individuals are both unified and interrelated. Therefore, in the Humanistic Buddhist faith, there is no opposition between time and space, nor is there any worry of life and death. What we seek to attain in passive terms is the absence of fear, confusion, and degradation, as well as the inability to become broken; in active terms, life can become happier, more peaceful, more tranquil, freer, and more liberated. Ultimately, the life and spirit in Humanistic Buddhism is entirely one of joy; they are within limitless time and space; they are also within the limitless relationships and achievements. However, all of this can only be obtained within the faith of Humanistic Buddhism.

10) Humanistic Buddhism does not necessarily require the attainment of Buddhahood. The Buddha had already said that everyone has the Buddha nature. Hence, what we now need is enlightenment. Once we enlighten ourselves, we can harmonize ourselves with all worlds and be able to get along with ourselves and all worlds. As in the "harmony within the Dharma realm," Humanistic Buddhism holds that

everything in the world can "be mine," and everything can be "not mine." The Dharma realm and I can be harmoniously integrated, which also means that I and sentient beings throughout the ten Dharma realms are all equal as part of the same body.

11) The faith of Humanistic Buddhism is simple, unique, the state of no birth and no death, and existence that is non-arising and non-ceasing. This is a faith seeking perfection, eternity, enlightenment, and liberation from affliction in life and in thought. Self-purification ensures that among all sentient beings, one will be like the famous maxim of the Olympic movement, "Jump higher, throw farther, run faster, and do better."

12) The goal of practicing Humanistic Buddhism is to reach the state of "the mind having neither worry nor obstruction, having no fear, and being away from confusion and delusion." We believe that through morality, charitable work, and compassion, we can enable ourselves to reach an even higher state. This is a state without affliction, without the fear of birth and death, and without sorrow or torment; everything will develop naturally in accordance with faith. This higher state belongs to us forever; there is no need for any deity to bestow it, for fulfillment of everything depends upon ourselves.

Whether it is this life or future lives, not remembering past lives, or even the confusion concerning birth and death or the lack of faith for liberation of self and others; none of these will occur, for after one is enlightened, one understands everything. We also believe that we can then recognize our original face (one's inherent Buddha nature) after enlightenment. This is the sacredness of Humanistic Buddhism. As for what has been spoken of in the past, such as the "three great incalculable kalpas," the "Eastern Buddha Land," and the "Western Buddha Land," if one can attain the wisdom of dependent origination, one will realize that these are all expressions of skillful means. When it comes to one's world, as well as liberation and freedom, the Buddha's power can provide a blessing, but everything is to be resolved on one's own.

13) Humanistic Buddhism means "One and others can all be integrated together." There is no difference between the mind, Buddha, and sentient beings. This is because one and time are both limitless; one and space are both infinite; and one and immeasurable sentient beings are coexistence.

14) Life is liberated right here in the cycle of birth and death; therefore, there is no cycle of birth and death. While there is the cycle of birth and death, that does not mean suffering is within the cycle of birth and death and happiness is outside of the cycle of birth and death. This is because the cycle of birth and death is also in the space of the world, and it can be elevated and can be kept far away. Nevertheless,

where exactly is such a world? It is still within the cycle of birth and death. Where is the cycle of birth and death? It is in space. What is known as the "harmony within the Dharma realm" exists everywhere and is present everywhere, as in the saying "One is all, and all is one." An expression that may serve for now is "The wise do not abide in the cycle of birth and death; the compassionate do not abide in nirvana." This describes the world of Humanistic Buddhism.

15) After a life attains enlightenment, it has the *prajna*[2] wisdom to handle itself. After one is enlightened, when facing oneself, it is like traveling in this world; one has limitless energy. After one is enlightened, one understands what is good and what is bad, what is right and what is wrong, and what is wholesome and what is unwholesome. One feels that none of these are anything special and bears in mind none of the five desires[3] and the six sense objects.[4] Is this not the liberation of Humanistic Buddhism?

16) The value of faith lies in the expansion of oneself, the refinement of oneself, the liberation of oneself, and the perfection of oneself. In my mind, this is the ultimate goal of Humanistic Buddhism, which must be accomplished by oneself. We must act as our own eminent benefactor; this is indeed like the Buddha.

2 In Sanskrit, and transliterated in Chinese as bore (般若), it means "wisdom."
3 Form, sound, smell, taste, and touch.
4 Sight, sound, smell, taste, touch, and dharmas (i.e., mental sensory data).

17) It is not just Humanistic Buddhism, since no religious truth can resolve the problems of others. Half of the world is a Buddha world, and half of the world is mara's world. This is like the saying "All life is only able to survive by relying upon slaughter." Consequently, since ancient times, the world has seen the calamities of war and the law of the jungle. Cycles like this do have to exist. It is just like how the tigers and lions would be unable to survive without small animals to prey upon for food. However, this is also not something that can be resolved by our individual strength. Only the power of each individual's karma can resolve things for each one of us. Even in the case of the Buddha, he is able to liberate himself and guide someone along the path of liberation, but he cannot liberate them on their behalf. Therefore, so-called "God's judgment" requires further deliberation. Where is he making this judgement? In Buddhism, all sentient beings judge themselves. It does not happen via an external power but is entirely incurred through the power of karma; one can only depend upon oneself for liberation.

18) Within the assembly, one can purify oneself, regulate oneself, and educate oneself. The meaning of gathering for joint practice is mutual respect in the performance of proper conduct, harmony in view through sharing the same understanding, economic harmony through sharing things equally, physical harmony and sharing possessions through living together, verbal harmony through praising, and

mental harmony through the joy of meditation and Dharma. When the Buddha first organized the religious order for commual practice, he made the six points of reverent harmony its foundation, which is also what we stand for in Humanistic Buddhism.

19) Humanistic Buddhism's view on faith is one of self-affirmation. Regardless of the distinctions others may make, our own faith is the most supreme. In the true meaning of faith, there are distinctions comparable to kindergarten, elementary school, middle school, and college. However, we are all students. If I am studying at the kindergarten level at this time, that does not mean I lack promise, for I have my greatness too. The current stage for someone else may be the pursuit of a PhD degree, but there is no difference whatsoever between that and my studying at the kindergarten level, as everyone has their own course of study. Within faith you have your greatness, and I have mine.

20) Life is eternal and does not die. This is inherent Buddha nature, it is sacredness, and it is Humanistic Buddhism. As humans, we aspire to transcend and expand; the purification and the refinement of faith is sacredness; having the power to transcend is Humanistic Buddhism.

The Main Shrine at Fo Guang Shan.
photo by Zeng Xiumei

Postscript

Trees Have Roots; Waters Have Sources

A Brief Description of My Relations and Hometown

Trees have their roots, and people have their origins. As human beings, we must endeavor to increase joy in the world for the sake of everyone in the world, and we also must ensure that life will sprout flowers and bear fruits as strong and sturdy as the peach. "Mother" is the source of life for every person, and she is also the harbor on which each person depends for their first contact with the human world. The conduct and virtue of the world's mothers in compassionately dealing with the world and wisely managing the household affairs all become the nutrients for life during our time on Earth.

When I was a child, someone asked me, "Where do you live?" I said, "In Xiannü Temple Town."

As a young person joining the monastic order in Nanjing, people would also frequently ask me where I was from, and I would say, "I am from Jiangdu District in Yangzhou."

Yes, I was born in a small town, Xiannü Temple Town, in Yangzhou, Jiangsu Province, China. It was about six miles from Yangzhou city. On my birthday in 1927, Sun Chuangfang, the commander in chief of armies for the League of Five Provinces, engaged in battle with the Northern Expedition forces under the order of Chiang Kai-shek of the Nationalist Party near our hometown. My mother said, "People were being killed outside while you were being born." I remember that I even asked my mother, "Could I be one of those people killed who then took rebirth after death?" Buddhist ideas had profoundly affected the common people, so this natural association with life that I made even at a very young age also shows how deep that influence had become.

The Venerable Master's family home in Jiangdu, China

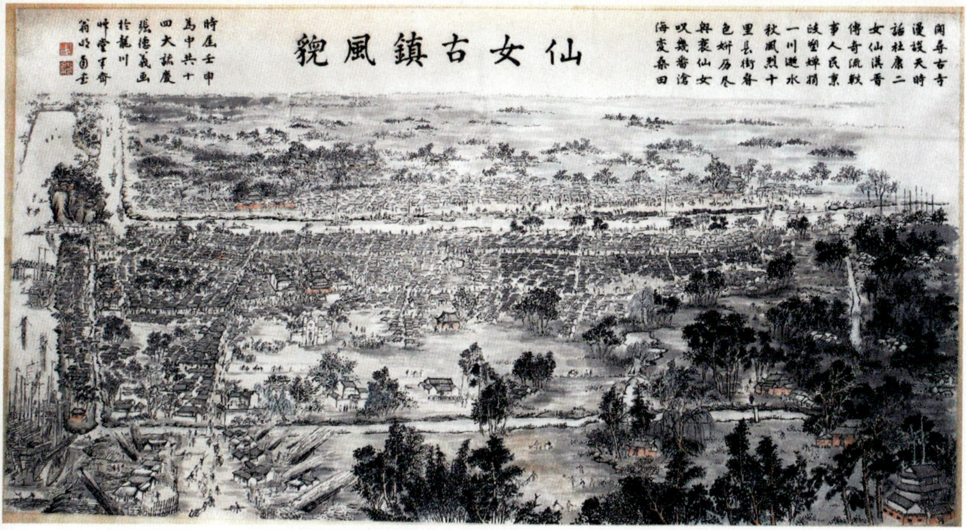

Old townscape of Xiannü Temple
Photo provided by Yangzhou Municipal Government

I was born and raised during that period when war raged all around, streets and alleyways were mostly destroyed, and rubble was everywhere. At the end of 1937, the Japanese Army had occupied Nanjing, and we suddenly lost contact with my father, who was doing business in Nanjing. In early spring of 1938, my mother took me to Nanjing in search of my father's whereabouts, and I met a monastic from Qixia Monastery who asked me whether I was willing to join the monastic order and become a monk. I answered, "Yes!" Thus, I joined the monastic order.

Since this had to do with the search for my father, the causes and conditions for my joining the monastic order could be regarded as having been bestowed by my father. "Trees have roots; waters have sources" means that every event and every person all have their origins. The family relations on my father's side and my mother's side are the source of my blood relationships, so I will trace back some events related to my family and my hometown, in order to show what I commemorate and feel thankful for in my life.

My Father, Mr. Li Chengbao

There have been many people in the past who compiled a family genealogy so as to record what has been passed down through the family. Even though I also would like to understand the circumstances surrounding my family in the past, my ancestors never served in any official post, nor was my family one of wealth and honor, nor were the members of my clan very numerous. It is for these reasons that I have no family genealogy, which became a matter of regret.

From a young age, I always wanted to understand anything connected to my father. It was said that twenty-eight days after my father was born, my paternal grandfather passed away. During my father's adolescence, when he was only fourteen years old, my paternal grandmother also passed away. My father was the only male heir, for he had no brothers. He did have an older sister, my aunt, who was married off to someone in Chenjiadian, a place three miles from us and which ought to have been under Yangzhou's jurisdiction. I only remember that when I was about seven or eight years old, my father once took me to visit her, but now I cannot remember what my aunt looked like. It was only after cross-strait family visits were permitted that I learned I had two older cousins, who were the sons of my aunt. They were office workers in Shanghai Municipal Government.

I heard that before my father got married, he managed an incense and candle store and had regular dealings with the temples. During his free time, he also enjoyed helping out at the temples as a volunteer. As a result, he could cook delicious vegetarian dishes. He was often invited by his friends to cook for vegetarian banquets, and he had quite a reputation. After

The Venerable Master reuniting with his mother and siblings for the first time after more than 40-odd years: (*first right*) his older sister, Li Suhua. (*first left*) his younger brother, Li Guomin, and his older brother, Li Guohua (*second right*).
1989

getting married, my father successively had a sauce, and a pickle shop, and then a clothing store. However, none of them were successful, and they went bankrupt one after the other. In order to support the family, my father could only work far from home.

The fragmented memories of when my father and I lived together were only from before I was ten years old. I do not have any clear understanding as to my father's age, I can only calculate it from the year of the Chinese zodiac that my parents were born in. My mother was born in the year of the tiger and was twenty-five years old when she had me. My father was born in the year of the rooster; thus, I know that when I was born, my father was already thirty.

I remember that when he was not working, he would occasionally return home for a visit. Since I had not seen my father for a long time and missed him terribly, I would start crying without any explanation as soon as I saw him; I could not stop no matter what. Later on, he had lived in Nanjing for a long period of time until the Sino-Japanese War erupted. Since we had no news of my father, in the first month of the Lunar New Year when I had just turned twelve years old, I accompanied my mother as she looked everywhere for my father's whereabouts. We did not find my father, but it was his blessing that enabled me to find the monastic path.

My parents raised us four kids. My big brother was named Li Guohua; my big sister was named Li Suhua; I was named Li Guoshen; and my little brother was named Li Guomin. My big brother never attended any school just like me, but he was very smart and read more books than me. I heard that my younger brother even served as a member of the Political Consultative Conference for Yangzhou. My older sister joined a group of refugees that made their way to Guangxi during the turmoil and chaos of war. She passed away at the age of eighty-seven. My big brother also lived to be nearly ninety, while my younger brother Li Guomin passed away when he was nearly eighty. Of the Li family and relatives of my generation, I am currently the only one alive.

My life has been strangely wonderful in this way. Besides having few memories of my father, I was separated from my family for forty years, including from my own mother. Even my residence at the seat of my lineage after joining the monastic order would only turn out to be a brief period of time. Truly, human life is like that of a passing traveler.

My Mother, Liu Yuying—The Grandma of a Big Family

My mother's maiden surname was Liu, and her given name was Yuying. She was born into a poverty-stricken family in Yangzhou's Xiannü Temple Town, and as a consequence she maintained hardworking and thrifty habits throughout her life. The relatives on my mother's side were more numerous. My maternal grandfather was named Liu Wenzao, and my maternal grandmother's surname was Wang, though she did not have any given name; Mrs. Liu, née Wang, was her name. The Liu family was moderately affluent, and among them, there were perhaps several dozen people. As a child, I did not know what their names either.

My maternal grandmother was the same as my mother, for she had three sons and one daughter, the latter being my mother. My eldest maternal uncle, Liu Yuting, served as the local constable for the village; my second maternal uncle, Liu Guisheng, was a hardworking farmer; and my third maternal uncle, Liu Yuhua, served as the township mayor and as commander of the local militia. All four of them passed away at a venerable age.

Having never studied and being illiterate, my mother could still recite lines of poetry that left one deep in thought; for example:

> *Wilted lotuses no longer possess the canopies holding off rain;*
> *Faded chrysanthemums still have their branches so proud in the frost.*

This is a couplet from Su Dongpo's [1037–1101] poetry that I heard her recite aloud decades ago. In fact, not only did she

Second right, the Venerable Master's mother, Liu Yuying; *from the left*; his third maternal uncle, Liu Yuhua, his second maternal uncle, Liu Guisheng, and his eldest maternal uncle, Liu Yuting.

Photo provided by Hsiao Pi-hsia Shigu

recite this verbally and mentally, but my mother even spent her entire life putting the meaning of these couplets into practice. Consequently, it was also no wonder that she could just about produce an impromptu comment on just about any topic from astronomy to geography.

My childhood was spent with my mother as we lived through hard times, yet my optimistic mother did not feel any hardship despite our poverty. I never saw her express any worry or sadness due to poverty. She often told us that a person must be able to be poor but not be destitute. If one sees the dazzling array of items on sale but has no wish to buy them, then they are considered a person of wealth. In view of this notion, throughout her life she never enjoyed buying, nor did she enjoy acquiring things. On many occasions when there was a bit more money in the house than usual, she would immediately exchange it for a lot of loose change and give it to people in need, making donation to form affinities. Her reasoning was, "A penny can hound a hero to death, yet a penny can save a hero too."

It often happened that the cupboard had very little food, but she was not perturbed in the slightest and went around surmounting difficulties and resolving disputes for others as usual. My mother's need for food and drink were very simple; in 1980 when I contacted her, my seventy-seven-year-old mother still looked healthy and strong. Very few people could believe that my mother was ranked among the "five black categories" during the Cultural Revolution (because of my being in Taiwan). Her monthly income during that time was only eleven Chinese Yuan, but my mother, who did not have enough to eat for her three meals, was as healthy and hardy as ever.

Later on, I had the opportunity to bring my mother to the United States so I could look after her. Filled with joy, I prepared for her all manner of vegetarian dishes as a way of showing my filial respect to my aged mother. However, who could have known that for every meal, her chopsticks moved this way and that way but always centered on only two condiments, fermented bean curd and pickled cucumber, which she paired with her porridge. Sometimes she would add a cup of tea, and these are the fine and delicious items she fancied the most. If you were to have a nutrition specialist come to inspect my mother's way of maintaining good health, her ability to remain healthy and live so long on such simple fare would probably become an inexplicable mystery in medical science. In my mind, it is because of my mother's lack of greed. She did not consider food and drink as nourishment; rather, it was her enthusiasm in helping others and her standing up for what is right that nourished her.

Throughout her life, there were a few events that made my mother proud. In 1990, my mother was finally able to come to Taiwan and visit Fo Guang Shan, which was founded by her son. At the Devotees' Gathering of twenty thousand people, everyone warmly cheered loudly to her, "Hello, Grandma!" She had never experienced such a scene in her life, yet she neither had stage fright nor became flustered. She happily waved both hands in a warm and lively manner as she greeted everybody. Then she gave everyone a short teaching in the Yangzhou dialect, and I acted as my mother's interpreter. She said:

> *Fo Guang Shan is indeed the Pure Land of Ultimate Bliss; heaven is here in the human world. I hope that everybody will practice well. In the past, Guanyin Bodhisattva attained enlightenment on the great Mount Gandha,*[1] *and I hope that everyone will gain enlightenment at Fo Guang Shan.*[2] *Everyone has been so good to me, but I have nothing to give you all, so I can only give my son to everybody.*

There was another event that made my mother proud. My maternal grandmother had given birth to four children, and all four of them were alive and healthy all the way to the time she passed away. Their ages added together amounted to more than three hundred and sixty years. My mother had herself given birth to four children, and the average of our ages was more than seventy years, while our ages added together amounted to two hundred and eighty-odd years.

1 In Sanskrit, "Incense Mountain."
2 In Chinese, "Buddha's Light Mountain."

The Venerable Master's mother, "Grandma," at the Fo Guang Shan Devotees' Gathering, when she said joyfully, "I give my son to everybody!"
From left: Venerable Tzu Chuang, the Venerable Master, Venerable Tzu Jung, Grandma, and the Very Venerable Hsin Ping.
February 25, 1990

In particular, it was during the Cultural Revolution period when so many people were scattered from their families, starved to death, hanged themselves, committed suicide, or were executed by firing squad. However, our family of the "five black categories" somehow managed to survive unscathed. My mother felt that only the reliance upon the light of the Buddhas and bodhisattvas ensured that we could come through it safe and sound. She often admonished her children and grandchildren:

> *A person cannot be blessed until they comprehend what blessings are and cherish them. The blessing of merit is like putting savings in a bank, which are not to be spent carelessly.*

The Venerable Master is his mother's audience.
1994

She was true to her words and diligently put them into practice her whole life. Staying happy with a simple life, being content, and even "deriving moral courage from poverty and destitution" constitute the best portrayal of my mother's life. Her dignified presence and the courage to stand up for what is right can be said to represent the two characteristics with which she was born.

One day, at Hsi Lai Temple's Buddha Hall in the United States, I said, "Let me light the incense for you to worship the Buddha."

My mother replied, "Why would the Buddha want our incense? Why would he want our flowers? The Buddha only wants the simple heart of us ordinary people." When I was with my mother, she usually held forth on the Dharma while I listened with respectful attention.

There was also one time at Hsi Lai Temple, I was giving a talk on *The Diamond Sutra*, and I did not know that my mother was sitting at the back listening. She waited until I came down to criticize me for speaking in such arcane terms. How could I have told everyone "no notion of self, no notion of others, no notion of sentient beings, no notion of longevity?" No notion of self is all that needed to be said. If one went on with no notion of others, then there is no one else to look upon or think about, so what would be the point of practice?

Upon hearing this from my mother, I was at a loss for words. At the same time, I also grasped that my mother's insistence on "having a notion of others" precisely clarified the Humanistic Buddhism that I was endeavoring to carry out. My mother explained the Dharma for us; it can be said that she was a classic of "the study of humanity," as she wanted us to see sentient beings and to bear sentient beings in our heart.

During her lifetime, my mother had experienced many wars, joys and sorrows, as well as partings and reunions. There were also several times that she faced a nation in crisis and the family being in peril. However, my siblings and I never saw my mother shed tears at all. During the July 7th Incident, the Japanese army launched the war against China on the Luguo Bridge in Beijing. In the winter of that year, the war had spread all the way to Nanjing, and my mother stood on a road in Yangzhou, watching her own home go up in flames from the deliberate destruction caused by the Japanese army. Being a young child at the time, I stayed close to my mother, and I saw with my own eyes how she appeared as if nothing had happened.

During the two periods of wartime, a lot of people died in every battle. As children, we would wait until after the battle was over and then count up the number of the dead as a game. One time, I counted up to a soldier who was still alive, so I ran home to tell my mother. My mother comforted the soldier, "Don't move, let me come and help you." She then found a door plank and asked a neighbor to take this soldier to the back. After some time had passed, I personally saw how this soldier, who had risen in rank and was equipped with a pistol at his side, came to our house to thank my mother for the kindness of saving his life.

My mother had always repaid the merest drop of kindness she received with a fountain. During the time of the great Tangshan earthquake [1976], due to the fear of danger, my mother had no choice but to leave Yangzhou for Shanghai and take refuge in her cousin's home, where she lived temporarily for several months. After I was reunited with her, she kept insisting that I send her cousin's family various items, such as a radio, television, refrigerator, and so on as a way of thanking them for the kindness of taking her in during that time. Since my mother attached great importance to repaying kindnesses, I later on established the Water Drop Teahouses everywhere at Fo Guang Shan's Taipei Vihara, the Nantai Temple, and many branch temples. Besides marking my gratitude to my teacher, Venerable Master Zhikai, for the "half bowl of salted vegetables," these teahouses are also related to my mother's spirit, which is the spirit of "Repay the kindness of a drop of water with a fountain."

My mother was innately embedded with a caring and motherly concern toward others. When I went to different places to propagate the Dharma, my mother would even help me educate my disciples. One time, she said to the venerables who were attending the University of the West:

> *There are so many of you in the monastic order, and you can have your opinions, but you must understand something about harmony! Since your venerable master's undertakings are great, the Dharma is great, and the aspiration is great, you too must follow him by making your aspiration great.*

There was one time when I praised her:

> *You are kind and compassionate, dear mother!*

She said:

> *If I were not kind and compassionate, would you have taken rebirth with me?*

My mother had her own view on life:

> *People must have good minds; it does not matter if you are unfairly treated by others. You see, I have been through the Northern Expedition, World War II, and the Cultural Revolution. It has been so much tribulation and hardship, yet I have lived into my nineties, nevertheless.*

In retrospect, when my mother was more than seventy years old, she lived at her home in Yangzhou, and she would go every day to the Grand Canal to bring water back home. After boiling it, she would first pour it into a bowl and then place one bowl after the other on a bench so that the teachers and students at a nearby elementary school could have some water to drink. Later on, everyone as one accord would call her "Grandma" as a way of expressing their respect. Who would have thought that the word "grandma" could span the strait

The Venerable Master's mother, Liu Yuying "Grandma."
photographed at Yuhua Vihara in Nanjing, China.

between the Mainland and Taiwan, and even resound throughout the world?

Every time I went to the United States to teach the Dharma, despite being extremely busy, I would still make time to see my mother for morning and evening visits, thereby fulfilling my filial duties to some degree. Every time I saw her tender and hopeful expression directed toward me, it felt unbearable. Therefore, although there were many matters that had not been dealt with, I would always sit with her for an hour or two and have small talks with her. Sometimes our chats would even go on until late into the night.

I remember in the April of 1994, the ban on cross-strait family visits had been lifted and I made my third trip to mainland China. My brothers coming from Yangzhou, my older sister coming from Guangxi, and my many cousins coming from Shanghai all arrived at the Yuhua Vihara in Nanjing to crowd around in front of my mother's bed. Seeing thirty to forty children and grandchildren all gathered together in one hall, my mother was inspired to recite a line of poetry: "A tree-full of peach blossoms from a single root." The superficial meaning is that although the sons and daughters are separate and in different places, they all come from the same family. The deeper meaning is hoping that the children and grandchildren will reflect upon the source when drinking water; importance must be placed on the roots at the base, for only when the roots are stable can the leaves grow in profusion on their branches. In this way, the flowers will bloom, and the fruits will ripen.

Trees have their roots, and people have their origins. As human beings, we must endeavor to increase joy in the world for everyone in the world, and we also must ensure that life will sprout flowers and bear fruits as strong and sturdy as the peach. More than a decade before, I was granted the favor through the good intentions of all my devotees and established the Grandmother's Memorial Library at Fo Guang University in Ilan. In this way, I wanted to ensure that everyone will continue to inherit and impart humanity's love and honor as well as the gratitude shared between self and others. "Mother" is the source of life for every person, and she is also the harbor on which each person depends for their first contact with the human world. The conduct and virtue of the world's mothers in kindly and compassionately dealing with the world and wisely managing the household affairs all become the nutrients for life during our time on Earth.

My Maternal Grandmother, Mrs. Liu, née Wang

What I cherish the most in my life is my maternal grandmother. When I close my eyes, the image of my maternal grandmother bowing to the Buddha with a kind and compassionate smile on her face remains clear and distinct. Venerable Master Taixu was also raised by his maternal grandmother. In his "Thoughts on My Fiftieth Birthday," there is a reference to his maternal grandmother in the line, "My maternal grandmother possessed rare virtue." I feel the same way regarding the fond memories of my maternal grandmother.

Everyone has a concept of an idol. My maternal grandmother was the person I most deeply respect in my life; she was also my idol. She never received any education and did not even have a personal name. However, she was decent, hardworking, honest, kind, and eager to help others. She never gossiped about others and was never critical of other people. These many excellent virtues of hers influenced my whole life.

The Venerable Master's maternal grandmother, Liu, née Wang, as painted by Li Zijian. The Venerable Master said, "This looks so much like my maternal grandmother."

In the winter, when there were snowflakes swirling about and before there was light in the sky, my hardworking maternal grandmother used to quietly get out of her bed so as not to wake me up from deep sleep with any noise. She alone would go into the garden to pick vegetables, and then take them to sell at the street market. After beams of sunlight were shining through the window, my maternal grandmother, all beaming with smiles, would bring back baked wheat cakes and deep-fried breadsticks fresh from the oven. She would call out to me, "Eat them while they're hot!" With the bone-chilling cold wind outside of the room, the baked wheat cakes and deep-fried breadsticks in my mouth were superior to any sumptuous spread of gourmet delicacies.

In the evenings, with the light of the oil lamp as small as a pea, my maternal grandmother would softly chant the sutra texts as she bowed to the Buddhas and bodhisattvas she so revered in her heart. The chanting of my maternal grandmother was more pleasing to the ear than flowing waters. In the scattered beams of light, her devout figure appeared like a kind and compassionate Guanyin Bodhisattva.

As I recall, my maternal grandmother said that her surname was Wang, and that she was eighteen when she married my maternal grandfather. After that, she went by the name of Mrs. Liu, née Wang. She was a devout Buddhist and was a lifetime vegetarian. Even now I am still not clear about which school of Buddhism she believed in. Now that I think about it, she ought to have belonged to the grassroots society of do-gooders.

Back then in my poverty-stricken hometown, we rarely saw any monastics. However, my maternal grandmother would often tell me:

> *The Triple Gem is the best and the Triple Gem is the most important; the merits of the Triple Gem are limitless, so a person should respect the Triple Gem.*

At the time, I did not understand what the Triple Gem was, for I only knew there was Mother Guanyin.

When my maternal grandmother went to participate in the offering ceremonies, I would occasionally accompany her. Because of this, I was able to learn *The Heart Sutra* by the age of four or five. I also knew about being a vegetarian, and I even competed with my older sister as to who was able to remain a vegetarian longer. Sometimes I did not accompany my maternal grandmother when she went out, but she would then bring back a bag of cakes and buns from the beneficent shrine. I would wait for her at the door to receive a share of the offered fruits she had received some fruit after it had been offered at the shrine demonstrates that one has a certain standing, equivalent to the usage of "benefactor" today.

The impression I got was that her attitude in bringing back things was one without any sense of superiority. She was very kind and amiable, serenely bringing us things to eat. She let us eat with dignity and warmth, rather than making us feel like she was giving us charity. Her encouragement to do good was non-utilitarian and unconditional. She would never say, "You have to study hard after eating this, or what will become of you in the future?" When she brought back the offerings of fruits, she was just happy to share them with us. I only understood later on that my maternal grandmother was demonstrating that giving must be done to the delight of self and other.

From a young age, I learned from my maternal grandmother diligence, decency, and courage. At home, even though I was not ranked as the eldest son, all of my family paid attention to me, my statements, and my ideas; all of which they could respect. Thinking about it now, it was my decency, maturity, and lack of bad behavior that enabled my family to accept me in this way. As for my propensity to readily be of service to others, this too I inherited from my maternal grandmother.

My maternal grandmother had three sons, and each of them had married and built up their careers, with each of them taking their own paths as well. Therefore, my maternal grandmother left behind any reliance upon them and became independent as early as possible. However, she had been an independent person all along, perhaps because my maternal grandfather died prematurely, which made my maternal grandmother see through the impermanence of the world. Naturally, she had strengthened herself from within. My maternal grandfather was a tailor and passed away when I was only five or six years old.

As I recall, my maternal grandmother faced the death of my maternal grandfather without being stricken by any intense alarm. I only remember that she cried softly and sang a long and drawn-out funeral address:

> *Why have you so callously abandoned me, for what should I do all by myself?*

The Venerable Master spent his childhood with his maternal grandmother at this small house.
Painted by He Datian

To grieve without becoming heartbroken gives one a sense of the longing between husband and wife for their deep bonds of love.

My maternal grandmother's home was very close to ours. She had been living alone very early on, but without the pessimism and loneliness some old folks have when living alone. Being in high spirits every day, she would go into the vegetable garden to work before daybreak. She would help her neighbors by relieving them of their worries and resolving their problems. Then she would go to the beneficent shrine for group practice. Whether it was inside the house or outside, the area was always spotlessly clean. I often felt that being in my maternal grandmother's home was like being in a fairy tale where fairies lived while multicolored clouds wafted about in all directions.

My character was more similar to my maternal grandmother's. When I was seven or eight years old, I was living with my maternal grandmother for long periods, and she was already more than fifty years old. Why would I live with my maternal grandmother? Because I liked her very much, and because the temperaments between the two of us, grandmother and grandson, were close. It was also a good experience for her too.

My illiterate maternal grandmother was a person of vision. She insisted that I receive an education and sent me to study. Studying in those days required four copper coins per day. One copper is equal to a penny. Each day, my maternal grandmother would give me four pennies to present to the teacher, and four pennies for me to have breakfast. A single baked wheat cake cost two pennies, and it took two cakes to feel full. So off I went to study before dawn had broken.

Unrest and poverty constituted a general portrayal of society at that time. The fighting and the migration of people later on made it impossible to maintain a complete learning environment. However, no matter where we migrated to, my maternal grandmother would always think of some way to find a traditional private school for me. As a juvenile, I did not understand the importance of studying all that much. This was because I liked doing housework, such as sweeping the floor, wiping the windows, and tidying up the kitchen. Doing this work filled me with energy.

My maternal grandmother was never harsh and brusque, for she always spoke in a soft and gentle voice to everyone. The education she offered us was one of encouragement. For example, when I was sweeping the floor, she would say, "How one tends the fire or sweeps the floor shows whether they have ambition or not." This makes one happy upon hearing it, and so one is inclined to do the sweeping even better and to have cleaner results. The average person considers sweeping to be a lowly task, but my maternal grandmother saw it as a way to judge character. Whether or not one is able to accomplish anything begins with how one sets about doing smaller tasks. If my maternal grandmother gave me some pieces of candy and then I gave one to someone else, she would look at me with a smile and praise me for knowing about sharing. This enabled me to enjoy giving throughout my life, feeling that "giving is more blessed than receiving."

Every night when I went to bed, she would still be doing her evening practice. She would sit straight on the bed in meditation, doing her Gongfu[3] practice. Her stomach would be making an avalanche of rumbling sounds, and sometimes the noise would even wake me up. I would ask her, "Grandma, why are the sounds from your stomach so loud?" She would say, "This is Gongfu!"

Before leaving mainland China, I once returned to my hometown to see her. I asked her, "Grandma, do you still have your Gongfu ability?" My maternal grandmother said, "Of course I do; how can Gongfu ability be lost?" At the time, she must have been more than sixty years old already. I thought that I understood something about the Dharma. It so happened that a Japanese airplane flew across the sky, so I said, "Grandma, the sound of the airplane engine is even louder, so can your Gongfu liberate one from life and death? Can it free one from affliction? Can it increase morality?" Upon hearing this, my maternal grandmother's face darkened. At the time, I thought of myself as a person who had received a modern education. I had studied at Buddhist colleges and was learning a lot from the Buddhist circle. None of the stomachs of the great monks I knew made noise. All of them stressed morality, loving-kindness and compassion, and wisdom.

It wasn't until several years later that I shockingly realized my ignorance and cruelty. My maternal grandmother's Gongfu ability was something she had spent several decades

3 In Chinese, 功夫 (gonfu) means skillful work achieved through diligent practice.

of effort during her life to achieve, and I destroyed the achievement of the faith she held in her heart. My pride came in exchange for her disappointment. It is something I really ought not to have done, and I deeply regret how I had treated my maternal grandmother.

Faith transcends language; in my opinion, an old lady's pious reverence, her sense that the deities are everywhere, her concept of wholesome and unwholesome karmas and their effects, and her ability to do good and help others are far more noble and saintly than the mind of some selfish intellectual whose only thought was the pursuit of personal gain. After all, my maternal grandmother was a person with the wholesome roots of faith. Although she was illiterate, she could recite *The Diamond Sutra*, the "Universal Gate Chapter on Avalokitesvara Bodhisattva" of *The Lotus Sutra*, and *The Amitabha Sutra* entirely from memory. There were many sutra verses that she could sing as well, and she also sang them very pleasingly.

My maternal grandmother maintained her independence, and I never heard her complain about her children being unfilial or lament about how bad the political situation or her fate was. No matter how dangerous or difficult circumstances or human affairs had become, my maternal grandmother would always patiently endure them like a solid mountain or remain calmly tranquil as a deep spring. My maternal grandmother's ability to be patient exerted a subtle influence upon my character. It enabled me to cross the ocean and reach Taiwan while still young in age. I did not fear the boundless future, only acting as I did for the sake of a heart filled with the zeal to propagate the Dharma. This character of having the ability to endure patiently was perhaps how my maternal grandmother influenced me.

After the Luguo Bridge Incident, the war came to my hometown of Yangzhou. The Japanese army was setting fires and killing people everywhere. My maternal grandmother's family was very big, and they would surely become targets of the ravages wrought by the flames of war. She gathered her family relations together and said, "We cannot all die together." What she meant by this was, "All of you must flee to the rear area as refugees; let me stay behind and I will look after our home." She was already planning to sacrifice herself, and although I was young, I still felt a great reluctance in my heart to part from her. I thought of my maternal grandmother like a deity in a great hall, so mighty and lofty.

It was just like that couplet from Du Fu's [712–770 CE] poetry:

> *Flames of war rage continuously for three months;*
> *Letters from home are worth thousands in gold.*

There was no telling how long the flames of war would rage. Was my maternal grandmother staying at home safely? Even though my mother was by my side, my little heart would still be constantly worrying about my maternal grandmother's safety. However, I dared not open my mouth and ask about it lest my mother become more anxious.

In order to take loving care of her family relations, my maternal grandmother vowed to protect the homestead, and she nearly lost her life in the inferno. After she fled from our hometown, she found us in our refuge of a "waterwheel shed." Two days later, I was accompanying my maternal grandmother on the return trip home when we unexpectedly encountered the Japanese army, who then flung her into the Grand Canal.

Fortunately, she was saved and brought back by helpful strangers. My maternal grandmother escaped from two great calamities of fire and water, so it seemed that she was protected by unseen deities. In my mind, this too was owing to my maternal grandmother's regular practice of helping others and doing good, for only in this way could such a miracle have occurred.

My maternal grandmother kept me company as we crossed through the flames of war. The two of us, grandmother and grandson, depended upon each other for our lives as we roamed everywhere fleeing the war. I saw the corpses, which made me think of a couplet:

Sadly the bones beside the Wuding River
Are still in dreams of their beloved ones.

The dead beside the road were all being eaten by wild dogs, a terrible sight. My maternal grandmother was afraid my mind would be harmed by this, so she told me, "Do not panic when facing death." That was about the time I learned not to be afraid. This meant not fearing ghosts, people, the dead, or the living. Besides the baptism of the times and the tempering of war, my courage and steadiness were also due to the example set by my maternal grandmother.

In 2007, Hanshan Temple presented the gift of the Peace Bell, for which I wrote a poem:

The earthly bonds across the straits are like a dream;
Family and close relatives cannot keep in contact.
From the ancient temple of Hanshan in Suzhou
The sound of the Peace Bell reaches Taiwan.

Hanshan Temple in Suzhou, China presented to Fo Guang Shan a reproduction of an old Tang dynasty bell, the Peace Bell, to commemorate the eternal bond between two brother temples. A Peace Dedication Dharma Service was held at Linkou Stadium.
September 9, 2007

In writing this part, I recalled my parting from my maternal grandmother under the willow trees, one that turned out to be forever. I could not help feeling a deep sense of loss. In those days with the havoc of war happening again and again and my father being away from home during those years, if it had not been for my maternal grandmother's support, my mother, who was constantly ill, would have found it impossible to raise us.

My maternal grandmother had one younger brother and two younger sisters. One of the younger sisters was a bhiksuni who joined the monastic order, and I called her "grand master." I also once stayed at her nunnery for a month. Then not long after I was born, I was accepted as the disciple of a bhiksuni. This was because according to the customs of my hometown, having a baby acknowledged as the disciple of a venerable master meant that it was comparatively easier for the child to grow up safe and sound. That I became a disciple of the venerable master after being born was surely what my maternal grandmother had especially intended for me as well. In my mind, it was my maternal grandmother's hope that I be guided toward the Triple Gem. In this way, I could be spared the heartless misery of war and be kept away from the torments of impermanence in the human world.

For those first few years after I joined the monastic order, I often imagined that the visage of Guanyin Bodhisattva worshipped in the Buddha Hall had been transformed into that of my maternal grandmother. The serene and warm sound of my maternal grandmother's voice often left me missing her, and when I awoke from dreams at midnight, my pillow would be wet with tears. I did not know in what year and what month I would be able to see my maternal grandmother again. I am ninety-three [2019] years old now, and my maternal grandmother passed away nearly seventy years ago. The smiling expression on my maternal grandmother's face, so plain to see, still remains etched in my mind even now.

I am grateful to my maternal grandmother; her kindness in raising and educating me cannot possibly be measured. Her benevolent example in word and deed, her righteousness and courage, and broadminded magnanimity of not arguing with others showed me how traditional women were brimming with great wisdom through their hard work, thriftiness, and patience. Through their efforts on behalf of family and relatives, what they adhered to is the heart of a bodhisattva who asks for nothing in return without complaint or regret. My maternal grandmother's spirit of kindness and compassion became deeply rooted in my innermost being. I am thankful to my maternal grandmother, for enabling me to forge a deep and profound bond with Buddhism; I am also thankful to my maternal grandmother, for enabling me to learn how to cherish life even as a child so that I could understand about hardworking diligence and the dedication of one's selfless enthusiasm. During my more than eighty years in the monastic order, I too have dedicated myself to Buddhism without complaint or regret so that I may enthusiastically propagate the Dharma for the benefit of sentient beings in the world.

My Hometown Yangzhou and the Seat of My Lineage

Yangzhou is the hometown of my parents; including my childhood and early teens, I spent some twelve years in total living in Yangzhou. When I was a bit older, I traveled and studied at Qixia Monastery in Nanjing and other famous ancient temples and Buddhist colleges for another twelve years. I arrived in Taiwan in 1949. It was not until seventy years later when I looked back on the past that I had a sense of how the local conditions and customs along the Yangtze River fostered within me the language and character of the Yangzhou people. The rains and grain of Taiwan also nurtured me, enabling me to "establish a foothold in Taiwan, and keep China in my heart, walking toward the world."

Before I turned fifty, all my work of propagating Buddhism had been focused on various countries throughout Asia, such as Hong Kong, Malaysia, Singapore, Thailand, the Philippines, India, Japan, and so on. It was not until the age of fifty that I went to the United States and made preparations to build temples and house monastics. By the age of seventy, I had been to Europe, Australia, South America, and Africa. In this way, I seemed to be moving farther and farther away from my feelings for my native land. Often people would ask me, "Where are you going?" My answers were always, "I am going back to mainland China," "I am going back to Taiwan," "I am going back to Hong Kong," "I am going back to the United States," "I am going back to Europe," or "I am going back to Australia"—even to the point that every stretch of land around the globe is a "hometown" that I would be going back home to.

My entire life had been deeply influenced by my maternal grandmother, along with the addition of the causes and conditions for the Buddhist faith. From a young age, I understood that human life in this world need not demand a rigid adherence to a certain person, a certain activity, or a certain place. In 1989, after a forty-year separation, I returned to Yangzhou for the first time. At the time, I was sixty-three years old. Someone asked me, "How do you feel?" I said:

Symbol of Yangzhou: the Five-Pavilion Bridge.
Photo by Venerable Hui Yan

> *Seeing the old ladies, I feel like I am seeing the shadow of my maternal grandmother; seeing the women and men, I feel like I am seeing the appearances of my mother and father; seeing the young people, I feel like I am seeing the figures of my classmates back then. This is the feeling I have upon setting foot in Yangzhou and returning home.*

Later on, I saw a document, the Local Annals compiled in 1696, which recorded how Taiwan in those days was once under the jurisdiction of Yangzhou. I could not help but feel delighted, because all along for the past seventy years, I had never really left Yangzhou.

I recall that it was April of 2015 and it was the 2,500th anniversary of Yangzhou city's founding. I was thankful for the Yangzhou municipal government for inviting me to attend to the Yangzhou Forum at the Jianzhen Library held over the course of three days. I gave a talk on "*The Heart Sutra*: The Perspective on Life and the Universe." More than ten thousand free tickets were put online, and within a few minutes all of these were completely gone. The audience included attendees from all parts of mainland China. There were even attendees who came from as far away as Inner Mongolia, which required a thirty-hour journey by car. Their determination to hear the Dharma was moving indeed.

Thinking back over my life, regardless of whether it was Xiannü Temple Town or Jiangdu, or even such famous cities as Yangzhou and Nanjing, all of them constituted the long and enduring causes and conditions linked in countless ways and so impossible to sever. An example of this is Xiannü Temple Town, which also has a long history and even great cultural

Celebrating the 2,500th anniversary of the city's founding, Yangzhou Municipal Government invited the Venerable Master to give a Dharma talk at Yangzhou Forum for the first time, on "*The Heart Sutra*: The Perspective on Life and the Universe."
Photo by Gu Yan

noteworthiness in various ways, including Buddhism, human affairs, and architecture.

As for Yangzhou, it had been a flourishing place several times historically. This was especially so during its rise to prominence under the "salt merchants," when many rich and prominent merchants came to be gathered there. Hence, Yangzhou also became a heaven that many people could dream about, as in the saying "To be born in Yangzhou; to take a wife from Suzhou; to eat in Guangzhou; to die in Liuzhou" or the verse "With a purse of ten million in cash; / Riding a crane into Yangzhou." The most beautiful lines are by the Tang poet Li Bai [701–762 CE], who wrote, "An old friend bids farewell to Huanghe Tower in the west; / going down to Yangzhou amid misty March's spring blossoms." Even now the spring blossoms in March are still there, but the people and events through a thousand years and more are no more.

I was born in Yangzhou, but I had never seen any lovely spring scene nor seen any degree of prosperity. On the contrary, I spent my childhood amid the flames of war and the roar of explosions from which I barely escaped death. I was young in those day and did not know the true appearance of Yangzhou. It was comparable to a verse composed a thousand years ago by Su Dongpo [1037–1101], who was moved by the beauty of Mount Lu:

It's a mountain range when viewed horizontally, a peak vertically;
Near, far, high, or low—how its appearance varies.
One cannot know the true nature of Mount Lu,
For one is on that very mountain itself.

Yet I was but a tiny pebble in Yangzhou. It was like that couplet in Venerable Master Taixu's poem "Thoughts on My Fiftieth Birthday":

My life is but a bubble on the sea;
I wish that one bubble could lift a myriad of sufferings.

I only hope that this life like a bubble upon the blue sea can be employed to take up the many sufferings of this human world.

In today's world, I myself am a lonely old man. However, saying that I am a lonely old man is also not completely true, because I have more than a thousand monastic disciples. It is like the saying "three parts guidance and seven parts friendship." When put this way, such joy is no less than that of secular families. Life is like an illusion, and worldly affairs alter

Fo Guang Shan hosts the Fo Guang Family Gathering, inviting the family members of Fo Guang Shan monastics to attend. The Venerable Master personally greets all his Buddhist relatives.
Photo by Zhuang Mei Zhao, September 10, 2012

with the vicissitudes of life. There is no need to become so worried and attached.

I always see the people of the world as my family members, which is why every two years at Fo Guang Shan a family gathering is held for the disciples. The parents of my disciples are my relations, so it is named the "Fo Guang Family Gathering." Each time we gather together, the event is especially warm and friendly. I really do have this cherished wish, that all men are my father, and all women are my mother. I only hope that all the people of the world can make affinities with each other and help each other, just like members of the same family. Then together we can accomplish good and beautiful deeds for the human world.

Besides my birthplace and the monasteries where I studied, the place upon which I have relied throughout my life is the temple where I joined the monastic order at Yixing Dajue Temple, the seat of my lineage; it is the homeland for my Buddhist

education. For more than fifty years now, I have built nearly three hundred temples and monasteries in various places around the world, where I propagate the Dharma and house monastics. In Taiwan, I established the Fo Guang Shan Monastery as our main headquarters. There are also North America's Hsi Lai Temple in Los Angeles, South America's Zu Lai Temple in Brazil, Africa's Nan Hua Temple, Europe's Fa Hua Chan Temple in Paris, Australia's Nan Tien Temple, New Zealand's Fo Guang Shan Buddhist Temple in Auckland, Japan's Hosui Temple, and Malaysia's Fo Guang Shan Dong Zen Temple among others. These are all regional headquarters in various places.

I am grateful for the various causes and conditions, and especially the government of mainland China, for enabling me to return to Xizhu Township in Yixing, Jiangsu. Hence, I could

Yixing Dajue Temple, the seat of lineage of Fo Guang Shan
Photos provide by Dajue Temple

restore the seat of my lineage, where I joined the monastic order. I gave it the name of Dajue Temple, the Seat of Lineage of Fo Guang Shan. The meaning here is that the temple is the family of the life of wisdom, which belongs to all Fo Guang Members around the world. It is the seat of our shared lineage and the ultimate source for the faith we inherit and impart.

I came to Taiwan when I was twenty-three years old, and the Taiwanese said I was an outsider from mainland China. I went back to mainland China at the age of sixty-three, yet the mainlanders said I was a monk from Taiwan. Who am I after all, a mainlander or Taiwanese monk? Having reached this point in life through a conflux of causes and conditions, I thought the description "global citizen" would best express my feelings now!

Many writers like to describe human life as "The Song of Life." I once composed many Buddhist songs for the sake of Buddhism's future.

Looking back on my childhood, I feel that it can be described by the lyrics in the first section of the song "The West":

Upon an ocean of suffering stretching boundless and vast,
Life is like a small boat drifting in the ocean's mist.

Regarding the great age of compounded miseries, I feel that this verse comes quite close. My youth was spent at Mount Qixia and Jiaoshan, a period of being nurtured by the Dharma. It could be represented by "Bodhi Tree," "Homage to the Triple Gem," and "The Gate of Faith." "The Gate of Faith" has the lines:

Large and plentiful fruit,
Must grow from the roots of faith;
An inexhaustible treasury
Must be entered through the gate of faith.

The young must have even more faith.

Upon arriving in Taiwan, the pace of life underwent a huge shift. Indications of my modest aspirations can be derived from "The Rhythm of the Buddhist Youth," "In Praise of the Buddha," and "Let's Take Refuge in the Buddha Now," up to "The Song of Dharma Propagators" and "Buddhism Depends upon Me." As an example, "The Song of Dharma Propagators" states:

Fellow Buddhists, let's
unite in our great
effort
And become the
vanguard for our
faith.
Going through waters
and treading upon
fires,
We dedicate ourselves to
being martyrs for the
faith.
Individual happiness is
not our wish;
'Tis only winning
glory for the noble
teachings.

Cherish endless causes and conditions; then there can be endless accomplishments.
Photo by Venerable Man Ch'ien

The lyrics to this song are an able expression of my frame of mind.

Then there is "Harmonize," equivalent to the five harmonies I advocate. One should begin with the harmony of joy within oneself, and then with the harmony of cooperation within the family, the harmony of respect between self and other, and the harmony of unity in society; then there can be the harmony of peace throughout the world. This is precisely my wish for the humanity. Please listen:

Harmonize all that is wrong,
Work for a peace that is strong,
And gain some respect from this earth,
For all of mankind we will serve.

The Brahma Net Sutra states:

> *All men are my father; all women are my mother. I have always been given life through them from life after life. Therefore, all sentient beings are my parents.*

This clearly shows early on how sentient beings are related through the connection of karma. Now this account has given a brief description of past events concerning my father, mother, and maternal grandmother, as well as my hometown of Yangzhou and the seat of my lineage. Even though the times we encountered were tumultuous and we experienced ordeals of various kinds, through poverty, war, and tribulation, we still were able to nurture patience and courage.

I hope from this everyone can gain some insight and experience some warmth in the human world, as well as cherish and protect all of the people, events, and encounters in life. Buddhism believes in the combination of causes and conditions. Causes and conditions are not a linear development; rather, they mutually influence one another. The causes and effects of things are all interrelated, echoing with one another in an endless multiplicity of layers. Only by understanding how to cherish endless causes and conditions can there be endless accomplishments! This too is an expression of my devout and sincerest hope.

The Venerable Master propagates the Dharma, keeping up with the times. He says, "Fellow Buddhists, let's unite in our great effort, and become the vanguard for our faith. For all of mankind, we will serve!"
Pictured are BLIA Young Adults enthusiastically welcoming the Venerable Master.
Photo by Wang Kunxian

At 93, the Venerable Master thinks the happiest things in his life is being "a monk who does not 'sponge off' Buddhism" and he takes "Buddhism depends upon me" as a guiding light for his endeavors.

The collage above is the Venerable at different stages of his life.

皆大歡喜
appily Ever After
41~50歲
心甘情願
Perfectly
Willing
21~30歲
佛教靠我
Buddhism
Depends on Me
31~40歲
老二哲學
The Philosophy
of Being Second

Afterword by Daniel Han

Venerable Master Hsing Yun Garners Admiration and Respect from People

The Buddhism that I know possesses the longest history among the great religions of the world, and it is endowed with a broad aspiration and tolerance toward every ethnicity and religion.

The Fo Guang Shan that I know propagates the Dharma everywhere throughout the world, and it holds a broad sense of solicitude and transformative power toward society. It was founded and is led by Venerable Master Hsing Yun whom everyone honors and respects.

On February 14th of this year while the second "Colorful Yunnan"[1] exchange event was being conducted at Fo Guang Shan, I went to the Great Enlightenment Auditorium in the Fo Guang Shan Buddha Museum to deliver a speech as a representative of the Kaohsiung municipal government. I said:

> There are three kinds of people in the world who garner my admiration and respect: The first kind is the philanthropist, for they help the disadvantaged of society with their selflessness; the second kind is the politician, for they dedicate their mental and physical efforts to the enrichment of the nation and the

1 A cultural exchange event about Yunnan Province, China; it included the exhibition of Yunnan's ethnic clothing and accessories, as well as a dance performance.

Kaohsiung Mayor Daniel Han and his wife, Lee Chia-fen, with the Venerable Master at Fo Guang Shan Dharma Transmission Center.
Photo by Zhuang Mei Zhao, Nov. 14, 2018

strengthening of the people; the third kind is the religious leader, in that they employ their selflessness to liberate themselves and all sentient beings.

Venerable Master Hsing Yun is indeed the kind of religious leader of which I spoke. At the age of twenty-three and a monk for eleven years, he came to Taiwan from mainland China and inaugurated a period of unprecedented prosperity for Buddhism in Taiwan. Over the course of his eighty-one long years as a monk, he has conferred benefits upon human beings in this world, and his influence extends globally.

Once more in the company of the venerables at Fo Guang Shan, I was fortunate to pay a visit to the newly completed Sutra Repository, and I saw many treasured examples of the *One-Stroke Calligraphy* written by Venerable Master Hsing Yun. Among these were the "Four Givings": the working principles of "giving people confidence, giving people joy, giving people hope, and giving people convenience." This is an article of faith for providing service that every organization should take seriously, which is so admirable! I think the working principles around "giving" constitute the core values within the Venerable Master's new book, *I Am Not a Monk "Sponging Off" Buddhism*: illuminating oneself; bringing light to the human world; loving-kindness, compassion, joy, and equanimity; and devotion through sacrifice. I am able to be among the first in having the pleasure of reading this book, and besides feeling so honored, I am also especially willing to recommend it to all readers.

I often encourage others to read books. In my family, I want my children to do a great deal of reading, so they develop a reading habit. When I was in the service of the Taipei Agricultural Products Marketing Corporation, I would personally select books every month and distribute them to the six hundred workers. A cash award was further given for writing about what was learned from reading, my hope being that my colleagues would change their temperament through their reading. Now I hold the post of mayor for the city of Kaohsiung, but I still recommend a good book every month, and after reading, I also conduct solicitations among the people of the city for essays on what they learned. It is my hope that the promotion of reading will bring about the enhancement of the cultural undertones for Kaohsiung and the dissemination of an atmosphere for scholarship. For myself, it is mainly by means of a wide range of reading that I transformed my views on life, and it is also owing to the instructive and philosophical nature of books that I successfully overcame many failures and setbacks.

I Am Not a Monk "Sponging Off" Buddhism includes ten articles by the Venerable Master. Within them, I see Venerable Master's selfless and lifelong dedication to Buddhism; I see how the Venerable Master embodies the humanistic Three Acts of Goodness, the code of moral principles of doing good deeds with one's body, speaking good words in one's speech, and thinking good thoughts in one's mind; the Venerable Master's good example of a silent revolution that he has established during these degenerate times; the Venerable Master's humanistic character that creates broad affinities for a positive future and sentiment with righteousness; the Venerable Master's free and easy magnanimity with which he meets hardship, setbacks, and the pain of sickness; and the Venerable Master's bodhisattva spirit, which "cannot bear the sufferings of sentient beings nor the decline of the noble teachings."

In the postscript "Trees Have Roots; Waters Have Sources—A Brief Description of My Relations and Hometown," I saw the life of the Venerable Master, from when he was born to when he joined the monastic order on up to his propagating of the Dharma throughout the world. It is a somewhat complete record of his life's circumstances and youth as well as the turning point that inspired the Venerable Master's initial resolve and vows. During his younger years and his period of maturity, he faced so many horrific hardships. As for the particularly harsh and domineering monastic education, so many people gradually gave up under the beatings and scolding, the blows and shouts. On the contrary, it was by undergoing such repeated ordeals that the Venerable Master kindled the greatest and purest loving-kindness. The Venerable Master regards patience as strength, in that trials and tribulations allow us to excel and foster courage and responsibility. This inspires us, for everyone possesses unlimited potential. By understanding self-awakening and self-contemplation, we can develop that most precious spirituality within human nature.

In having the pleasure to read the Venerable Master's works, I feel deeply excited, for after all, these are pearls of wisdom coming from a monk approaching one hundred years of age, whose entire life has been tempered by undergoing all kinds of hardship. Thus, every sentence in the book constantly resonates with my spirit. Here I will quote a few sentences from this book so as to share what I have gained from reading them, but I also do so in the hopes that my humble remarks will lead others to follow suit.

1. The Venerable Master says, "The meaning of life's existence cannot be separated from everyone as a whole, and it cannot be separated from contributions to society; otherwise, one is nothing but a rice bucket or a clothes rack. What value is there in that?"

My life has not been a smooth journey either, and I have experienced countless difficulties along the way. There was a seventeen-year period when I stayed alone in the mountains and let my mind settle down as the clouds rolled by. Only in this way did I gain some realizations somewhat akin to the Venerable Master's. By perceiving one's real feelings, the chessboard of human affairs can be clearly seen. Therefore, I hope to take my own hero's journey, and even if the figure of that hero remains alone, the "complex mind and the simple heart" can always be preserved. This tranquility gives me the ability to spare no effort when dealing with public matters, and when facing the ever shifting and changing tumult of political

Kaohsiung Mayor Daniel Han and his wife, Lee Chia-fen, came to Fo Guang Shan to visit the Venerable Master. Mayor Han spoke of himself as a Buddhist, expressing gratitude toward *The Heart Sutra* for bringing peace to his mind and helping him transcend low points in his life. He recited *The Heart Sutra* and wished all Fo Guang Members well.

Photo by Zhuang Mei Zhao, Nov. 14, 2018

circles, I never forget the spirit of compassion that is loving-kindness and magnanimity.

In the year that the Venerable Master first arrived in Taiwan, he was penniless without a single possession, was snubbed everywhere, and suffered various kinds of unfair treatment; to be able to go from that predicament to his propagating of the Dharma around the world as the Buddha's Light shines throughout the five continents is absolutely no coincidence. The aspirations and vows made by the great personages of the age and their unconditioned giving to the world can be compared to the sun of human wisdom shining everywhere, or like the sweet rains that provide moisture to all things. Then again, in response to my keeping a low profile for seventeen years, I perceived that we have the ability to follow our real feelings so that we can have a chance to serve society and confer benefits upon the people. That would be the greatest merit for human life as well as a way of cultivating the bodhisattva path.

2. The Venerable Master says, "After a person is born, a person's inherent nature has an inclination, which may be a source of energy for faith. But I make a distinction concerning faith; that is, I should have faith in what is good and not in what is bad; I should have faith in what is wholesome and not in what is unwholesome; I should believe in what is true and not in what is false."

I think faith is the source of a person's willpower and realizations about life, which are able to help us see through to the essence of life and seek out a standard for observing human affairs and things. We find ourselves constantly surrounded by what is good or bad, right or wrong, and we must be clear about what is true or false. In this, we absolutely should have the central values that faith establishes in us.

I remember that before the election, I did go to Fo Guang Shan to pay homage to the Buddha. During the Dharma service at that time, I gathered together with the Buddhist disciples. As for offering a blessing, I made an impromptu recitation of *The Heart Sutra* to encourage everyone. *The Heart Sutra* kept me company as I pulled through the deepest valleys of my life. The great wisdom of Avalokitesvara Bodhisattva's "mind without worry and obstruction" let me appreciate how there must be "the freedom of taking and letting go" in life, for no matter at what level one is living, one can cultivate anywhere and anytime. Every single person can have the sunlight within their hearts so that together we can illuminate each other and join together in increasing the radiance of the world.

3. The Venerable Master says, "Tribulation can nurture us mentally and physically, and adversity can increase our strength, but joy alone constitutes the most important treasure in human life."

I recall the phrase "The world is breakable, but passion cannot be broken." During the electioneering process, I once made the rounds on a dozen or more stops in one day and did not even have any time for meals. My weight decreased from 154 pounds to 132 pounds, and on many occasions, I became exhausted and vomited owing to my electioneering, much to the detriment of my health. But what supported me in continuing to complete the daily election itinerary was the enthusiasm and confidence demonstrated by the many city residents of Kaohsiung when they came out to see me. This motivated me to roll up my sleeves once more and put forth more vigorous efforts. After I assumed the office of Kaohsiung's mayor, I became filled with gratitude that I could shoulder the ardent hopes of its 2.78 million residents and join with the city government team and the city's residents in creating the future of "a soaring Kaohsiung and a rising south."[2] For this reason, I am profoundly touched by the Venerable Master's unswerving determination and sense of responsibility with which he made the vow "I will have Buddhism depend upon me" at the age of twenty-three. It is just like my taking on the forging of Kaohsiung's three mountain districts of Gangshan, Fengshan, and Chishan into "a mountain of gold, mountain of silver, and mountain of reliance" for the sake of the city residents.

---

2 Kaohsiung is located in southern Taiwan.

I am elated because now that *I Am Not a Monk "Sponging Off" Buddhism* is published, I can have a heart-to-heart talk with the Venerable Master as I read through the book. I have found this book to be profoundly moving for me; every word and every sentence offer infinite sparks of realization. The book deserves to be read carefully again and again and should always be kept handy on the desktop, so one can open it and browse through it from time to time. I once encouraged young students to "establish a foothold in Taiwan, keep China in the heart, take a broad view of the world, and tame the universe." The Venerable Master's moral conduct as demonstrated in this book—how he positively exerts himself, puts demands upon himself, makes painstaking and patient efforts, dares to innovate, and works everywhere for the sake of others—deserves of study and emulation by young people.

I think that Taiwan's ability to have such a great religious teacher like Venerable Master Hsing Yun and its ability to have the most magnificent Buddhist temples on a global scale, such as Fo Guang Shan and the Fo Guang Shan Buddha Museum, that bless and protect the mass of people, represent merit for everyone in Taiwan. This is something that we should cherish!

Former Mayor of Kaohsiung

Chinese Editor's Remarks

Venerable Master Hsing Yun's Blessing

At the beginning of 2016, we began editing the *Complete Works of Venerable Master Hsing Yun*, comprising altogether more than thirty million Chinese characters in three hundred and sixty-five volumes under twelve major topics. With the Venerable Master being an author and an editor himself, our editorial team for the *Complete Works* were able to receive the Venerable Master's guidance at all times and were naturally able to resolve many problems with ease.

In October of that same year, owing to his brain hemorrhage and surgical treatment, the Venerable Master was granted the blessings of the Triple Gem and accorded the protection of the Dharma guardians, so his restoration to health was extraordinarily successful. In the face of the concern for him coming from all quarters, the Venerable Master said, "I haven't taken ill, nor is there any pain; I am simply inconvenienced a little bit." During his convalescence, the Venerable Master continued rendering his *One-Stroke Calligraphy,* and he inaugurated the Seeds of Hope Project to help young people and teenagers successfully attend school. He gave instruction on *Buddha-Dharma: Pure and Simple* to those who came seeking teachings from him, and he initiated the propagating of Dharma teachings through speeches and Buddhist music.

Because of the Venerable Master's concern for the nation and society along with the needs of the people, he published a series of articles in the *United Daily News* and the *China Times*, such as "Enemies—They Can Become Friends by Stimulating Our Potential, so There's Nothing to Fear," "I Can Call Myself a Taiwanese-Chinese Monk," "I Am Not a Monk 'Sponging Off' Buddhism," and so on, lending his voice for the sake of the people's happiness and well-being and for the sake of justice and fairness in the world. It was also because of these articles that an enthusiastic discussion was touched off in the media and society. This led to a large-scale response on the part of readers, at home and abroad, who sent in droves of letters requesting the publication of a book. Thus, this is why the book *I Am Not a Monk "Sponging Off" Buddhism* came to greet the public.

Throughout his life, the Venerable Master has placed a dual emphasis on understanding and practice, becoming the finest example for all who have set their minds on the study and practice of the truth. After repeated discussions, the editorial group decided to make "I Am Not a Monk 'Sponging Off' Buddhism" the central focus and compile a book of Dharma essentials that were "spoken by the Buddha and are needed by the people—all that is pure, good, and beautiful" for the sake of both monastic and lay practitioners as well as interested people in society. Within the Buddha's light and the Dharma waters,[1] all people will be able to turn affliction into *bodhi* and turn darkness into light; by conducting ourselves in this way, we are able to walk along the road of hope and joy.

Practice is the only way to assess the truth. This entire book is composed of ten essays focusing on the Venerable Master's

1 Buddha's light relates to wisdom, and the Dharma waters relate to purification.

upbringing, faith, aspiration, teaching, and realization. These are divided into three units—"For Buddhism," "The Progress of Faith," and "Diligent Efforts Will Not Be Wasted"—which relate in detail to the nearly hundred-year course of the Venerable Master's life. In order to promote Humanistic Buddhism, he begins with his initial resolve and then experiences all kinds of disasters and calamities to reach a lifetime of joy and happiness, and throughout it all "even if there are millions upon millions of obstacles, [he] will still go forward!" Adhering to the principle of "not 'sponging off' Buddhism," the Venerable Master has committed himself to not depend upon Buddhism for making a living and has vowed to have "Buddhism depend upon [him]" and to "glorify Buddhism." He has become a person who is able to give, who enhances the beauty and goodness of the world, and who is willing to devote himself through sacrifice.

Generally, most often, people mistakenly believe that the cultivation of Buddhism is something like a steep and perilous peak that is difficult to climb, or it is like a thousand-foot-deep valley where one fears slipping and falling. In his essay "My Progress of Faith," the Venerable Master employs the insights from his own experience to enable us to understand and believe in Humanistic Buddhism. Spiritual cultivation begins with living, and as long as we can "have loving-kindness, compassion, joy, equanimity, and the mind without abiding," we will give rise to limitless Dharma joy and meditative bliss and be in possession of a completely different human life.

The postscript "Trees Have Roots; Waters Have Sources—A Brief Description of My Relations and Hometown" was selected for inclusion at the end of the book, and this essay enables the reader to seemingly accompany the Venerable Master as a youngster to experience that time of war and join with his

Courageously realize that "I am Buddha" and life will be different.

maternal grandmother in fleeing through the chaos of armies in the midst of battle. One comes to realize the liberal view on life and death, "Do not panic when facing death."

One could say that besides being a paragon of encouragement for everybody, *I Am Not a Monk "Sponging Off" Buddhism* is also a treasury for spiritual cultivation that helps us to join in as practitioners of Humanistic Buddhism. It is also a blessing that the Venerable Master offers to the world, as he wishes fervently for everyone to be able to improve themselves, develop the harmony of joy within themselves, the harmony of respect between self and other, the harmony of cooperation within the family, then onto the harmony of unity in society and the harmony of peace throughout the world.

The *Complete Works of Venerable Master Hsing Yun* (shown partially).
Photo by Su Shaoyang

Acknowledgments

Like all of Fo Guang Shan International Translation Center's endeavors, this project benefited from the contribution of many people. We would like to thank Venerable Tzu Jung, President of the Fo Guang Shan International Translation Center (FGSITC); Venerable Yi Kong, President of Fo Guang Shan Culture Council; Venerable Yi Chao, Executive Director of FGSITC; and Venerable Hui Dong, Abbot of Hsi Lai Temple; for their support and leadership.

Robert H. Smitheram provided the translation; Vanessa Wang, Jeanne Tsai, Leann Moore, and Selena Zeledon edited the texts; Venerable Miao Hsi, Tom Manzo, Shujan Cheng, and Olive Chen proofread the texts; Charles Kao, Founder of the Global Views-Commonwealth Publishing Group, and Jude Thomas Manzo, PhD, Yale University, each wrote a foreword; Daniel Han, Former Mayor of Kaohsiung, wrote the afterword; cover and book designed by Yin Chiu; Amanda Ling, Flora Liu, and Kathy Stull prepared it for publication.

Our appreciation goes out to everyone who supported this project from conception to completion.

Fo Guang Shan International Translation Center

Fo Guang Shan International Translation Center is dedicated to translating and distributing quality translations of classical Buddhist texts as well as works by contemporary Buddhist teachers and scholars. We embrace Humanistic Buddhism and promote Buddhist writing that is accessible, community-oriented, and relevant to daily life. On FGSITC.org you can browse all of our publications, read them online and even download them for FREE, as well as request printed copies for you or your organization.

Donors

600 copies	Jia Peir Wang & Alice Wang
390 copies	San Diego Buddhist Association
300 copies	Guang Ming Temple
250 copies	Fo Guang Shan Miami Temple
230 copies	Echo Tsai
200 copies	溫哥華佛光山、IBPS New York、C Jim & Julie Y Chen、Dennis Wang & Derek Wang
150 copies	Min Shun S Chang & Jia Bee Chang
105 copies	三寶弟子
102 copies	Vic Wu & Chu-Fen Wu
100 copies	American Buddhist Cultural Society, Fremont、Guam Buddhism Society、Michael Lu
65 copies	Eva Su-Jen Chen、Jonathan Ma
50 copies	佛光山中美寺、林玉梅、林如蓉、張淑美、Adam S. Chou & Pei Pei Wu Chou、Te Ming Chung、Linda Tung

30 copies	崔中寶 & 劉湘麗
25 copies	葉春福閤家
20 copies	國際佛光會達拉斯協會、王雪香、曹笑蓮、曾文中、潘靜秋閤家、蔡和裕、馮文安
13 copies	Yu-Tung Kuo
12 copies	劉綺華、Tien Lun Ho、Pi-Yun Hung、Arturo Ortega & Louvenia Ortega
10 copies	佛光山法水寺、吳敏、吳翠芳、孫添寿、張世平、林桂屏、林翠英、楊紅霞、楚顏靜、熊懋蘭、留許秀琼、蔡玉、蔡雪鈺、謝嬌琴、郜瑜、郭奕秀、錢綺鑾、陳慧嘉、陳桂標、陳森、陳漢中、陳漢國、陳瑞華、陳達憲、陳達舜、黃文飛、黃明智、黎康、Venerable Miaowei、Chinghsiang Chang、Kaiwei K. Chang 、Erwan Erwan、Ann Fornaro、Dorinda Tang Ha、Jack Hsu Family、Paul Hsu、Shih-Hou Lin、Chun Liu、Ming Lu、Yu Oshimura、Ching Pan、Johnny Vuong、Peter Yang、Bruce Zhou
8 copies	知空法師、馬迪雅、Denyse Olsen
6 copies	賴麗娥
5 copies	妙哲法師、丁淑萍、方藹美、史嘉瑜、余天慶、李昭琪、洪亳寓、孫惠美、徐家治、莊芳齡、陳月婣、陳若君、陳若珊、陳若茵、陳思揚、

陳珠錦、陳張瑜華、陳許曉芹、陳進、陳慧娟、陳麗輝、陳寶寶、陳豔玲、馬淨亞、留平敏、留芳芳、留婉婉、留港財、留榜石、留聯泰、張于震、張永爵、張婉薇、張樑溪、張麗郡、梁永峯、傅碧珠、黃小英、蔡瑞莊、謝孟樵、謝睿展、謝睿陽、蘇頌雅、蘇錦浪、關潔儀、How Keat Chan、Mimi Ho、Dean Isensee、Karyn Lam、Yukki Law、Cheryl L. Malone、Bee Toh Siow、Kathy Stull、Albert Tam、Jerome & Bernice Tan、Nghia Tran、May Yen

4 copies 妙安法師、知居法師、吳寶琴、林育陞、林育寬、林淑玲、林復興、洪再興、陳俊榮、陳麗夙、黃瑞菊、黃燕卿、薛雲、薛蓉、Woei Ling Lee、Jorden McNally、Yvonne Tan

3 copies 妙諦法師、滿機法師、郭志雄、陳明枝、麥陳淑瑛、盧冠嘉、Benjamin Cho Wai Fung、Ng Mui Lee、Jing Liu、Travis Sababria、Sang Ping Yeo、Winnie Zhang

2 copies 永餘法師、安加法師、妙聖法師、知成法師、知意法師、知榮法師、知德法師、道融法師、滿方法師、覺機法師、江國琴、何美儀、吳坤榮、李岳勳、林彥鈞、林恩悅、姚銓浩、姚寶寶、洪允昕、洪允萱、洪莊媚、洪綺梅、翁柏雅、郭依眞、郭建俊、郭建輝、陳蓮友、許然娟、黃子睿、黃心妤、黃家和、黃達滔、葉晉塱、葉慶華、葉澔臨、葉熹瞳、葉賴佩兒、鄧玉英、鄭嘉慶、鄭鳳鸞、盧美子、蘇宇維、蘇辛涵、蘇頌元、蘇簡笑怡、Jit Shiang Ang、

Wesley Bachur、Carlita Ramona Bautista、Genevieve Ramona Bautista、Bert Graham、Thomas Halbert、Ting Lai Houang、Sarah Kwok、Minh Le、Carl Chinq Lee、Michelle Liang、Esther Man、Nathaniel Rich、Lydia Sung、Tam N. Ton Tam、Audrey E. Tan、Kaylee L. Tan、Nolan M. Tan、Poh Lan Tan、Victor Tsuen、Jenny Tsueng、Liting Wang、Chung Seong Wong、Eva Yang、Queenie Zhang

1 copy

心畫法師、永印法師、如定法師、有五法師、有紀法師、妙信法師、慧津法師、慧覺法師、吳佩芳、李如珍、李時傑、李楚洲、金曉慧、林景德、姚金榮、姚羊宋卿、姚陳玲、姚子祺、姚家祺、紀爭威、郭恩至、郭恩霏、郭恩霖、陳吳清香、陳致光、黃玉招、梁力仁、梁友平、梁王平、梁秀平、梁峻瑋、梁珮璇、梁華平、梁敏平、梁麗蓉、游秋桂、葉秋鳳、楊海榮、羅安迪、羅瑞恩、Asher Barr、Clarisse Chan、Lillian Chang、Vee Kee Chong、Yee Heon Chong、Ngoclan Diep、Alexandre Ducrocq、Breyette Fazio、Alex Fisher、David Gofton、Alec Hirang、Petr Hora、Zarahjane Isip、Lisa Lam、Philip Lee、Christopher Link、Griffin Link、Alexander Liu、Charles Liu、Adam Nasiry、Naomi Roberts、Kara Selinger、Swee Hong Tan、Amy Tay、Stephen Victor、Eva Wan、Mark Wan、Aric Wu、Rachel Wu、Sandra Wu、Winston Wu、Cin Dee Yeo、Cin Hwee Yeo、Shin Loong Yeo、Mimi Yip、Tommy Yip

Thank you to everyone and their families who donated to support the printing and distribution of this book. With the help of supporters like you, we will continue our best efforts to spread the Buddha's teaching around the world.